Frank Stella **Unbound**

Frank Stella

Mitra Abbaspour, Calvin Brown, Erica Cooke

Princeton University Art Museum
Distributed by Yale University Press, New Haven and London

Unbound

LITERATURE AND PRINTMAKING

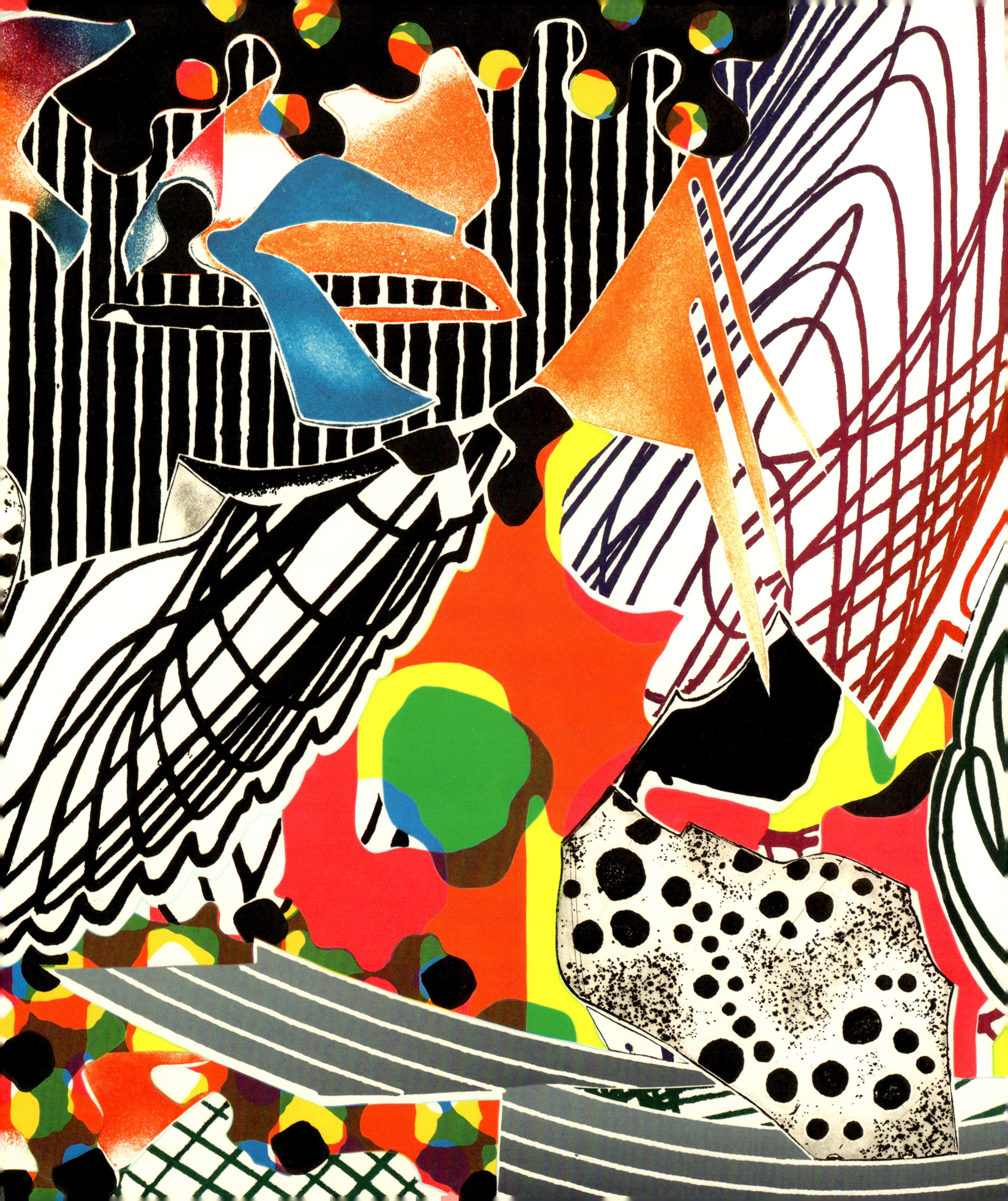

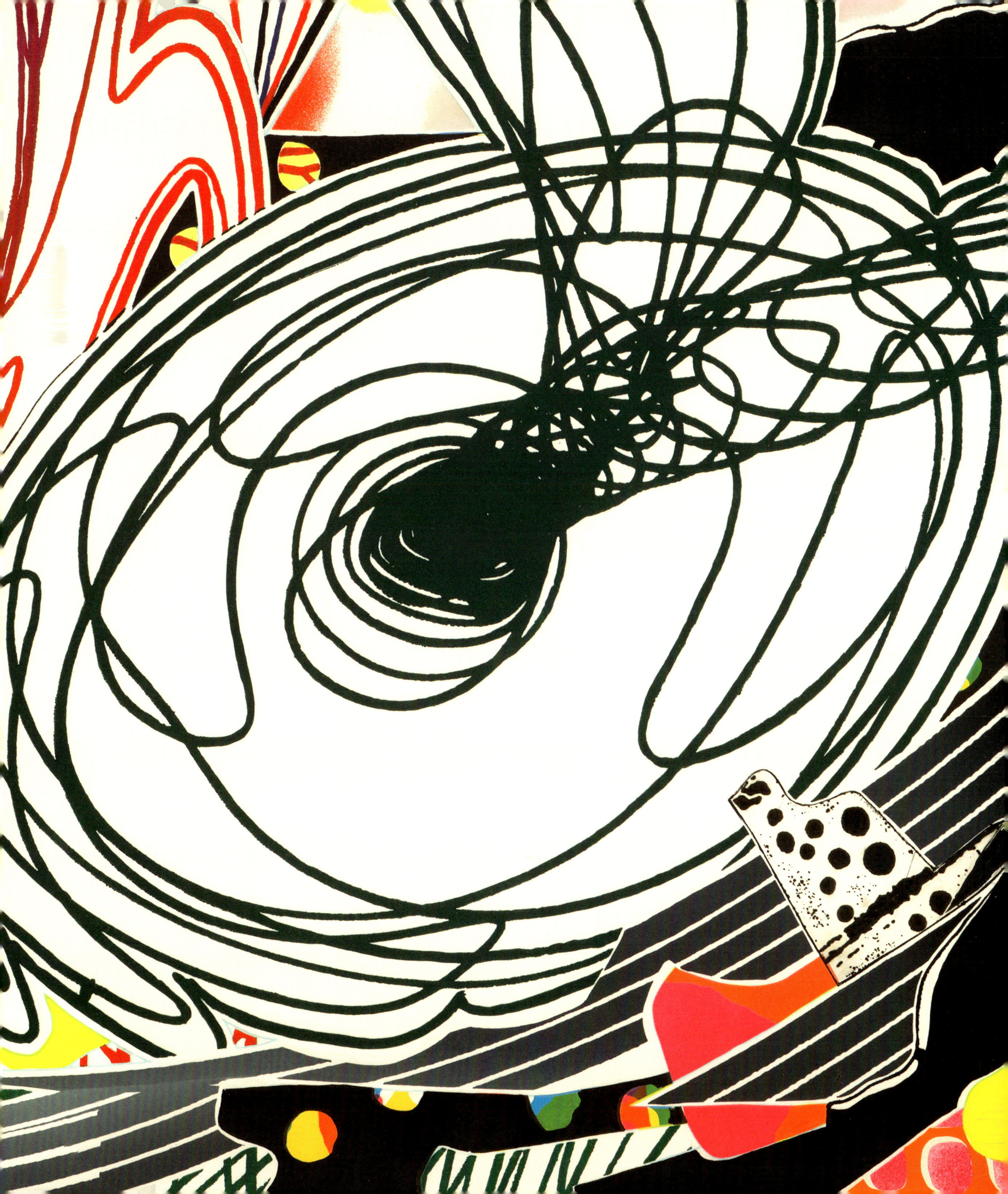

This book is published on the occasion of the exhibition *Frank Stella Unbound: Literature and Printmaking*

Princeton University Art Museum
Princeton, New Jersey
May 19–September 23, 2018

Museum of Contemporary Art Jacksonville
Jacksonville, Florida
October 6, 2018–January 13, 2019

Frank Stella Unbound: Literature and Printmaking was organized by the Princeton University Art Museum and has been made possible with generous support from the Barr Ferree Foundation Fund for Publications, Department of Art and Archaeology, Princeton University; the Andrew W. Mellon Publications Fund; the National Endowment for the Arts; Preston H. Haskell, Class of 1960; the Douglas A. Hirsch and Holly S. Andersen Family Foundation; Susan and John Diekman, Class of 1965; the Julis Rabinowitz Family; Theodora D. Walton, Class of 1978, and William H. Walton III, Class of 1974; Stacey Roth Goergen, Class of 1990, and Robert B. Goergen; Nancy A. Nasher, Class of 1976, and David J. Haemisegger, Class of 1976; and William S. Fisher, Class of 1979, and Sakurako Fisher, through the Sakana Foundation. Additional support has been provided by the Judith and Anthony B. Evnin, Class of 1962, Exhibitions Fund; the New Jersey State Council on the Arts, a partner agency of the National Endowment for the Arts; the Allen R. Adler, Class of 1967, Exhibitions Fund; Lynn and Robert F. Johnston, Class of 1958; Ivy Lewis; Blair Moll, Class of 2010, through the Bagley and Virginia Wright Foundation; and the Partners of the Princeton University Art Museum.

Produced by the
Princeton University Art Museum
Princeton, New Jersey 08544-1018
artmuseum.princeton.edu

Curtis R. Scott, *Associate Director for Publishing and Communications*
Janet S. Rauscher, *Associate Editor*

Designed by Margaret Bauer, Washington, D.C.
Proofread by Jane Friedman
Color separations and printing by Meridian Printing, East Greenwich, Rhode Island
Typeset in Transit Pro and printed on Sterling Premium Matte Cover

Distributed by Yale University Press
P.O. Box 209040
302 Temple Street
New Haven, Connecticut 06520-9040
yalebooks.com/art

Printed and bound in the United States of America

ISBN (Princeton University Art Museum)
978-0-943-01253-7

ISBN (Yale University Press)
978-0-300-23699-6

Library of Congress Control Number:
2018935132

Front cover: *Feneralia*, 1995 (detail of plate 28); **Back cover, pp. 4–5:** *The Monkey Rope*, 1993 (detail of plate 26); **Title page:** illustration from Daniel Sheets Dye, *A Grammar of Chinese Lattice* (detail of p. 44, figure 8); **p. 8:** *The Butcher Came and Slew the Ox*, 1984 (detail of plate 9); **p. 12:** *Then Came a Dog and Bit the Cat*, 1984 (detail of plate 4); **p. 30:** *Cantahar*, 1998 (detail of plate 40)

p. 65: Frank Stella quoted in Rubin 1987, 142; **p. 74:** Stella 1989; **p. 100:** Stella 2000b, 87

Contents

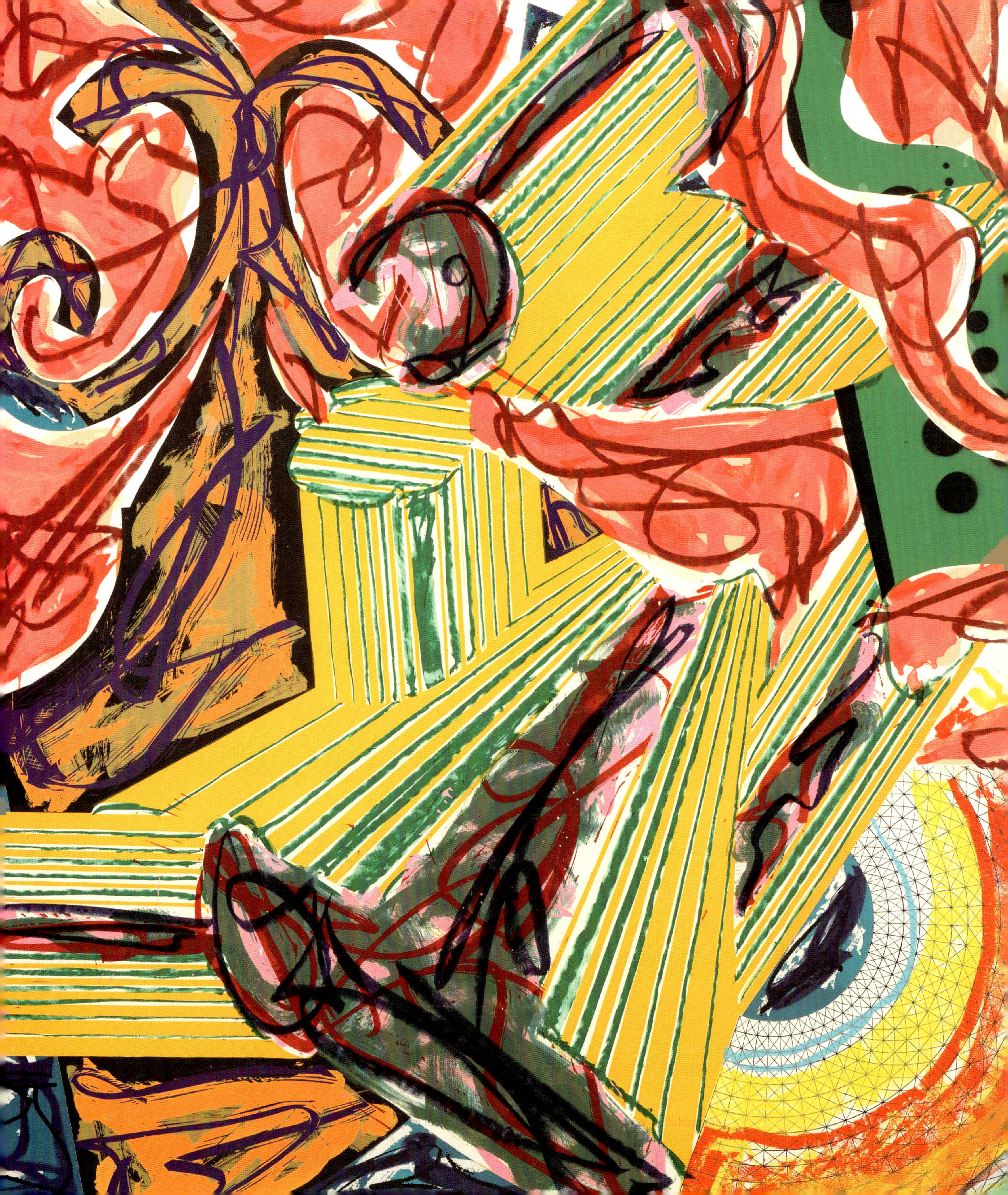

James Christen Steward

Foreword and Acknowledgments

Frank Stella Unbound: Literature and Printmaking commemorates the sixtieth reunion of Princeton alumnus Frank Stella, Class of 1958, one of the most celebrated and influential artists of our time. Stella's formidable career was launched in the year following his graduation, in the Museum of Modern Art's seminal exhibition *16 Americans*; in the decades that have followed, he has carried the modernist heritage of post–World War II abstract art into the twenty-first century and has made numerous contributions to how we define abstract art. Indeed, Stella's impact has been described as "something like Dylan's on music and Warhol's on more or less everything."

In 1983, the Princeton University Art Museum recognized Stella's twenty-fifth reunion with an exhibition of highlights from the artist's body of prints: *Frank Stella: Fourteen Prints, with Drawings, Collages, and Working Proofs*, curated by Judith Goldman. Beginning where that exhibition concluded, *Frank Stella Unbound* considers closely the four major series of prints Stella made between 1984 and 1999, each of which was titled after a literary work. The first exhibition to focus exclusively on the vital role that literature played in the artist's groundbreaking explorations of the print medium during these decades, *Frank Stella Unbound* explores the interconnected role of narrative structures and abstract composition in works that became crowning achievements in Stella's graphic oeuvre and transformed his visual language and working methods in all media.

While previous studies of Stella's prints have concentrated primarily on his technical innovation in the medium, this project offers a critical new perspective on the artist through its examination of his interdisciplinary processes, literary approach, and interest in the lessons of art history as critical factors for his artistic development. This study is thus driven by Stella's own interest in art history, knowledge rooted, in part, in his studies at Princeton and in his voracious and widespread appetite for the arts pluralistically. Stella's writings about art—its narrative capacity and formal innovation—date from his senior thesis on Ottonian sculpture, and he solidified these ideas in later writings that inform the perspective on his work offered so thoughtfully and incisively here by Haskell Curator of Modern and Contemporary Art Mitra Abbaspour, Associate Curator of Prints and Drawings Calvin Brown, and Erica Cooke, a doctoral candidate in Princeton's Department of Art and Archaeology.

The success of this exhibition can be credited to the pride Stella's alma maters—Phillips Academy, Andover, Massachusetts, and Princeton University—feel for this extraordinary artist. Loans from the Addison Gallery of American Art at Andover and from Princeton alumni provided the forty-one prints included here. Our great friend Preston Haskell, Class of 1960, has generously lent half of the exhibited works, including his complete set of Stella's *Illustrations after El Lissitzky's Had Gadya*. Our thanks extend also to John Gutman, Class of 1983, and to longtime friend and Princeton resident Rysia de Ravel d'Esclapon for loans from their collections. Additionally, the conceptualization, development, and final outcome of *Frank Stella Unbound* emerge from an enduring partnership between the Art Museum and the Princeton University Library—a partnership that builds on a history of collaborative exhibitions that in recent years has included *"Remember Me": Shakespeare and His Legacy* (2016), *By Dawn's Early Light: Jewish Contributions to American Culture from the Nation's Founding to the Civil War* (2016), *Princeton's Great Persian Book of Kings* (2015–16), and *Cartographies of Time* (2011). We are also delighted that the exhibition will travel to the Museum of Contemporary Art Jacksonville, and thank Director Caitlín Doherty and Curator Jaime DeSimone for their energies in assuring that Stella's work will be seen there as well.

Like all complex loan exhibitions and scholarly undertakings, *Frank Stella Unbound: Literature and Printmaking* is made possible by the generous support of many, including the Barr Ferree Foundation Fund for Publications, Department of Art and Archaeology, Princeton University; the Andrew W. Mellon Publications Fund; the National Endowment for the Arts; Preston H. Haskell, Class of 1960; the Douglas A. Hirsch and Holly S. Andersen Family Foundation; Susan and John Diekman, Class of 1965; the Julis Rabinowitz Family; Theodora D. Walton, Class of 1978, and William H. Walton III, Class of 1974; Stacey Roth Goergen, Class of 1990, and Robert B. Goergen; Nancy A. Nasher, Class of 1976, and David J. Haemisegger, Class of 1976; and William S. Fisher, Class of 1979, and Sakurako Fisher, through the Sakana Foundation. Additional support has been provided by the Judith and Anthony B. Evnin, Class of 1962, Exhibitions Fund; the New Jersey State Council on the Arts, a partner agency of the National Endowment for the Arts; the Allen R. Adler, Class of 1967, Exhibitions Fund; Lynn and Robert F. Johnston, Class of 1958; Ivy Lewis; Blair Moll, Class of 2010, through the Bagley and Virginia Wright Foundation; and the Partners of the Princeton University Art Museum.

I would also like to particularly thank individual members of the staff here at Princeton who have made exceptional contributions to the success of this project. In planning the exhibition and related programming, I especially thank T. Barton Thurber, Associate Director for Collections and Exhibitions; Chief Registrar and Manager of Collections Services Alexia Hughes; Manager of Exhibition Services Michael Jacobs; Head of Installations Todd Baldwin; Preparator John Walako; Associate Director for Education Caroline Harris; Mellon Curator of Academic Engagement Juliana Ochs Dweck; and Student Outreach and Programming Coordinator Cara Bramson. This visually rich and engaging volume was shepherded to publication by Curtis Scott, Associate Director for Publishing and Communications, and owes a great deal to the talent and efforts of Jeffrey Evans, Manager of Visual Resources and Photographer; Visual Resources Imaging Specialist Emile Askey; Manager of Collections Information Cathryn Goodwin; and Associate Editor and Interpretive Manager Janet Rauscher, without whom this publication could not have taken such beautiful and probing form in so short a time. Beyond the Museum, I also thank book designer Margaret Bauer for once again lending us her exceptional talents, and Danny Frank at Meridian Printing.

Frank Stella's artistic journey from Princeton into the world has been a long one, rich in evolution. As he once observed on the occasion of a major retrospective of his work, "It's about what you make, what you learn from it and what it suggests. And move on." We are delighted and honored to share with you these glimpses into Stella's journey, and to invite you to share with us this important occasion on which we celebrate the work of a remarkable American artist.

James Christen Steward

Nancy A. Nasher–David J. Haemisegger, Class of 1976, Director
Princeton University Art Museum

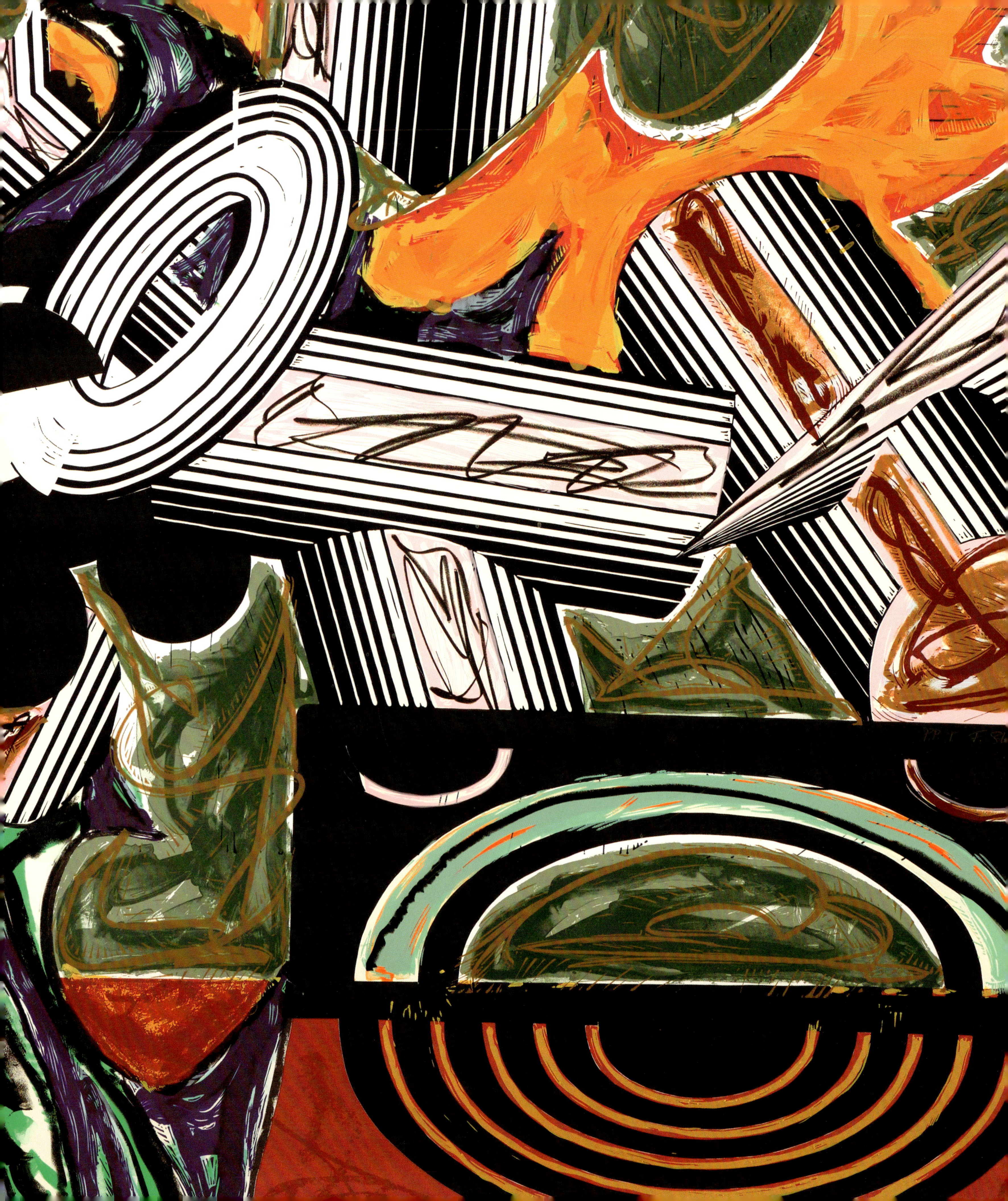

Mitra Abbaspour and Calvin Brown

> **The question we must ask ourselves is: Can we find a mode of pictorial expression that will do for abstraction now what Caravaggio's pictorial genius did for sixteenth-century naturalism and its magnificent successors? The expectation is that the answer is yes.[1]**

Graphic Imagination: Frank Stella and the Literary Print

In 1984, Frank Stella issued the above challenge—a call to advance the expressive potential of abstraction—over the course of six lectures that he delivered as that year's Charles Eliot Norton Professor of Poetry at Harvard University.[2] Stella was the first visual artist to garner this distinction in twenty-seven years, and the lectures cemented his position as a defining figure of postwar American art.[3] The artist donned this mantle with confidence, tracing a path in his heavily illustrated talks from the regimented linear perspective of the sixteenth-century Renaissance painters, through the "audacious naturalism" of the Baroque masters who extended illusion outside the picture frame, and onward to a parallel relationship between the groundbreaking removal of figures from the early twentieth-century abstractions of Cubism, Constructivism, and De Stijl and the explosion of scale (and therefore pictorial space) in the mid-century work of the Abstract Expressionists.[4] Concluding with an extended introspective view of his own practice, Stella pondered whether the historical arc of Euro-American art could reveal a path for the continuing evolution of pictorial expression. His meditation on history and obsession with progress was fitting for an artist who had achieved a remarkable degree of recognition in the twenty-five years since his graduation from college as a member of Princeton's Class of 1958—an early mid-career retrospective at the Museum of Modern Art (1970), residency at the American Academy in Rome (1982), a traveling retrospective of his prints organized by

1. Stella 1986, 4.

2. Transcripts of Stella's Norton Lectures were published the following year as *Working Space* (Stella 1986).

3. Previous Norton Lecturers included T. S. Eliot, Igor Stravinsky, and Buckminster Fuller; Stella's appointment made him the first visual artist to deliver the lectures since the painter Ben Shahn in 1956–57. The shift from Shahn to Stella represented, according to Robert Storr, the "evolution from illustrative liberal humanism to efficient abstract positivism in educated art taste" (Storr 1985, 11). For an account of Stella's lectures and their significance, see Kimball 1983; Russell 1984; Tomkins 1984; and Storr 1985.

4. Paraphrased by Stella in 1995 in Stella 2000b, 82.

the University of Michigan (1983)—and was poised to embark on a new chapter of his career.[5]

Concurrent with his preparations for the Norton Lectures, Stella's formal approach to his work underwent a radical transformation; the drawn gestures, fields of color, and cut-out shapes of his previous compositions were no longer discretely confined elements, packed together within a shallow picture plane, but rather sprung from the surface as illusionistic, geometric volumes, layered atop one another to create three-dimensional reliefs. During the same period, he was at work on a group of technically innovative, ambitiously scaled prints inspired by El Lissitzky's illustrated publication of *Had Gadya,* the traditional Passover song. Critical to this mid-career metamorphosis in Stella's aesthetic vocabulary and in his working methods were two elements: the artist's use of literature as interlocutor as he worked through the challenges of abstraction and, equally important, his enthusiastic adoption of printmaking, a medium that ultimately impacted his practice in all modes as his work began to integrate processes of painting, printmaking, and sculpture. In his prolific, influential, and innovative career as a printmaker, Stella contributed to technical innovations in the medium—and, more generally, to the discourse surrounding the late modernist avant-garde—through his exploration of the pictorial, narrative, and expressive potential of abstraction in the final decades of the twentieth century. Stella's accomplishments in the print medium—particularly the technical feat of his prints and the generative nature of his collaboration with master printer Ken Tyler—and his engagement with narrative subjects have drawn the attention of scholars; however, the particular dynamic between literature and printmaking in his work has yet to be explored.[6]

Over the fifteen years between 1984 and 1999, all of Stella's prints were titled after, and therefore drawn into a dynamic exchange with, literary works, including a compilation of *Italian Folktales*, collected and retold by Italo Calvino; the American epic *Moby-Dick*, a novel by Herman Melville; and the illustrated encyclopedia *The Dictionary of Imaginary Places,* a compendium of fictional geographic locations. These four series represent a crowning achievement in Stella's graphic oeuvre, and it was with them that printmaking became a central mode of his practice. Indeed, printmaking transformed Stella's working methods in all media to such an extent that by 1995 he would remark on his drive to advance the potential of representing pictorial space by stating that he saw the future of painting "through the eyes of printing."[7] *Frank Stella Unbound: Literature and Printmaking* contends that consideration of the particular relationship between printmaking and literature provides fertile ground for consideration of the ways in which Stella expanded the possibilities of printmaking as an art and extended the historical trajectory of abstraction in the modern era.

5. Survey exhibitions of his prints were held at both of his alma maters: Phillips Academy, Andover, Massachusetts, and Princeton University, the latter in conjunction with his twenty-fifth reunion. See Axsom 1983; and Goldman 1983.

6. On the technical innovations developed in the prints on which Stella and Tyler collaborated, see Tyler 1987, 21; Axsom 1983; Axsom 2016; Engberg and Stella 1997; Armstrong 1987, 35; Gilmour 1986, 121–27; and Hansen 1995, 79. On his engagement with narrative subjects, see Auping 2015; and Kantor 2015. Kantor employs the descriptor "narrative turn" for four bodies of work, including *Illustrations after El Lissitzky's Had Gadya, Italian Folktales, The Moby Dick Prints*, and a series of sculptural reliefs titled after the philosophical writings of Heinrich von Kleist. The last of these does not describe a discrete volume; for this reason, and given our focus on printmaking, we include instead *Imaginary Places*.

7. Stella 2000b, 84.

Frank Stella, Ken Tyler, and the American Print Renaissance

Printmaking was largely abandoned as a fine-art practice in the United States following World War II, when painting dominated the landscape of American art.[8] This changed with three innovative printmakers who opened independent studios: Tanya Grosman's Universal Limited Art Editions, East Islip, New York, in 1957; June Wayne's Tamarind Lithography Workshop, Los Angeles, in 1959; and Kathan Brown's Crown Point Press, Oakland, California, in 1963. Leading a print renaissance, these master printers partnered with established artists to create print series collaboratively, fundamentally transforming the role of printmaking in modern art.[9] Stella's introduction to the field came in 1967, at the height of this resurgence of printmaking, at the invitation and urging of Ken Tyler.[10] Having trained as a master printer at Tamarind, Tyler distinguished himself from that workshop through his embrace of industrial materials and mechanical apparatuses, as well as a willingness to combine multiple printmaking processes in creating a single work. To pursue his vision, in 1965 Tyler established his own workshop on Melrose Avenue in Los Angeles, where he was joined the following year by partners focused on the publishing side of the enterprise. Their studio, Gemini G.E.L. (Graphics Editions Limited), brought Tyler's unconventional attitude of unlimited technical possibilities to collaborations with such leading artists as Josef Albers, Jasper Johns, and Robert Rauschenberg. By many accounts, however, he worked most radically in partnership with Stella.[11] Tyler's ambition was the revival of printmaking not only as a fine-art practice but also as a medium that could command the scale, complexity, and place in artistic discourse traditionally reserved for painting and sculpture. In 1974, Tyler broke with his partners at Gemini to move across the country again, opening his own studio—Tyler Graphics—in upstate New York, where he was geographically closer to the artists with whom he worked and thus could focus on his goal of expanding the technical potential for printmaking as a fine art.

Stella had little firsthand experience with—or inclination toward—printmaking when Tyler urged him to try his hand at lithography, stating that he considered printmaking fundamentally tied to the skill of draftsmen working in the service of reproducing paintings.[12] Despite Stella's early reticence, almost immediately—in his first three print series for Gemini, *Star of Persia, Black Series I*, and *Black Series II*—the artist found in printmaking an opportunity to explore ideas that would have been untenable in his painted canvases. In the *Star of Persia* series, for example, Stella created variations, as color lithographs on graph paper, of a set of chevron-dominated compositions that he was unable to execute as paintings, as bolts of cotton duck were not available in dimensions wide enough to accommodate the thirteen-foot height of the proposed structures

8. In the 1890s and continuing into the twentieth century, technically sophisticated, innovative printmaking held a central place for avant-garde artists in Europe; however, with few exceptions, printmaking in the United States was confined to traditional intaglio and lithographic techniques, printed in black and white (rather than color), and generally was perceived as a commercial or reproductive process.

9. Previously, American print studios predominantly fulfilled custom print orders, remaining distant from the development of the image. For a thorough history of the shift represented by collaborative printmaking in the 1960s, see Hansen 1995.

10. In 1967, Stella moved to Los Angeles, prompting an invitation from Tyler to collaborate. See Guberman 1995, 105.

11. See note 6 above.

12. Stella was not alone among artists whose first efforts in printmaking were dedicated to the reprisal of earlier paintings but who, through experimentation, would go on to generate technical innovations that would revolutionize practices of fine-art printmaking. Paul Gauguin's self-published zincographs known as the *Volpini Suite* (1889) and Edvard Munch's portfolio of eight etchings and drypoints published by Julius Meier-Graefe (1895) are two examples of such early efforts. For comments by Stella on the subject of printmaking as a reproductive medium, see Stella 2000b, 81.

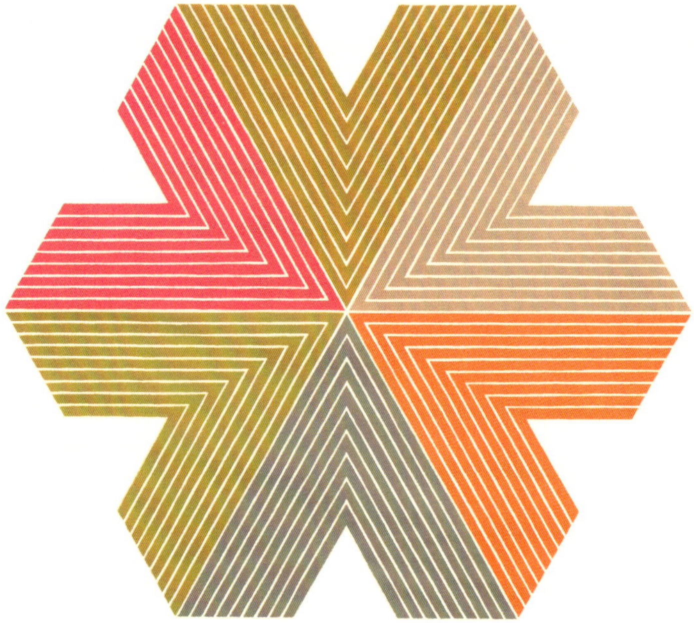

(*figure 1*). Beginning with the *Black Series*, the artist produced scaled versions of all of his striped paintings from the period 1958–65 as crayon lithographs, which, when printed, were intended to be bound into loose-leaf binders for presentation as albums.[13] Through this book-like format Stella not only reconstituted the dispersed striped works in bound volumes but in doing so also resuscitated the serial methodology of the paintings' creation, in which the artist determined a set of variables and explored the range of possible compositional variations they provided. These initial print projects established a template for Stella's engagement with the medium until 1982, giving the artist the opportunity to study his work as a sequence of formal experiments with line, shape, mass, color, and space. In the same way that the Norton Lectures reveal Stella's metacognition on his place in the arc of art history, the album project can be read as a self-guided retrospective that aligned with his expectation, early in his career, that the primary utility of prints lay in their capacity for reproducing paintings.

In 1982 this hierarchical relationship between paintings and prints—with paintings occupying the higher position—shifted as Stella began two series of prints, *Circuits* (1982–84) and *Swan Engravings* (1982–85), that he developed in dialogue with a series of metal-relief paintings also titled *Circuits* (1980–84). In the paintings, Stella's geometric, gestural language was rendered as shapes and planes that were painted, die-cut, and etched into corrugated aluminum and steel

13. Several complete sets of five of the striped paintings series were realized in this format: *Black Series I* and *Black Series II* (1967), *Aluminum Series* and *Copper Series* (1970), and *Purple Series* (1972). The lithographs sold well, but collectors preferred to purchase the prints individually rather than in albums, and the bound presentation was dropped. See Axsom 1983, 60.

Figure 1 Frank Stella, *Star of Persia I*, 1967. Seven-color lithograph (aluminum) on English Vellum Graph paper, 66 × 78.7 cm. National Gallery of Art, Washington D.C. Gift of Dr. and Mrs. Maclyn E. Wade (1979.75.2)

sheets, which he then assembled at various angles to create wall-mounted reliefs. The painted reliefs thus foreground their integration of the technical processes and formal concerns of painting, sculpture, and printmaking. The printed series *Circuits* and *Swan Engravings* were equally radical in their dissolution of the boundaries among various printmaking techniques—intaglio, engraving, woodcut, stenciling, and screenprinting might all be combined in a single image. To create these technically innovative prints, Stella collected scrap metal from the manufacture of his sculptures, plywood backing boards from which the shapes that formed his relief paintings had been cut, and photo-etched templates from industrial manufacturing jobs—all from the workshops of his fabricators—and brought them to Tyler Graphics, where they were recut and assembled into large multimedia compositions. Stella considered these various elements "found drawings," and when inked and printed they resulted in a complex montage of textures that mimicked the appearance of traditional woodcut or intaglio prints.[14] For example, the creation of *Pergusa Three* (*figure 2*) included sinuous paths excised from a sheet of plywood, strips of photolithographic lace (industrially made to be embossed along the borders of mass-produced tablecloths), and etched magnesium plates cut from scraps of Stella's own reliefs—all of which was printed on enormous sheets of handmade, hand-dyed paper.

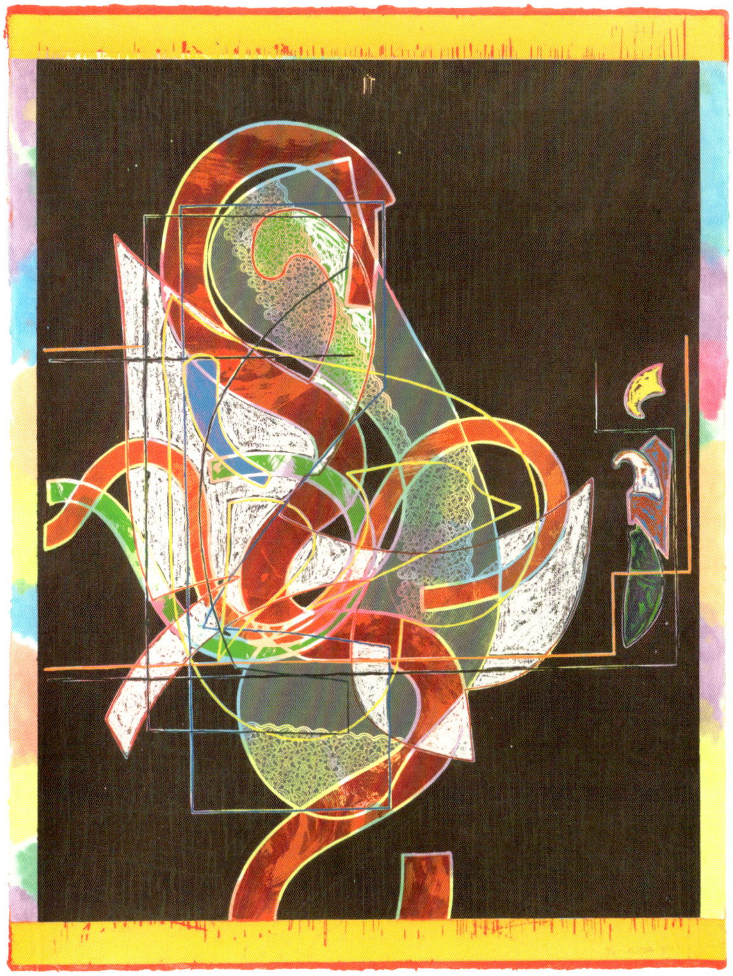

14. As related by the artist at length in Stella 2000b, 81–82.

Circuits and *Swan Engravings* thus systematically dismantled the formal boundaries between printmaking and the practices of painting and sculpture; they also addressed the practices at the core of the era's artistic discourse: assemblage, the use of readymade forms, and the conflation of the artist's hand and mass-produced patterns. For Stella, printmaking was no longer about

Figure 2 Frank Stella, *Pergusa Three*, 1983. Relief print and woodcut, 169.5 × 131.4 cm. Whitney Museum of American Art, New York. Gift of Joyce and Judge Steven Robinson (91.22.1)

reproduction but a means of formal experimentation that could be developed concurrently with his paintings, untethered from a single process or medium. Moreover, now that his print projects were liberated from merely reproducing previously developed series of paintings, Stella turned to specific works of literature over his next four bodies of prints, as conceptual scaffolding for the development of his theories on abstraction and pictorial space. The four works of literature Stella chose are narratives reliant on exaggeration, fantastical events, and imaginary space—the literary equivalents of expressionistic drama, pictorial illusion, and abstraction—and these texts laid the foundation for the artist's fifteen-year exploration of the narrative potential of purely abstract forms.

Illustrations after El Lissitzky's Had Gadya, 1982–84[15] plates 1–12

Stella gave the first of these series, which consists of twelve geometric abstractions developed through multiple techniques, the deceptively literal title *Illustrations after El Lissitzky's Had Gadya*.[16] In 1919, the Russian Constructivist El Lissitzky, who would become one of the most influential abstract artists of the early twentieth century, designed an integrated program of typography and pictures for a children's-book version of the song *Had Gadya*, traditionally sung at the end of a Passover Seder (***figure 3***). Stella, who had seen the gouache illustrations for the book at the Tel Aviv Museum of Art, created a series of prints in dialogue with Lissitzky's energetic arrangements of arcs, angles, and layered geometric planes. Strictly correlating his print cycle with Lissitzky's design program, Stella titled each of his prints after one of Lissitzky's—he also created a print for each side of the cover. However, whereas Lissitzky's pictures illustrate the central characters in the story, Stella's prints refer only to Lissitzky's fracturing of space and dynamic arrangement of colorful geometries.[17]

Lissitzky had been inspired by scenes from scripture integrated into the architectural structures of wooden synagogues that he visited on his travels through Eastern Europe, and his designs for the *Had Gadya* reflect a commitment to bringing a modern visual language to subjects of Jewish cultural heritage. Stella, decades later, was interested in the use of abstraction to maintain the expressive strength of a figural scene that did not rely on the drama of the represented narrative—in other words, in how the abstract image could create a self-sufficient pictorial dynamism. Therefore, during a period when Stella was thinking deeply about the most influential artistic antecedents to his own practice, he chose to echo not Lissitzky's revolutionary non-objective abstractions (for which he is better known) but an overtly figural set of illustrations with references to folk culture. Specifically, in responding to the lessons he absorbed from

15. Stella's prints are assigned the date on which the entire series was published; the dates of these section headings indicate the years during which he worked on each series.

16. While printed in New York, the series *Illustrations after El Lissitzky's Had Gadya* was published in 1984 by Waddington Graphics, London.

17. Stella had often used titles to intimate a latent symbolic weight in his paintings; however, up to this point in his work his prints were replicates of paintings, and subsequently took their titles from the works they mimicked, or, in the case of the *Swan Engravings*, the materials from which they were composed.

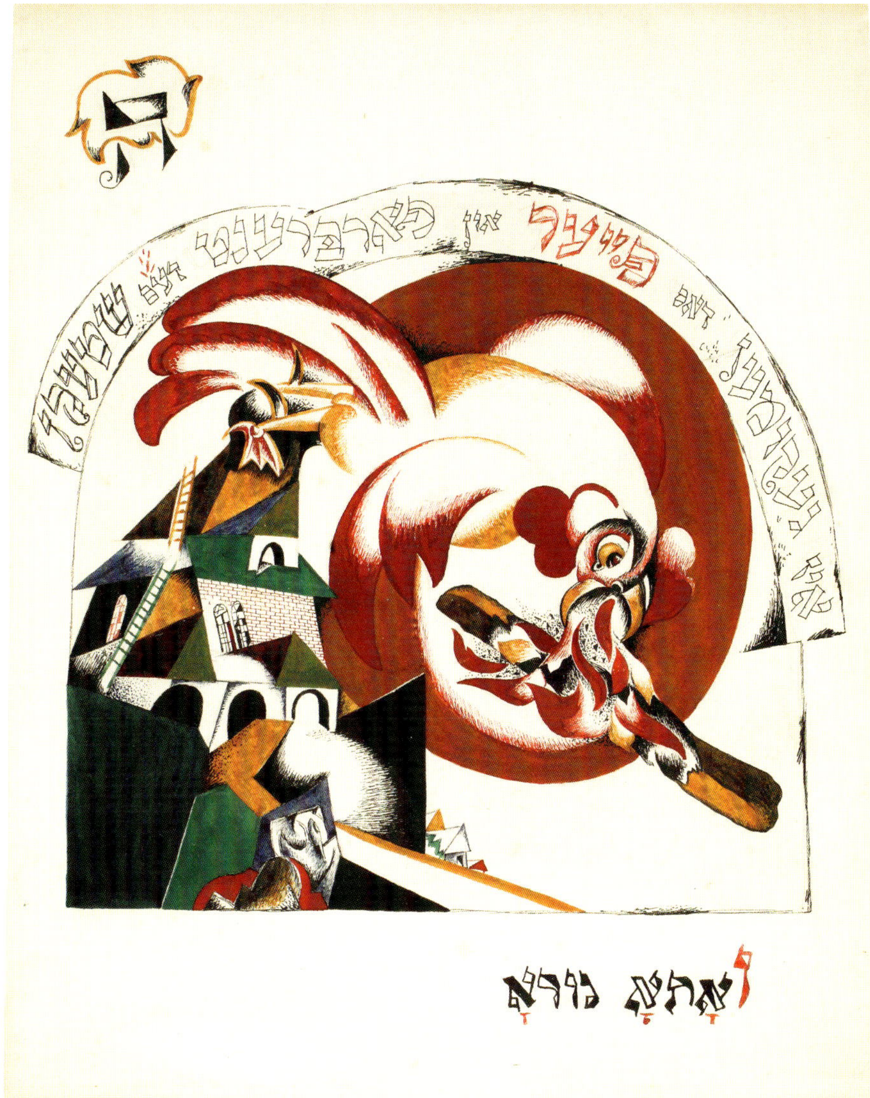

Lissitzky's *Had Gadya*, Stella selected a source whose structure aligned with his practice and interests at the time. The *Had Gadya* provided a compelling drama that developed in a serial fashion through exaggerated (and thus abstracted) animal behaviors, allowing Stella to experiment with a sequence of compositions that convey the expressive power—dynamism, drama, and spatial illusions—of arrangements of purely formal elements. In creating a print cycle of *Illustrations after El Lissitzky's Had Gadya,* Stella tipped his hand, revealing the significance of literature at this moment in his artistic evolution: parables, fables, and fiction are forms created to represent the morals, experiences,

Figure 3 El Lissitzky, *Then Came a Fire and Burnt the Stick*, from the series *Had Gadya*, 1918–19. Gouache and India ink on paper, annotated in Aramaic and Yiddish, 28 × 23 cm. Collection of Tel Aviv Museum of Art, donated by Israel Pollak, Tel Aviv, with assistance from the British Friends of the Art Museums in Israel, London, 1979

and emotions that drive—and yet exceed—the framework of literal accounts of historical records. In these genres of literature, Stella found works that provided narrative subjects, formal structures, and, most importantly, examples of imagined (illusory) space through which he could represent the natural world without illustrating it.

The publication of the *Had Gadya* prints constituted a technical watershed in Stella's printmaking. The artist installed a complete print shop, with a flatbed offset lithographic press, on the ground floor of his Greenwich Village home. Here, he crafted full-scale collages from which a team of printers developed, proofed, and editioned the *Had Gadya* prints, experimenting with intricate combinations of offset lithography, linocut, and screenprinting on hand-painted paper, as well as with the addition of printed and hand-cut collaged elements that occasionally protrude beyond the edges of the rectangular background sheets to heighten the layered three-dimensional effect of the prints.[18] In the *Had Gadya* prints, the illusionistic volumes of cones and cylinders represent a spatial depth that vies for visual impact with the material space created by collaging together layers of paper, playing illusionistic space against the physical extension of built space in front of and outside of the frame—and vice versa. Working from his home studio allowed Stella to play an active role in every step of the printmaking process, precisely at the moment that he was writing his Norton Lectures, a contemplation on the academic and artistic evolution of depictions of pictorial space through the history of painting.

Even when cut-paper elements extend beyond the rectangular border of the print, it is the stereometric renderings of cones and pillars, which Stella copied from a nineteenth-century L'École des Beaux-Arts architectural-drawing manual, that communicate the spatial rupture of the frame (***see p. 37, figure 5***).[19] This formal idiom, introduced in the lively compositions of the *Had Gadya* prints, became the central motif of a series—titled *Cones and Pillars* (1984–87)—of forty-eight metal high-relief paintings, to which Stella assigned titles from the collection of two hundred Italian fables published by Italo Calvino. In this way, the *Had Gadya* prints acted as the prelude to Stella's next painted series, comprising the first instance in his career in which formal solutions to pictorial problems were developed in prints before they appeared in paintings. Completion of the twelve-part sequence established by the design structure of Lissitzky's *Had Gadya* not only gave Stella a new set of formal elements that he would translate into painted-metal reliefs, it also clearly established the generative potential of working on prints and on three-dimensional paintings concurrently.

18. For a discussion of Stella's studio print shop, see Guberman 1995. For a discussion of the advantages of an offset lithographic proofing press, see Gilmour 1986, 77–79.

19. Monduit 1889.

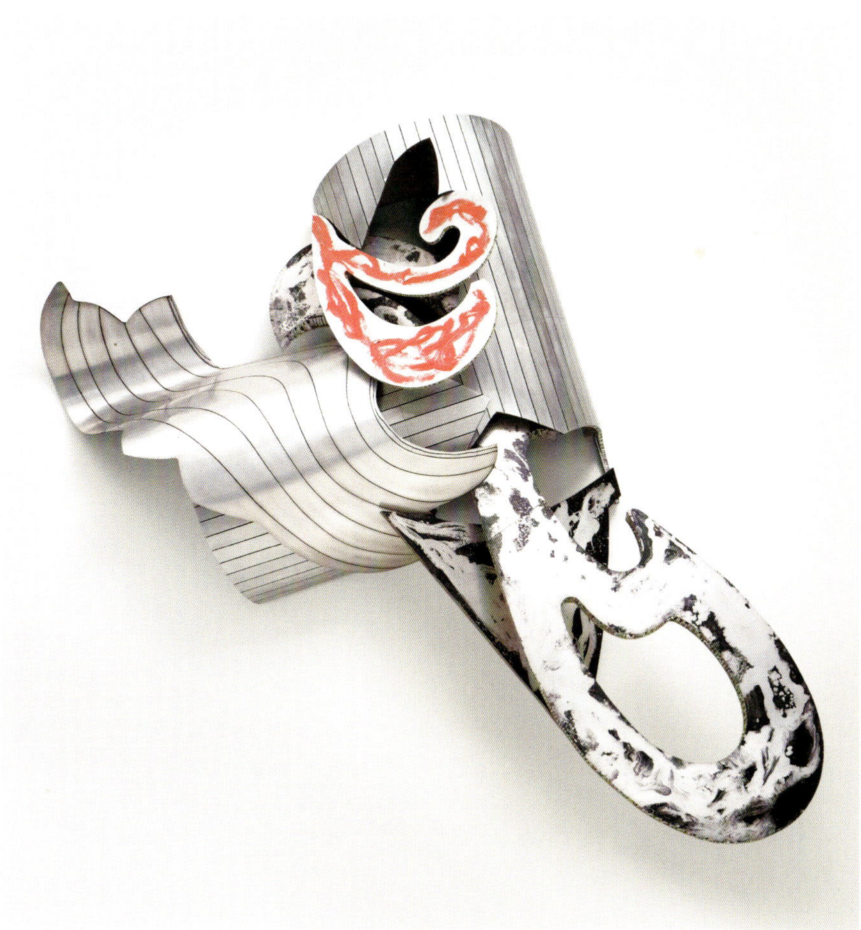

The Waves, 1985–89 plates 18–19

The creative cross-pollination between painted reliefs and prints that occurred in Stella's *Had Gadya* and *Cones and Pillars* was fully integrated in his next and largest body of work: a series of 266 works created in conversation with Herman Melville's novel *Moby-Dick* (1851), which the artist developed over twelve years (1985–97). Here, in one series, Stella worked across genres, creating painted reliefs, freestanding sculptures, and four groups of prints in multiple states and variations, titled after each of the 135 chapters and appendices of Melville's epic saga, as well as its epilogue. Throughout the wildly diverse and innovative compositions, one of the few unifying elements is a distinctive wave-whale form, the undulating white shape seen in *Loomings* (***figure 4***), one of Stella's earliest painted reliefs from the *Moby Dick* series, and repeated as a central element in many prints, including *Jonah Historically Regarded (Dome)* (***plate 23***). Variations of this

Figure 4 Frank Stella, *Loomings (3X)*, 1986. Ink and oil paint on etched magnesium and aluminum, 361 × 412.8 × 111.8 cm. Walker Art Center, Minneapolis. Gift of Joan and Gary Capen, 1987

fluid shape first appeared in several of the *Had Gadya* prints and reoccur throughout the works in the entire *Moby Dick* series.[20] To these were added a series of latticework patterns borrowed from a book on Chinese decoration (***see p. 44, figure 8***), as well as contours of cast-iron rain gutters copied from an architectural manual.[21] The *Moby Dick* series is so expansive and varied that it—much like its titular whale—is difficult to comprehend in its totality. Its significance also echoes its progenitor in time span and scope—it occupied Stella for twelve years, cutting a path through his entire artistic practice, and thus offers the most comprehensive opportunity to examine the artist's working process, intellectual investment, and evolving engagement with abstract compositions as a means to activate space, incite drama, and engage viewers.[22] For *Moby Dick*, Stella produced and published four individual print series, each with its own distinct graphic qualities and engagement of pictorial space: *The Waves*, *Moby Dick Engravings*, *Moby Dick Domes*, and *Moby Dick Deckle Edges* (***plates 18–26***). These discrete bodies of work provide touchstones for exploring Stella's pursuit of an ongoing language of abstraction.

The first, *The Waves*, was developed over a period of four years and utilized many of the same methods that Stella had evolved in the *Had Gadya* prints; however, the series represents two important shifts related to the depiction of pictorial space: a dramatic increase in scale and the building up of the print with multiple levels of collage. Scaled comparably to Abstract Expressionist or Color Field paintings, these towering prints relate to their viewers as physical spaces and must be viewed from a distance to fit within a single field of vision. Comprising the most complex prints the artist had made to that point, *The Waves* combines lithography, linoleum block printing, and screenprinting with added hand-coloring, metallic foils, and marbleized paper, which provides an aqueous effect appropriate to the theme. With these prints, Stella was once again working in his home studio and was able to fully engage with daily routines of proofing and printing, alongside the construction of maquettes, sculptures, and painted reliefs, as part of his creative process. For *The Waves*, Stella and his team developed ever more intricate and time-consuming approaches; creating *The Quarter Deck* (***plate 18***), for example, involved a printed base sheet, two levels of collage in multiple papers, hand-marbling, and fifty separate press runs.[23] Additionally, in collaging layers of media together, the process of creating *The Waves* parallels Stella's assembly of his painted reliefs. The *Waves* prints were begun in 1985, concurrent with the earliest of the *Moby Dick* painted reliefs, and, as with the *Had Gadya* prints, printing was executed and coordinated in Stella's Jones Street studio. While the graphic innovations that Stella's team of printers achieved were exceptional, the artist returned to Tyler Graphics to explore the possibilities of handmade papers and to expand the range of technical processes available to him.

20. As observed in Leider 1990, 172.

21. Dye 1937. For the cast-iron rain gutters, see Leider 1990, 176.

22. Gilmour 2001; and Dimock 2014.

23. For complete print runs and elements for all of Stella's prints, see Richard H. Axsom with Leah Kolb, *Frank Stella Prints: A Catalogue Raisonné, Erratum and Printing Sequences (Catalogue Numbers 00–315)*, online supplement to Axsom 2016, www.jordanschnitzer.org/s/stellaprintsequences.

Italian Folktales, 1988–89 plates 13–17

That printmaking could serve as a medium for developing the compositional possibilities of an abstract formula of fixed elements and limited variables — as had Stella's much earlier series of striped and geometrically shaped paintings — was brought to the foreground in the print series *Italian Folktales*, on which the artist collaborated with Tyler Graphics. For this group of eight editioned intaglio prints, Stella reprised titles and compositional elements from three of his painted reliefs named after Calvino's *Italian Folktales*. Unlike the evolution of earlier prints that shared titles with Stella's paintings and thus replicated their compositions, for the *Italian Folktales* prints each sculptural relief provided only a set of formal elements — shapes and textures — that became the jumping-off place for a sequence of prints. The relationships between compositional elements in *Bene come il sale* (***plates 13–16***), for example, are explored in a sequence of five prints: one full-color image and four variant states. Throughout this series, Stella experimented with the contrast between figure and ground by manipulating both the density of ink and the process of wiping the assembled plates before printing them on handmade paper dyed in pastel shades. Seen together, these prints make visible Stella's creative methods, revealing how adept he had become at altering the expressive qualities of an image purely through his manipulation of the plates at various stages in the printmaking process.

For the *Italian Folktales* prints, Stella and Tyler further developed the innovative mixed-intaglio techniques with which they had experimented in the *Circuits* and *Swan Engravings* series. Stella also revised pictorial shapes and themes related to three of his recently completed *Cones and Pillars* painted reliefs; he then etched them onto various irregularly cut magnesium and copper printing elements, assembling them like a jigsaw puzzle to form a single plate. This assembled plate was inked and printed on enormous sheets of handmade paper, hand-dyed in pastel shades. Stella often referred to this working method as "building the print," a fitting description for the process of gathering a variety of elements of different processes into one matrix. Whereas Stella had contrasted stereometric drawings with collage to create tension between illusionistic and material space in the *Had Gadya* and *Waves* prints, from *Italian Folktales* forward he would construct a printing plate in which pictorial and material depths were integrated graphically, as the inked relief elements of the printing plate revealed a single embossed impression when run through the press. This method would become essential in the production of all of Stella's prints that followed, especially those from the next bodies of work in his expansive *Moby Dick* series.[24]

24. As discussed by Stella throughout his 1995 lecture "Melrose Avenue," concerning the relationship between painting and printmaking in his work. See Stella 2000b.

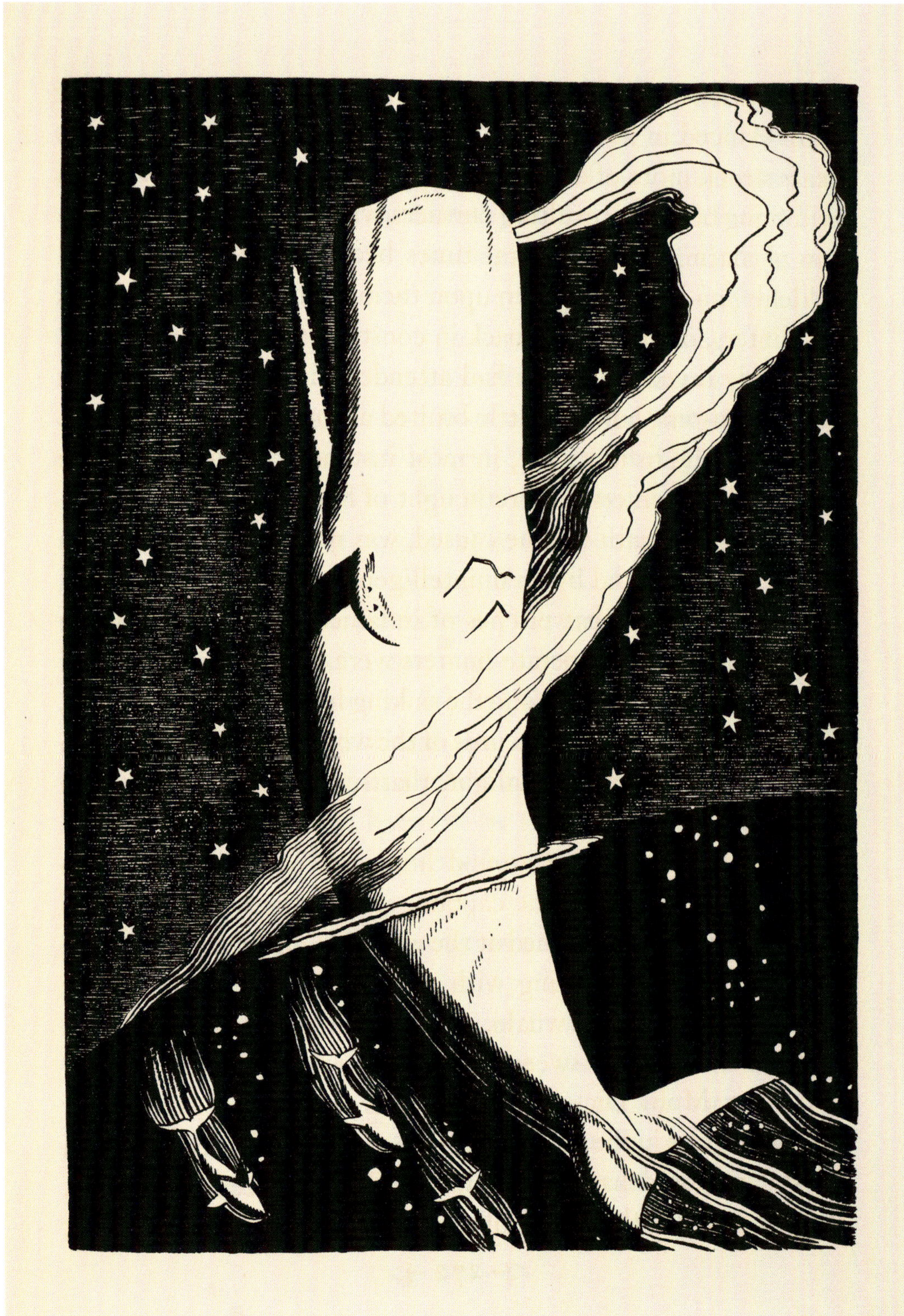

Figure 5 Rockwell Kent, illustration from Herman Melville, *Moby-Dick; or, The Whale.* Chicago: Lakeside Press, 1930. Graphic Arts Collection, Rare Books and Special Collections, Princeton University Library

Moby Dick Engravings, 1989–91 plates 20–21

Stella also worked on the remaining three series of *Moby Dick* prints in close collaboration with Tyler, and in each they advanced the complexity of the printing matrix. In the *Engravings* both the printing plate and each image's composition were based on intricate, multipart assemblages of elements from various sources and media. For these works, Stella constructed elaborate collages to arrive at his final compositions; Tyler and members of his workshop of skilled printers would analyze these works and translate their components into an elaborate combination of printmaking processes, devising the sequence of press runs that would be necessary to re-create the collages as prints. Tyler Graphics maintained an archive of discarded proofs and plates from previous Stella projects, from which the artist would cut and build his collages. Lines, shapes, and textures from these sources were enlarged, drawn by hand on sheets of transparent Mylar, then photographically transferred to lithography plates and printed for use in the collages and prints.

The *Moby Dick Engravings* variously combine intaglio techniques, including etching, aquatint, drypoint, Carborundum mezzotint, and engraving, printed on custom-made papers in a predominantly black-and-white palette. Muted blue-green accents are used to strategically highlight the circular mandala that surrounds the undulating wave-whale form at the center of each composition and to heighten the illusion of receding planes within the frame. The *Moby Dick Engravings* feature the strongest visual presence of the wave-whale form, resonating with both the central figure of the story and the distinctive wood-engraving illustrations created by Rockwell Kent to accompany the deluxe three-volume 1930 edition of the novel (***figure 5***).[25]

25. Melville 1930. The novel was popularized in the trade edition that was published as a single volume, complete with Kent's illustrations (New York: Random House, 1930).

Moby Dick Domes, 1992 plates 22–23

The *Moby Dick Domes* were printed from the same combination of plates as the *Engravings*, with two critical exceptions: each individual plate was inked by the printers in vivid color, and an etched, concave magnesium dome was fit to the exact location of the circular mandala at the center of the *Engraving*, thus rendering this portion of the composition in a repoussé, convex domed relief (***see p. 48, figures 10–13***). In order to achieve this effect, both the printing plate and the thick, handmade paper were created with corresponding domed surfaces. Tyler and his team developed a custom-built printing press to accommodate Stella's desire to rupture the surface of the image and to build pictorial space into the material space and experience of the print. In the same fashion with which Stella had once dissected the various shapes and planes of his paintings, transformed them into metal elements, and reassembled them as a sculptural relief, in the *Domes* he merged the illusion of three-dimensional space with its physical manifestation. The result is a series of technological feats in printmaking: three-dimensional color engravings embossed and printed on a single sheet of paper.

Moby Dick Deckle Edges, 1993 plates 24–26

For the nine prints of the *Moby Dick Deckle Edges*, Stella and Tyler combined all of the mixed-media printing techniques from the previous series to evolve a new working method. Stella added a host of new textures and patterns to his growing lexicon of "readymade" source materials, including benday dots enlarged from photo-offset reproductions of his own paintings, a honeycomb pattern from plastic construction fencing, and computer-generated volumetric renderings of his photographs of swirling cigar smoke (***figure 6***). Each of these visual elements was cut, folded, stapled, and taped together to form intricate collages that became patterns for the printing plate. Tyler then worked with Stella to translate the finished collages to print, selecting which elements to render in intaglio or lithographic processes and determining how to assemble the plates from multiple pieces that had been individually created. The resulting plates were hand-inked in riotous colors in order to replicate each of the corresponding elements from the maquette in the final printed image. As the plates were proofed, Stella would make changes to his collages and incorporate the alterations back into the prints, immersing himself in the process as he would in developing the final composition of a painting or sculpture. The final impressions have a frothy, accidental appearance that exactly imitates the overlapping layers of patterned materials in the original collages, an effect that Stella heightened by cutting away the margins to match the edges of the image, exaggerating the effect of the irregular edges of handmade paper for which the series was named.

Imaginary Places, 1994–99 plates 27–41

Over a period of five years, Stella developed the last of his series devoted to a specific literary text: *The Dictionary of Imaginary Places*. The *Imaginary Places* prints utilize nearly every process known in Western printmaking, fitting a dazzling variety of techniques, including lithography, screenprinting, etching, digitally enhanced engraving, mezzotint, woodcut, and relief printing, into unified compositions. For each print, planographic processes (lithography and screenprinting) were employed first, followed by woodcut, relief printing, and heavily embossed

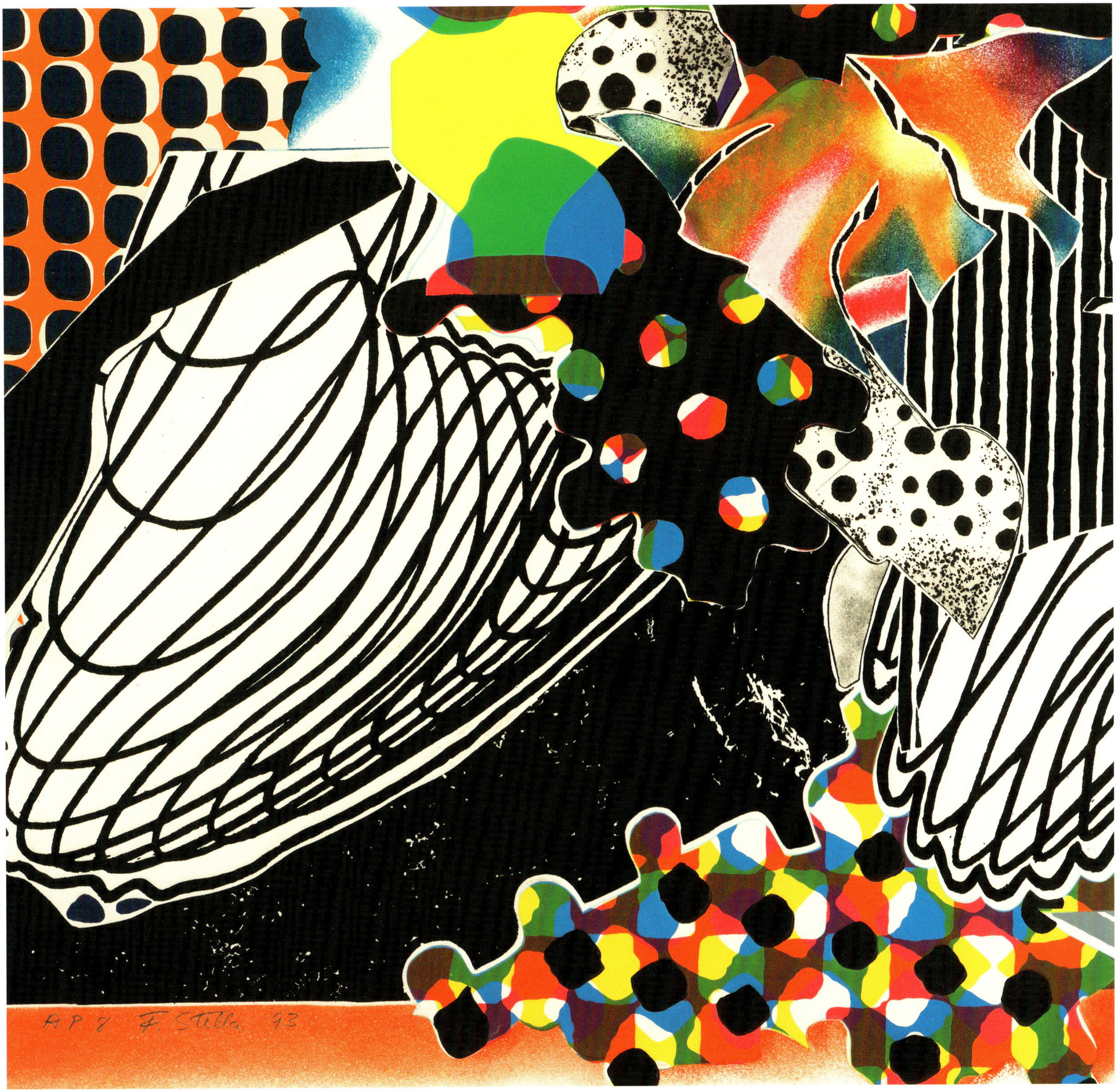

Figure 6 Detail of plate 26, *The Monkey Rope*

intaglio impressions from as many as fifty shaped, etched, and engraved metal plates that were inked by hand and assembled on a carved plywood baseplate for printing—all onto a single sheet of handmade paper.

The text, first published by Alberto Manguel and Gianni Guadalupi in 1980, is difficult to categorize. It is structured as a reference book, an encyclopedia of geographical places that exist only in world literature; however, the entirely fictional nature of its subjects also renders it in the realm of fantasy. Compiled in the spirit of a Victorian Baedeker, the book is complete with scholarly descriptions, maps, and captioned illustrations of fictional locations created by authors from the sixteenth to the twentieth centuries. Melville has fourteen entries, all drawn from his novel *Mardi, and a Voyage Thither* (1849), a fictional travelogue that includes a detailed description of the invented island of Juam. Stella chose Juam, described by Melville as imposing upon first view—a topography of sharp reliefs, where "a dark green pile of cliffs present a range of steep, gable-pointed projections, as if some titanic hammer and chisel had shaped the mass"[26]—as the title for the most complex and technically challenging print from *Imaginary Places* (**plate 38**). He developed the work over two years and also published a small edition of prints from an intermediate state, *Juam, State I* (**plate 37**).[27] For the print, Stella first assembled a disparate range of found and fabricated printing elements, including a large section of flattened honeycombed aluminum, a spiral cut from stainless steel, and shapes produced by pouring molten aluminum and bronze to create, as he would say, "frozen gestures"[28] of the drips and pools as part of the print's matrix. As in all of Stella's intaglio prints made after the *Swan Engravings*, these pieces were fit together on a plywood baseplate, individually inked, and printed in a single impression. The various media of the printing plates ensured that certain lines and planes were embossed with different degrees of relief, and thus spatial depth was both embodied and depicted in the printed image.

26. Manguel and Guadalupi 1980, 190.

27. For a detailed description of the printing of this spectacular work, see Engberg and Stella 1997, 18–31.

28. Stella 2000b, 86–88.

Conclusion: Graphic Art as We Never Imagined It

By the time he published *Imaginary Places*, Stella's work in printmaking was so thoroughly integrated into his practices as a painter and sculptor that it becomes difficult to clearly delineate his work by medium. In 1995 the artist delivered a set of lectures describing the relationship between painting and printmaking in his oeuvre, in which he declared his ambition:

To make a print in which the paper . . . is made into a pictorial surface so that the graphic apprehension of a print is, and must be, a pictorial apprehension as well.

This development could signal the end of graphic art as we know it. On the other hand, it could well be the beginning of graphic art as we never imagined it.[29]

Here, in Stella's vision of printmaking's potential, he summarized exactly what was so radical and innovative in his approach to the prints of these four literary series: that in printmaking he was able to merge illusionistic space and built space and to marry the narrative power of pictures with the challenges of abstraction.

These 1995 lectures became Stella's treatise on printmaking, and they provide a response to the call he had issued in his Norton Lectures, just over a decade prior. While the ostensible subject of Stella's Norton Lectures was painting, the core of his analysis was both more oblique and more focused on the particular subject of depicting space—illusionistic space, material space, and experiential space—through art. The painted and engraved sculptural constructions of the *Circuits* reliefs physically manifest—and therefore easily lend themselves to—Stella's exploration of pictorial space and the possibilities for illusionistic drama in abstraction. Printmaking, a medium driven by the impression of the image on a sheet of paper, may seem an unlikely focus for a consideration of Stella's charge to "find a mode of pictorial expression" that would break through the literal flatness of the painted surface to create a "working space," a pictorial space that engages the viewer in the experience of abstraction, as Caravaggio had in figural narrative painting.[30] However, it was at precisely this moment, in 1984—when Stella cited Caravaggio and Rubens as his artistic ancestors and undertook the *Had Gadya* after illustrations by the abstract master El Lissitzky—that he embarked on a deep exploration of the dramatic, expressive, narrative potential of abstraction. Later, describing this moment of inspiration, he explained:

Abstraction didn't have to be limited to a kind of rectilinear geometry or even a simple curve geometry. It could have a geometry that had a narrative impact. . . . You could have a sense of an abstract piece flowing along and being part of an action or activity.[31]

Frank Stella Unbound takes on this exploration, positing that the formal characteristics and historical models of literature and printmaking served as an essential framework for Stella as he considered the development of abstraction as well as his own place, among those artists whose work he most admired, in the history of art.

29. Stella 2000b, 91.

30. Stella 1986, 4, 35. *Working Space*, the title of Stella's published Norton Lectures, derives from his extended discussion of working space as the site in which a picture is composed: "What painting wants more than anything else is working space—space to grow with and expand into, pictorial space that is capable of direction and movement, pictorial space that encourages unlimited orientation and extension. Painting does not want to be confined by boundaries of edge and surface. It knows from the experience of Caravaggio that if its working space is perceived as real and palpably present, the depicted action will have a chance—it will have room to move and breathe" (Stella 1986, 35). *Frank Stella Unbound* makes the case that it is in printmaking, as much as in painting, that Stella developed techniques of breaking the bounds of edge and surface, and of creating compositions in which the pictorial space is experienced simultaneously as visual illusion and as real, tangibly present material.

31. McCartney 2014.

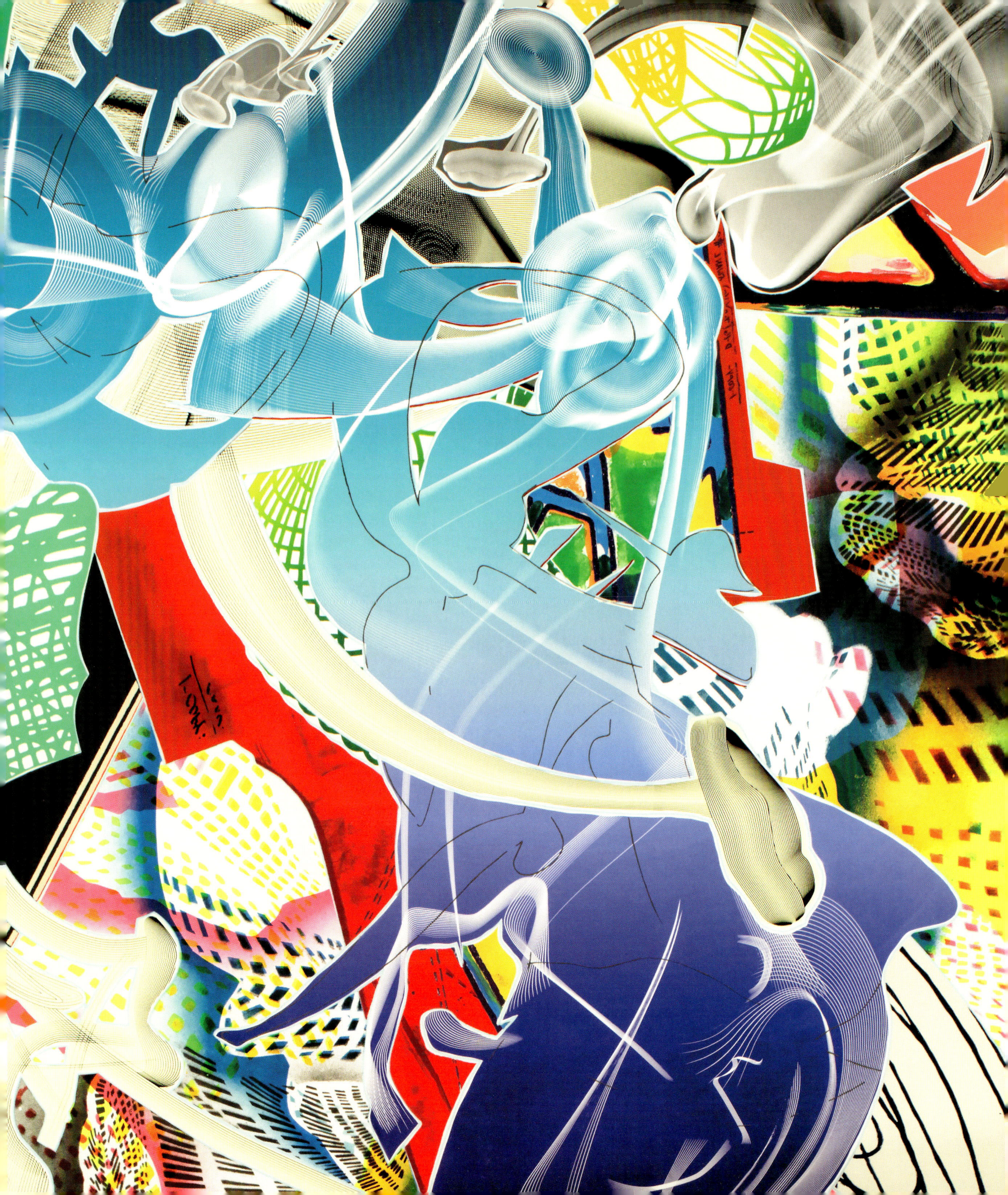

Erica Cooke

> You could tell a story with the shapes. It wouldn't be a literal story, but the shapes and the interaction of the shapes and colors would give you a narrative sense.[1]

Making Literary Impressions: Stella on Abstraction and Its Narrative Foundations

The American artist Frank Stella began to thoroughly connect his artistic production to literature during the 1980s.[2] Specifically, between 1984 and 1999 the artist executed four ambitious print series, each titled after a specific text: the *Had Gadya* (The Only Kid), a moralizing folk song in Aramaic and Hebrew that traditionally is sung at the end of the Passover Seder; *Fiabe italiane* (Italian Folktales), an anthology compiled and retold by Italo Calvino in 1956; Herman Melville's *Moby-Dick*, an iconic American tale first published in 1851; and *The Dictionary of Imaginary Places*, an encyclopedic documentation of fictional terrains selected from literary sources by Alberto Manguel and Gianni Guadalupi and published in 1980. Disparate in their narrative structures and content, these texts share the common trait of enabling Stella to reunite abstract art with elements that had become neglected following the rise of formalism in the mid- to late twentieth century: pictorial illusionism, metaphorical content, and shaped surfaces. Stella's fascination with literature during and following the early 1980s must be understood as his means of overcoming the ways in which formalism limited the experimental scope of abstraction. Ironically, the artist's earliest work was, and continues to be, perceived by art critics, curators, and art historians as an apex of formalism in abstract art.

Stella was only twenty-three years old in 1959, when the Museum of Modern Art (MoMA), New York, exhibited four of his Black Paintings (1958–60)

1. Stella, quoted in McCartney 2014.

2. Hobbs 2011, 20. Hobbs argues that the titles for Stella's early works were "a parody of the Abstract Expressionist penchant for using suggestive titles." He describes art historians repeatedly taking the artist's bait and mistakenly giving these titles too much weight. Brenda Richardson, for example, claims that Stella's *The Marriage of Reason and Hell* refers to J. D. Salinger's story, as well as William Blake's *The Marriage of Heaven and Hell*; Hobbs, however, claims that this title—given to Stella by the artist Carl Andre—underscores both artists' involvement in "the parodic game of discerning the enormous gaps between painted forms and ascribed content." I agree—references to literature in the titles of Stella's early

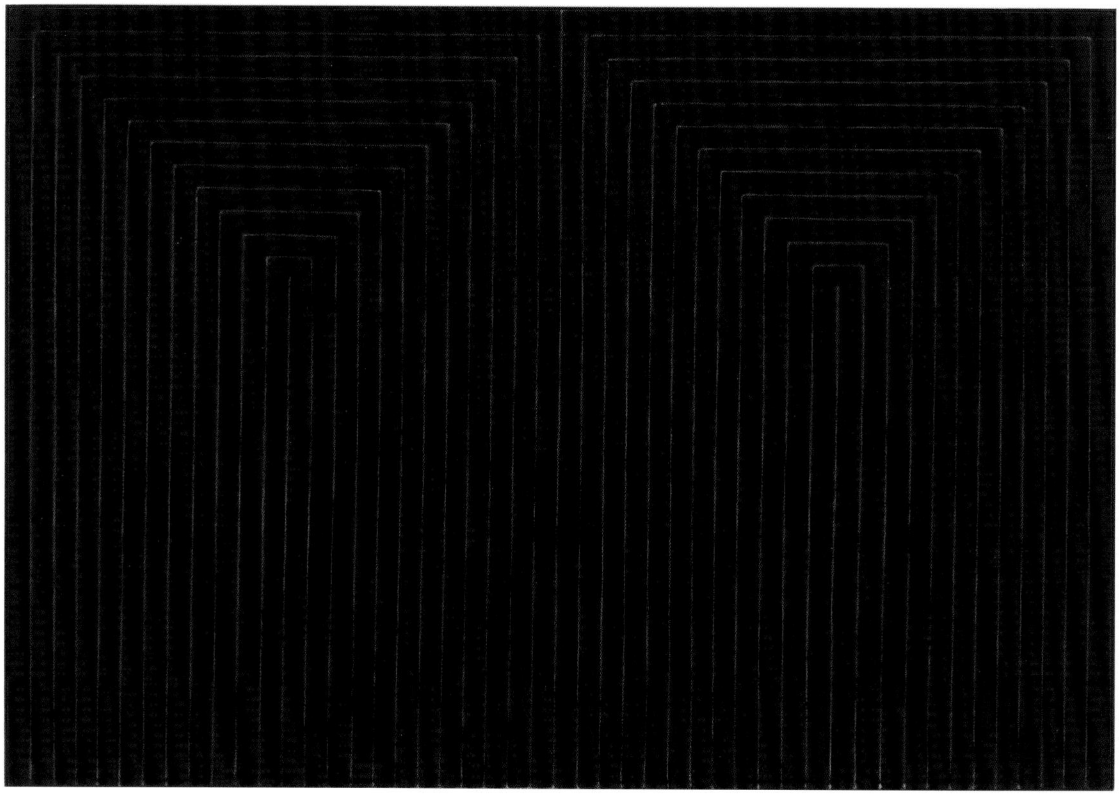

(*figure 1*).[3] These auspicious works, constituted by black stripes painted in symmetrical patterns that reinstate the rectangular shape of the canvas itself, precipitated ongoing debate over their meaning, or lack thereof. The art critic Hilton Kramer, for example, praised these works for their "radical refusal to allow anything suggesting expressionist feeling, organic form, or subjective fantasy."[4] In a similar tone of reductivist celebration, others lauded the Black Paintings for their "monochromatic literal flatness," evincing their appeal to modernist logic and its embrace of only the bare necessities of painting.[5] Stella's subsequent transformation of details—the shape of a canvas, the sheen of a pigment, the symmetry of a composition, the character of a brushstroke—only solidified his seminal status in the new formalist aesthetics that gripped American abstract art in the 1960s. As the art critic Philip Leider wrote: "Stella was crucially interested in keeping his pictures flat because he was crucially interested in making abstract pictures that could survive as post-Pollock art... completely consistent non-referential abstract painting."[6]

The Museum of Modern Art—the very same institution that hosted Stella's debut, and one of the leading museums of his day—granted the artist his first retrospective in 1970.[7] In the exhibition's press release, curator William S. Rubin

works should not be cited as examples of his forging substantial connections between abstract art and literature, which occurred much later in the artist's career.

3. These four paintings from 1959—*Arundel Castle*, *Die Fahne hoch!*, *The Marriage of Reason and Squalor*, and *Tomlinson Court Park*—were included in the group exhibition *16 Americans* (1959), curated by Dorothy Miller. This exhibition was the fifth in the American series and included such diverse artists as Jasper Johns, Louise Nevelson, J. De Feo, Ellsworth Kelly, and Julius Schmidt. MoMA acquired *The Marriage of Reason and Squalor* that year, marking the first purchase of Stella's work by a museum.

Figure 1 Frank Stella, *The Marriage of Reason and Squalor, II,* 1959. Enamel on canvas, 230.5 × 337.2 cm. The Museum of Modern Art, New York. Larry Aldrich Foundation Fund (725.1959)

remarked: "Stella opened one of the few genuinely new paths for abstract art since the Abstract Expressionists," the preceding movement in American painting that thrived in New York City during the 1940s and 1950s.[8] Though seemingly premature, Rubin's assessment of abstraction's history and future vis-à-vis Stella's nascent oeuvre suited the museum that employed him; with its 1936 exhibition *Cubism and Abstract Art*, MoMA had been the first major American institution to produce a narrative model for interpreting early twentieth-century art. Curated by MoMA's founding director, Alfred H. Barr, this ambitious survey, and the illustrative chart published on the catalogue's cover, showcased a sequential evolution of artistic styles—of forms begetting forms—organized into five-year periods from 1890 to 1935 (***figure 2***).[9]

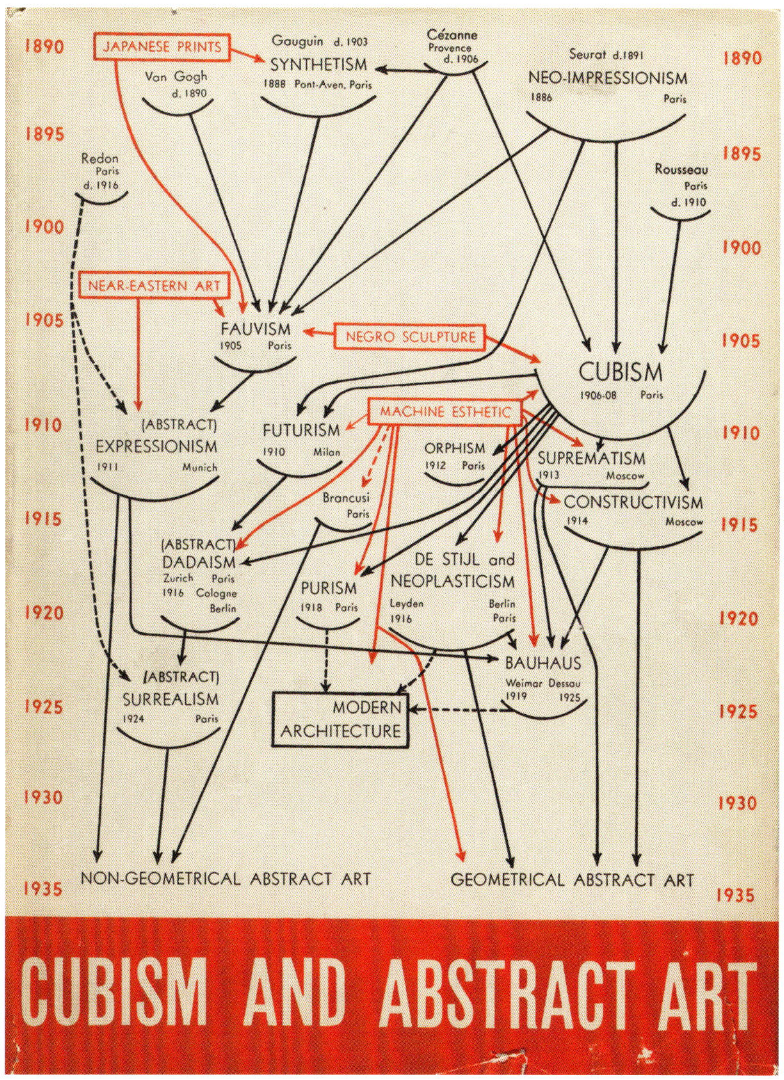

Figure 2 Jacket with chart prepared by Alfred H. Barr Jr., for the exhibition catalogue *Cubism and Abstract Art*, 1936. The Museum of Modern Art, New York, Photographic Archive

4. Kramer 1970. Kramer's list is notable for explicitly describing qualities associated with Abstract Expressionism.

5. De Duve 1990. In his introductory section, De Duve analyzes the prevalent doctrine of Modernism put forth by the art critic Clement Greenberg around mid-century, which argued that painting since Édouard Manet had advanced by nakedly disclosing its unique properties. He positions Stella's early black and aluminum paintings within this Greenbergian lineage of medium specificity, as perhaps the ultimate culmination of painting for mid-century modernism.

6. Leider 1970, 45.

7. *Frank Stella* (1970) traveled to four venues: the Hayward Gallery, London; the Stedelijk Museum, Amsterdam; the Pasadena Museum of Art, California; and the Art Gallery of Ontario, Canada.

8. Museum of Modern Art, New York, press release for the exhibition *Frank Stella*, March 24, 1970, accessed January 2018, https://www.moma.org/documents/moma_press-release_326673.pdf.

9. Museum of Modern Art 1936.

At the time of Stella's 1970 retrospective, Barr's teleological chart of modern art's development, though disputed, continued to inform the contextualization of artists whose work was presented at MoMA, as evidenced by Rubin's determination to periodize Stella—and the artist played his part willingly. During these formative years, his personal relationships with influential art critics, historians, artists, and curators—Michael Fried, Barbara Rose, Carl Andre, and Rubin, to name a few—undoubtedly contributed to his substantial presence in the art world at such a young age.[10] In fact, according to the art critic Harold Rosenberg, Stella—the "art-critical painter"—necessitated steady coupling with that era's "history-revising critic."[11] These critics, Rosenberg surmised, rescued the artist's formalist compositions from being perceived as "conventionally decorative."[12] In effect, these early works were dependent on discourse to furnish the viewer "with clues on how to 'read' them," amounting to what Rosenberg pointedly called "the most professorial paintings in the history of art."[13]

From the vantage point of the 1980s, Stella bemoaned this illustrative momentum in painting—the very quality that Rosenberg had associated with the artist's early work. "What we are left with is illustrated space which we read; what we have lost is created space which we could feel," claimed the artist in his series of six Norton Lectures, delivered at Harvard University in 1983 and 1984; he then traced this "created space which we could feel" through its elliptical manifestations, from the cave painters of Lascaux to Caravaggio to Pollock.[14] He thus rooted abstract art within a historical labyrinth of antecedents that dispenses with linear narrative in favor of networked growth. Likewise, in his production Stella jettisoned the straightforward march of stylistic progression, instead recovering characteristics that had been systematically purged from abstract art by the ideological apparatus of art critics, curators, art historians, and artists who supported formalism.

The Recovery of Illusionism: Had Gadya plates 1–12

Stella found an unexpected cure for his diagnosis of abstract art as "space-blind": illusionism.[15] He intimated that the project of modernism, as advanced in the postwar period by art critics such as Clement Greenberg, was at fault; its ideological bias for medium specificity led too many artists to oversimplify and reduce the spatial condition of abstract painting.[16] To recuperate the "sensation of real presence and real action" in abstract art, he proposed a return to techniques for rendering pictorial three-dimensionality that had been deafened within modernism's wholesale dismissal of illusionism: first, the depiction of volume and mass; second, the creation of interior space; third, the foundational link to everyday

10. Stella and Fried were undergraduate classmates at Princeton University (in the Classes of 1958 and 1959, respectively). Stella and Rose were married from 1961 to 1969. Stella and Andre were in high school together, a year apart, at Phillips Academy, Andover, but never exchanged a hello; they properly met in New York City in June 1958, and Andre often used Stella's studio to work on large-scale sculpture. Rubin was one of the first art critics to write about Stella enthusiastically, in the late 1950s, and became the artist's close friend and avid supporter (he was named MoMA's chief curator of painting and sculpture in 1969).

11. Rosenberg 1970, 108.

12. Rosenberg 1970, 106. Rosenberg borrowed this phrase from Stella, who claimed that his paintings were "so strongly involved with pictorial problems and pictorial concerns that they're not conventionally decorative in any way" (quoted in Rubin 1970, 149).

13. Rosenberg 1970, 106.

14. Stella 1986, 43. For more on these lectures, see p. 13 in this volume.

15. Stella 1986, 46.

16. Greenberg argued specifically for flatness in painting—the very quality that Stella would come to abhor. Greenberg wrote in 1961: "Flatness alone was unique and exclusive to [painting] . . . Flatness, two-dimensionality, was the only condition painting shared with no other art, and so Modernist painting oriented itself to flatness as it did to nothing else." Greenberg 1973, 69.

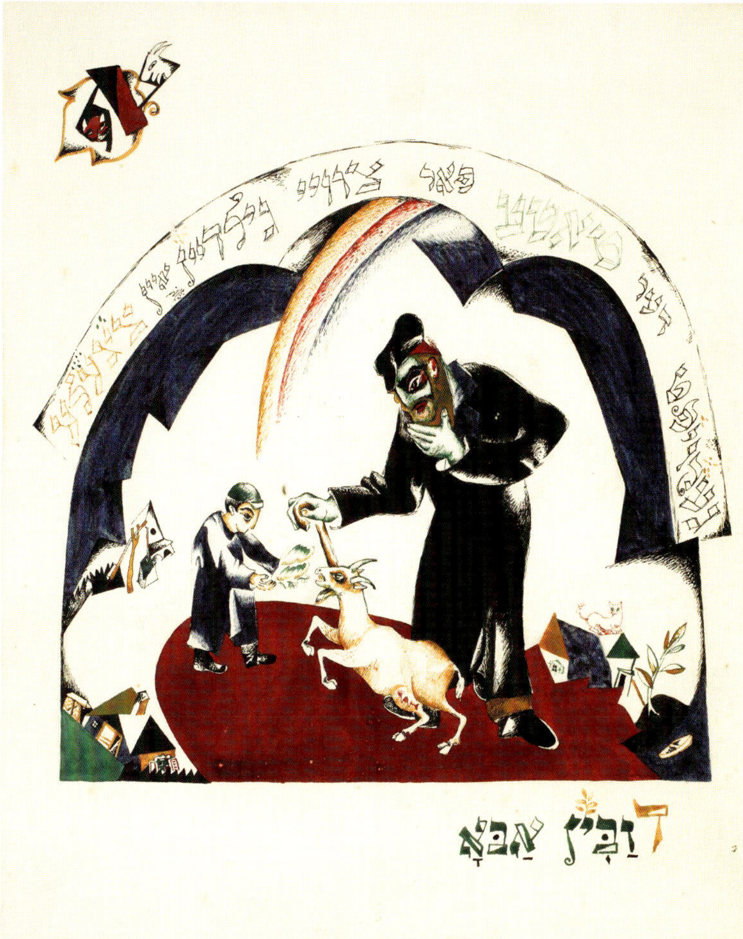

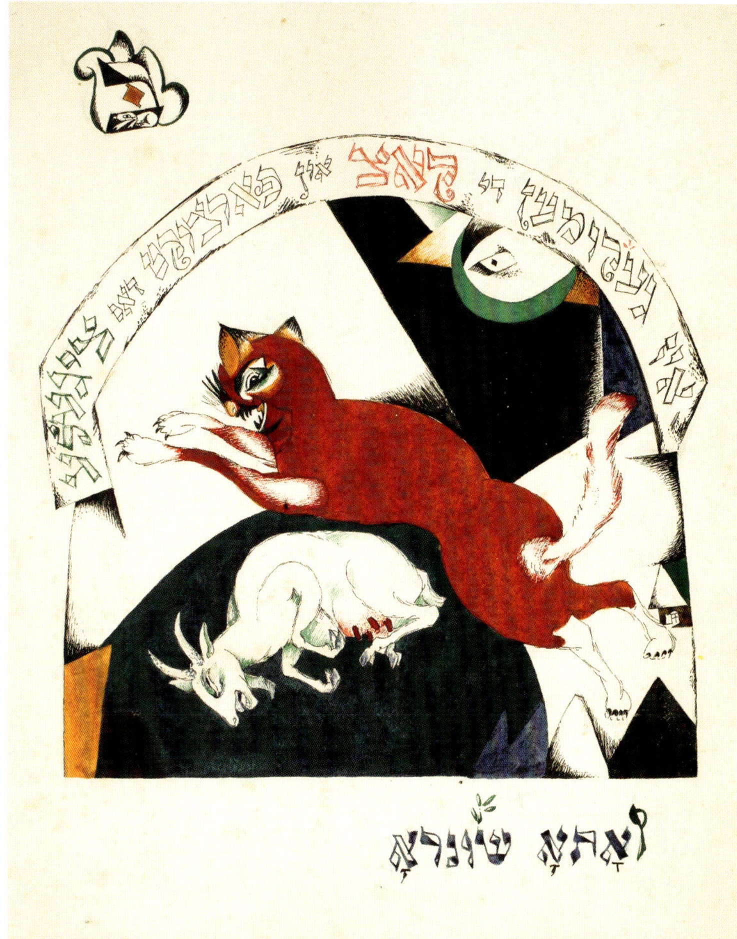

associations.[17] Although elements of these illusionistic techniques surface throughout Stella's oeuvre, the artist's exploration of them significantly advanced in his print series *Illustrations after El Lissitzky's Had Gadya*.

Passover's celebration of the story of Exodus gives way to the common reading of *Had Gadya* as an allegory for religious struggle, its symbols evoking the enemies that the Jewish people defeated throughout history.[18] In 1982, Stella began work on a print series inspired by this redemptive folk song. He had been led to *Had Gadya* through a display of work by the Russian artist El Lissitzky at the Tel Aviv Museum of Art in 1981; on view was a series of gouache paintings that illustrate the song, produced in 1919 as a source for a lithographic book edition (***figures 3–4***).[19] Infused with figurative imagery, symbols of Jewish culture, and text written in the Hebrew alphabet, these watercolors exemplify the less-known early phase of Lissitzky's career, before he engaged with abstract painting and gained status as an avant-garde modernist artist. It was this artist in his former

17. Stella 1986, 97–98.

18. Moshenson 1986, 4. To paraphrase Moshenson: the goat (kid) represents the Jewish nation, and the other characters symbolize its enemies: the cat is the Kingdom of Assyria; the dog, Babylon; the stick, the Kingdom of Persia; the fire, Greece; the water, Rome; the ox, Muslims; the slaughter, the Crusaders; and, lastly, the Angel of Death, the Turks who conquered the land of Israel and prevented its redemption until the holy one intervened.

19. Friedberg 1986–87, 294.

Figures 3–4 El Lissitzky, *One Small Goat Papa Bought for Two Zuzim* and *A Hungry Cat Ate up the Goat*, from the series *Had Gadya*, 1918–19. Gouache and India ink on paper, annotated in Aramaic and Yiddish, 28 × 23 cm. Collection of Tel Aviv Museum of Art, donated by Israel Pollak, Tel Aviv, with assistance from the British Friends of the Art Museums in Israel, London, 1979

years—the Lissitzky who still signed his works with his given Hebrew name, Elixir—to whom Stella paid homage in the title for his series of prints: *Illustrations after El Lissitzky's Had Gadya* (1984).

Populated with folkish depictions of humans, animals, and objects, Lissitzky's version of *Had Gadya* explicitly refers to each of the song's ten verses in ten corresponding watercolors titled with the lyrics: *One Small Goat Papa Bought for Two Zuzim, A Hungry Cat Ate up the Goat, Then Came a Dog and Bit the Cat, Then Came a Stick and Beat the Dog*, and so on. With the introduction in each watercolor of a new character that capriciously destroys the character introduced in the previous work, Lissitzky's series underscores *Had Gadya*'s cumulative action, which interlinks species in the great circle of life. Despite its universal applicability, this series is in fact charged with geopolitical bias. Lissitzky had integrated symbols of the Communist revolution and the victory of the Russian masses, with the intention of persuading the Jewish people of Communist redemption from czarist rule.[20] He therefore distilled *Had Gadya* to its messianic essence—as a metaphor for disrupting the existing order to create a new order—and applied it to the zeitgeist of Russia in the early twentieth century.

Similar to the way in which Lissitzky reworked *Had Gadya* as his response to the political moment of 1919, Stella reworked Lissitzky's version as his means of exploring pictorial space in abstract art during the 1980s. While Stella retained Lissitzky's holistic approach of one image per verse, giving each print the title of a verse, his non-figurative compositions do not illustrate *Had Gadya*'s narrative in the straightforward manner that Lissitzky's figuration had. Rubin explained:

> *It is . . . [important] to conceive of the overall vocabulary of shapes—the cylinders (or pillars), the cones, the "Mickey Mouse," the grilles, the wave-form, etc.—as a kind of cast of characters that may be used interchangeably to act upon one another, to tell a story whose events are more pictorial than literal.*[21]

The diversity and overall inconsistency of the ways in which these shapes "act upon one another" across twelve prints—ten verses plus a front and a back cover—dismiss the sequential unfolding of cumulative action detailed in the verses (as well as in the prints' titles) and depicted through Lissitzky's characters. Nevertheless, scholars, critics, and curators have praised Stella's *Had Gadya* as the first instance in the artist's career in which his abstraction exhibited the possibility for storytelling, and the artist certainly courted this interpretation of "abstract narrative" with his pointed use of the word "illustrations" in the full title of his *Had Gadya* series.

Stella's shapes in *Had Gadya* intimate narrative action through their highly charged relationships. What happens behind, in front of, and around each shape—more shapes, diversified mark-making, framing edges—bespeaks

20. Perloff 2004, v. Perloff documents the stylistic shifts from the 1917 version to the 1919 version, noting that the latter introduced several elements to highlight Lissitzky's interest in the song as a "parable of the Russian Revolution."

21. Rubin 1987, 135.

pictorial drama: "divergences, movements through space, clashes, fusions, metamorphoses, confrontations, obliterations, and all manner of happenings," as Rubin describes.[22] The intense degree of relational activity within the flat picture plane creates the sense of interior space, one of the aspects of traditional illusionism that Stella deemed relevant and salvageable for abstract art in the late twentieth century. Among the shapes responsible for rendering this illusionistic space in *Had Gadya* are drafting templates, specifically the striated cone and truncated cylinder, that Stella appropriated from a late nineteenth-century manual for stereometric measurements (***figure 5***).[23] While these two-dimensional figures were once commonly deployed by architects, engineers, and stone cutters to test their geometric configurations (such as domes and vaults) for structural soundness, more advanced computer drafting systems were in use by the time Stella created these prints. The artist's citation of these antiquated methods for construction deepened his earlier examination of architecture as a metaphor for painting and printmaking.

Stella developed his "idea of building a painting, actually constructing an object for the deliberate purpose of painting on it" as early as the 1970s, when he thoroughly explored the book *Wooden Synagogues* (1959)—a visual chronicle of these religious buildings in Eastern Europe that had been destroyed by the Nazis during the Third Reich.[24] These synagogues, which were perennially rebuilt over the centuries due to the impact of the harsh winter climates, compelled Stella to embrace the notion of craft and construction in his painting. The artist's *Polish Village* series (1970–73) marks the pivotal moment when he rejected the traditional surface of a canvas in favor of an architectonic "object." Works in the series, such as *Pilica II* (***figure 6***), emphasize the artist's innovative deployment of industrial materials, such as pressboard, corrugated cardboard, and Masonite, as well as his radical exploration of interlocking planar surfaces.[25] Akin to oversized jigsaw puzzles—whose piecemeal assembly is still visible even when the puzzle is complete—these paintings underscore Stella's combination of the formal language of abstract art with the structural expression of material construction—a combination previously manifested by, and most often associated with, the Russian avant-garde artists of the early twentieth century, including Lissitzky.

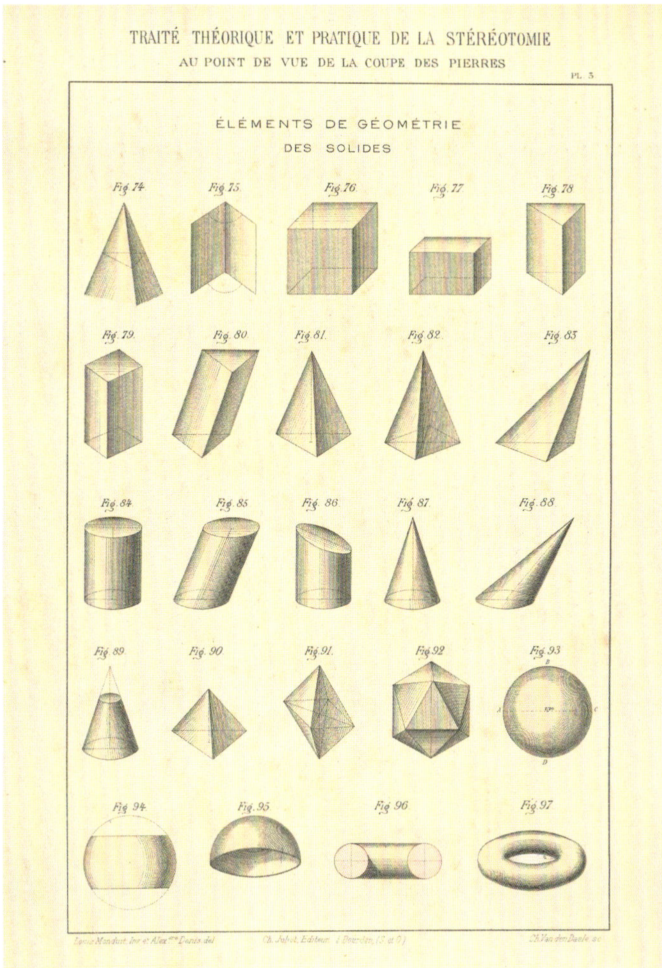

Figure 5 Illustration from Louis Monduit, *Traité théorique et pratique de la stéréotomie: Au point de vue de la coupe des pierres*, 1889. Marquand Library of Art and Archaeology, Princeton University

22. Rubin 1987, 135.

23. Axsom 2016, 270. This manual is Monduit 1889.

24. Quotation from Stella 2000b, 89. See also Salus 2010, 144. Stella received this book from the architect Richard Meier, his close friend and studio-mate in the late 1950s, and read it during an extended hospital stay in 1970—he created a group of 40 drawings during this stay and later made more than 130 large-scale painted constructions.

25. Chanin 2002, 3. Stella claimed to have captured the spirit of local craftsmanship behind synagogue roofs and their inlaid zigzag woodwork: "I invented a word—I think I invented the word; there certainly can't be this word—interlockingness, <laughs> whatever that means, but it was about the carpentry and about the craftsmanship that went into the joining and building of the wooden synagogues and basically of the structure that was built."

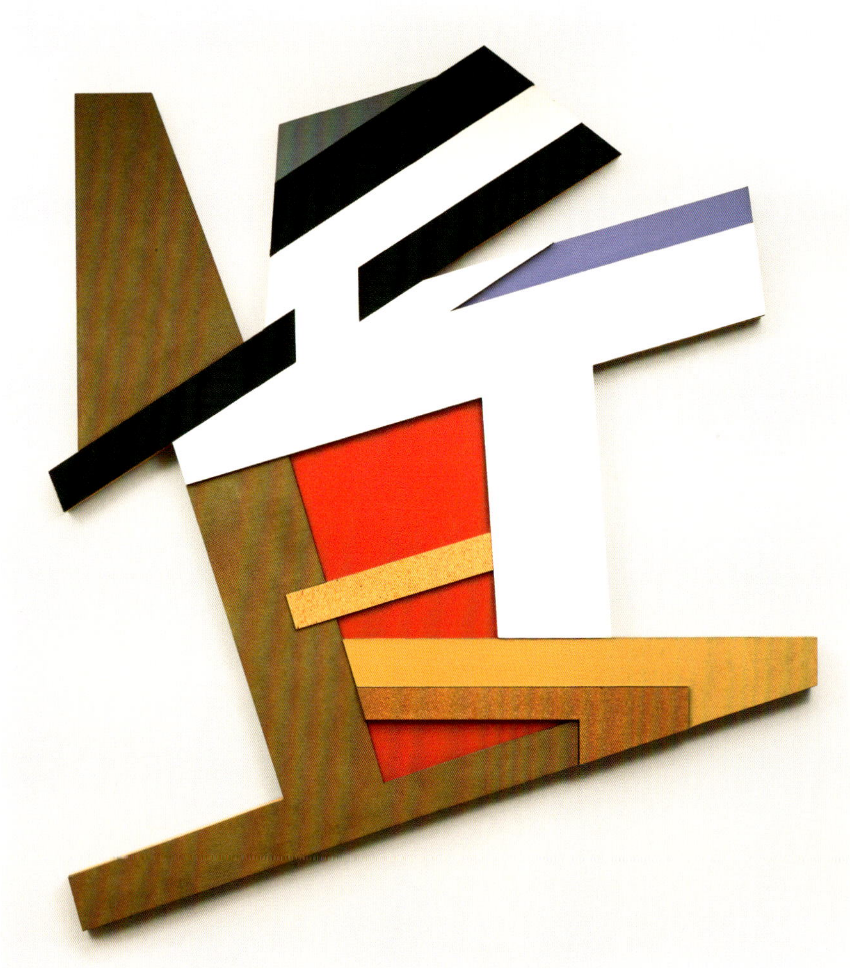

Leider's assessment of certain phases in Stella's work as an "unpremeditated encounter with some earlier point in abstraction" clearly applies to the artist's relationship to Lissitzky. Stella's first encounter with the Russian artist, however, occurred long before his 1981 visit to the Tel Aviv Museum of Art. As early as 1970, Stella unwittingly initiated a conceptual exchange with Lissitzky—in the moment that he opened his copy of *Wooden Synagogues* and consumed in photographs the very buildings that Lissitzky had visited during the 1910s, drawing inspiration for his illustrated versions of *Had Gadya*.[26] In essence, Lissitzky and Stella—in episodes more than fifty years apart—evolved distinct modes of abstraction in response to the very same architectural forms.[27] Dismissing these artists' interest in wooden synagogues as merely coincidental overlooks a persistent intergenerational feature of abstract art—that its imagery is grounded in external phenomena. Both artists, at these transitional moments in their careers

26. Abramsky 1966, 182. Lissitzky went on a joint expedition, on behalf of the Jewish Historical and Ethnographic Society of St. Petersburg, to document old synagogues in Belarus and the Ukraine. He was specifically chosen for the trip because of his background in architecture and engineering. Lissitzky and fellow artist Issachar Ber Ryback engaged in a variety of activities—collecting inscriptions, making rubbings, drafting plans, and producing colored drawings—during their visits to nearly two hundred synagogues over the course of two years (1915–16).

Curator Batsheva Goldman-Ida claimed that these visual records, specifically of eighteenth-century decorations on synagogue walls, guided Lissitzky's Jewish illustrations toward abstraction; such characteristics as "flatness" and details like "anthropomorphic animal faces" most clearly surfaced when Lissitzky painted *Had Gadya* for the second time, in 1919. Goldman-Ida 2014,135.

27. It is unclear whether Stella was or is aware of the fact that he and Lissitzky—separated by more than half a century—evolved aspects of abstraction in response to the same synagogues.

Figure 6 Frank Stella, *Pilica II*, 1973. Mixed media assemblage on wood, 281.3 × 240.7 cm. The Phillips Collection, Washington, D.C. Acquired 1974

(Lissitzky in the 1910s, Stella in the 1970s), devised motifs and compositions from careful observation of the world, especially its material construction.

Stella's second and more explicit encounter with Lissitzky — when he saw the artist's work in Israel during the early 1980s — inspired him to extrapolate the folk song's mode of storytelling and to develop a narrative series based on the "buildable print."[28] In a literal sense, Stella constituted this "buildable print" throughout *Had Gadya* by layering printmaking techniques, such as screenprinting, offset lithography, and linocut, with collaged elements to render three-dimensional effects;[29] in a conceptual sense, he referred to the act of building in these prints through depictions of measuring tools and drafting instruments. Specifically, the artist's stereometric renderings of cones and pillars in his *Had Gadya* series served as the foundation for his subsequent series of high-relief paintings, aptly named *Cones and Pillars* (1984–87), as well as for numerous print series thereafter. Stella's *Had Gadya* thus signified the beginning of his pictorial vocabulary for exploring "abstract narrative" and its insistence on multidimensional space.

28. Stella 2000b, 86.

29. For an exploration of these processes, see p. 20 in this volume.

30. Calvino 1980, xv. Despite the extensive documentation and cataloguing of Italian narratives in the late nineteenth century, Calvino felt by the middle of the twentieth century that his native country lacked a popular master collection of tales akin to those gathered and retold by the Brothers Grimm in Germany.

31. Nerucci, cited in Calvino 1980, xxi. It is important to remember that these folktales are rooted in oral traditions, having existed solely in collective memory until individuals, chiefly folklorists, put to paper what had been orally passed down for generations.

32. Calvino 1980, xxi.

A Novel Syntax for Illusionism: Italian Folktales plates 13–17

Italo Calvino's self-prescribed mission of anthologizing folktales in Italy exceeded the bounds of mere transcription.[30] Whereas exacting repetition saturates the domain of the folk song, with its static lines and rhymes, localized enrichment commands the field of the folktale, with its probing of human vicissitudes and destinies — a characteristic that Calvino acknowledged in the introduction to *Italian Folktales,* which quotes a Tuscan proverb: "The tale is not beautiful if nothing is added to it." Every author therefore weighs convention against invention in selecting "what is woven and rewoven into [the folktale]."[31] Calvino overtly complied with this decentralized model of authorship for his compendium, electing to act as yet another "link in the anonymous chain [of authors] without end."[32] Like the author before him (and the author to follow), he blended narrative elements — words, descriptions, and plotlines — that were proprietary to him, modified from other authors, and uniform to the genre. What distinguishes Calvino's version of each tale is his selection and arrangement of mostly preexisting elements — that is, his diversification of repetition.

Approximately three decades after Calvino's publication of *Italian Folktales*, Stella likewise adhered to this serial matrix when repeatedly engaging these tales in the visual realm. First, the artist titled forty-eight relief paintings in his *Cones and Pillars* series after individual stories from the book (***figure 7***). Soon after, he selected three of these relief paintings and translated their three-dimensional forms into two-dimensional imagery for eight prints, each referring to the source painting in its title: *Bene come il sale (As Dear as Salt)* (***plates 13–16***) exists in four state editions, or five print variations, of the same image, which mirrors its namesake's composition; *La penna di hu (The Peacock Feather)* comprises a color edition that likewise mirrors its namesake's composition, as well as a black-and-white edition that reconfigures the basic shapes within that composition and repositions them along a vertical axis; and *Giufà e la berretta rossa (Giufà and the Red Cap)* (***plate 17***) stands alone as a singular print, departing from its source painting to the greatest degree, with only a handful of shapes that tenuously relate to the painted iteration.

These prints for *Italian Folktales* (1988–89) return to Stella's original mode of sequencing his prints after paintings.[33] This order in production, from the modernist point of view, privileges the source painting and relegates the print(s)

33. Axsom 2016, 224. This was his "default setting" during the first phase of his printmaking career (from its inception in 1967 to approximately 1980). Rubin also notes: "In his earliest prints, Stella did little more than record the catalogue of his paintings—in smaller format." Rubin 1987, 135.

34. For further discussion of Stella's ordering of media, see p. 16 in this volume.

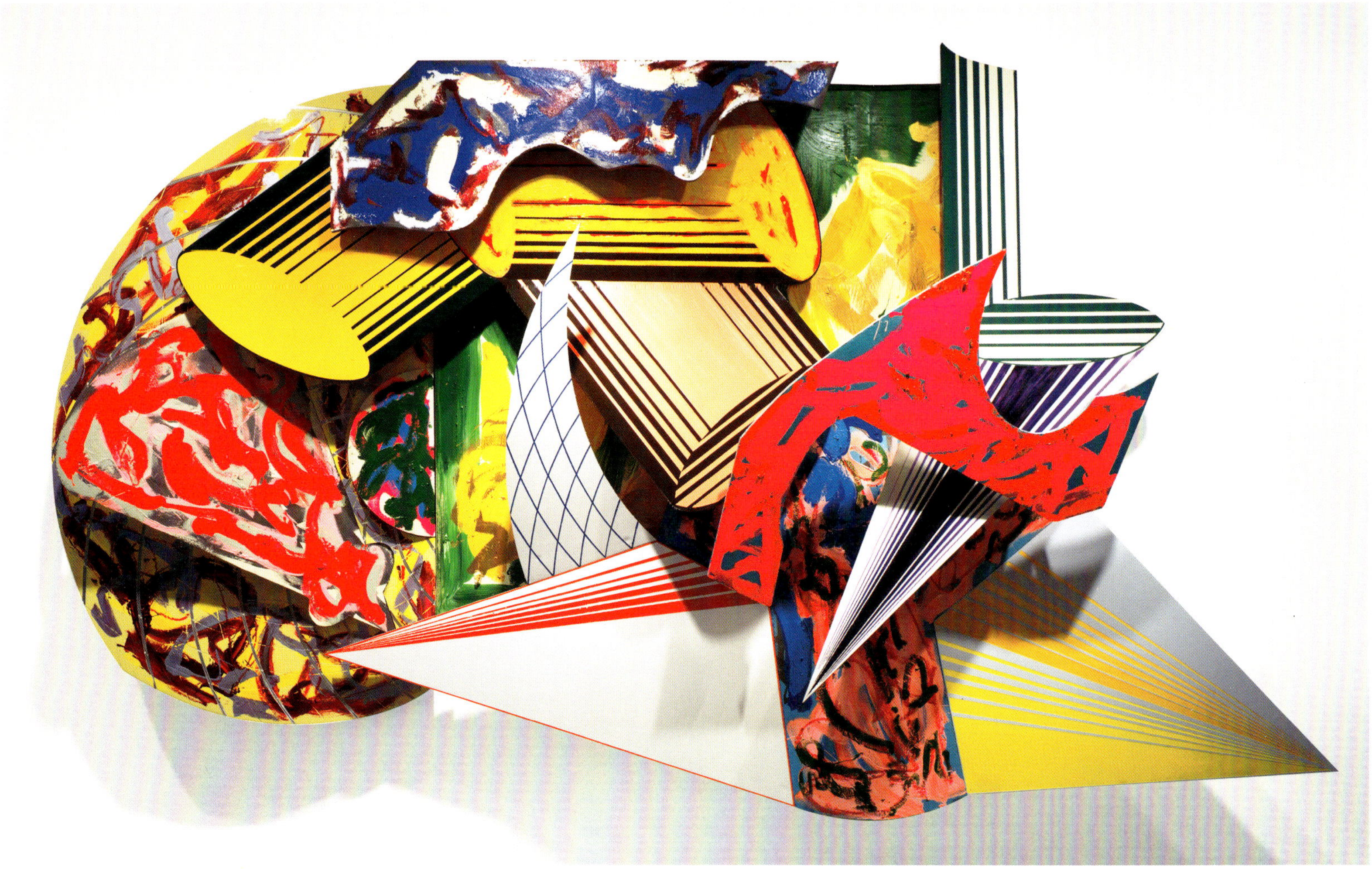

Figure 7 Frank Stella, *Giufà, la luna, i ladri e le guardie*, 1984. Synthetic polymer paint, oil, urethane enamel, fluorescent alkyd, and printing ink on canvas, and etched magnesium, aluminum, and fiberglass, 293.3 × 491.1 × 61 cm. The Museum of Modern Art, New York. Acquired through the James Thrall Soby Bequest (509.1984)

to a secondary and/or documentary status; it also ranks the foundational print above subsequent states of that print.[34] Stella, however, dispensed with this clichéd hierarchy for his works tethered to Calvino's anthology. He treated painting and prints, foundational or made as an edition, on equal footing. The artist achieved qualitative equilibrium among these works by honoring the principle of repetition with variation — the very principle responsible for each folktale's manifestation over time. As if under the operative spell of this genre, Stella retold *Bene come il sale* again and again through a mystifying blend of narrative (in)consistency; he repeated a collaged shape of overlapping architectural tools and geometric forms for all of the works titled after this folktale. Although this collaged shape is the compositional denominator for the six works, it seems to surface anew in every print due to its varied contextualization: both in dimension (relief and paper) as well as with types of mark-making (such as multicolored cross-hatching, monochromatic gestural strokes, and nebulous rainbow stains).[35]

Stella's method of repetition with variation is not always as conspicuous as the collaged shape that announces itself throughout *Bene come il sale*. For example, the artist's two works titled after *Giufà e la berretta rossa* substantially deviate from each other in composition; both painting and print, however, manifest a similar impression of recessional depth and projective space through overlapping, intersecting, and fragmented neighboring shapes that range from drafting tools like the French curve to geometric forms such as the circle and the cone. Illusionism thus arises from these ambiguously layered planes that lack a static background to anchor figure–ground relations. Although Stella eschewed the mathematical model of strict linear perspective commonly associated with illusionism since the Italian Renaissance, his version of illusionism adopted another centuries-old approach to pictorial space.[36]

As the art historian and curator Robert Hobbs explains, Stella took interest in painting from the Baroque period because the pictorial elements in these works achieve the effect of "moving forward and breaking through the picture plane as well as receding behind it into deep picture space."[37] Ultimately, the artist cultivated this type of illusionism — multidimensional and gradually sensed rather than measured and immediately readable — to expand the possibilities of how viewers experienced abstract art in the late twentieth century.[38] "By 1970 abstract painting had lost its ability to create space," claimed Stella in his Norton Lectures:

> *The space in painting became available to eyesight alone, but unfortunately not to eyesight in a pictorial sense, but to eyesight in a literary sense. In a word, it became available to the eyesight of critics rather than that of artists, to the critical, evaluative faculty rather than the pictorial, creative faculty.*[39]

35. For example, the painting *Bene come il sale* projects from the wall, approximately five feet at its farthest point, and thus creates three-dimensional volume in a commonly two-dimensional medium. Simultaneously, the colored parallel lines of graded width running along these projected "cones" and "pillars" signify volume in a three-dimensional form that is already volumetric, a gesture that renders these graphic techniques for shading and modeling useless — but of conceptual interest when considering Stella's movement between two and three dimensions.

36. The mathematical model — developed by the Renaissance mastermind Leon Battista Alberti — locates the viewer as "a Subject in a composed space, not merely a random witness," writes the art historian Donald Preziosi. "Subject and Object are captured and fixed along the centric ray passing back and forth between point of view and vanishing point. The distance between the two is a fully articulated space, rendered either explicitly or implicitly as architectonic — the chessboard of the urban stage." In rejecting this model, Stella also rejected the perspectival ideal that the viewer must exist in a fixed relationship to the work of art. Preziosi 2010, 58.

37. Hobbs 2011, 30. The author details the experiential force of the giant's head in Caravaggio's *David and Goliath* (1610), which Stella had praised during his Norton Lectures.

A Metaphorical Return to Figuration: Moby Dick plates 18–26

Stella's decision to revisit Melville's *Moby-Dick*—a book that he had read in his youth—was fueled by repeated encounters with beluga whales at the New York Aquarium in Brooklyn. In the artist's words from 1989:

> *The idea of the whale reminded me of Moby Dick, so I decided to go back and read the novel and the more I got into it, the more I thought it would be great to use the chapter headings of the novel for the titles of the pieces.*[40]

Indeed, Stella created at least one work for each of the 135 chapters, producing 266 unique works of art in total over the course of twelve years, from 1985 through 1997.[41] The artist's reflections on his engagement with *Moby-Dick* are significantly biographical: Stella once spoke of the book's appeal with reference to his own frustration elucidating abstraction for a general public. According to the art historian Pat Gilmour, Stella insisted, "it had been difficult to establish abstract art at all. People wanted to see themselves in pictures. One of the reasons he had chosen the great white whale as a subject was to address abstraction's inability to tell a story."[42] This purported inability is often related to a stylistic resistance to figuration, suggesting that stories depend upon viewers "seeing themselves" (or some correlative of themselves) in the picture. Presumably, this figure lures the viewer into modes of self-identification that are not merely literal (e.g., "that looks like me," "that point of view is mine") but also conceptual. This figure, for example, acts as a cohesive element within the pictorial space, providing foundational contingency for relationships among compositional elements; it therefore enacts conceptual orientation of the self in formalist terms (e.g., "that compositional unity reflects my will to organization," "those juxtapositions reveal my inner turmoil").

Stella's claim that abstraction cannot tell a story hinges on this belief—that the loss of a relatable figure prohibits the viewer from these modes of self-identification; however, the artist's decision to tether his abstract work to *Moby-Dick* arguably does tell a story—the story of abstraction overcoming its "inability" by capturing the spirit of first-person narration.[43] The "great white whale" in *Moby-Dick* represents limitations in the quest for human knowledge; escaping visibility as it slides beneath the ocean's surface, offering only partial views of its body, this ephemeral creature cannot be accounted for with certainty—especially because in 1851, when the novel was initially published, much of the American public had never seen a whale firsthand. However, the whale does not simply vanish from the mind's eye because it cannot be fully grasped by human sight; in fact, its evasive status magnifies its pervasive existence in the imagination. The "great white whale" is continuously multiplied

38. Whereas Alberti diagnosed artists who did not follow such compositional organization as suffering from horror vacui (fear of the empty), Stella (dis)qualified those who followed the Albertian prescription as falsely assuming actual vision to be measurable and transparent. See Stella 2000a, 57–69.

39. Stella 1986, 43

40. Stella 1989.

41. Wallace 2000, 4.

42. Gilmour 2001, 418.

43. Stella, cited in Tomkins 1984, 54. Abstract art can locate "a viable substitute for the human figure," as Stella once said.

as a fictive image(s), awaiting the first-person narrator to project his or her desires onto it, and ultimately to inhabit its boundless form. As Stella explained, "The whale is an image for me, but it's an image waiting to be filled up. And also it's a number of images, and then there's the business of combining the images."[44] For *The Waves* (1989)—the first of four print series within his magnum opus—Stella did not illustrate the book's chapters for which the prints in this series are named; rather, he forged a formalist link between the troubling nature of the first-person narrative presented in *Moby-Dick* and the search for "a viable substitute for the human figure" in abstract art.

There is not one *Moby-Dick*, but two, as the poet Charles Olson first hypothesized in his groundbreaking book *Call Me Ishmael* (1947).[45] To reprise his theory of the two *Moby-Dicks*: in May 1850, Melville had nearly completed his "whaling voyage," reprising his formula of writing sea tales that derived from his personal experiences working on ships; this "first book did not contain Ahab. It may not, except incidentally, have contained Moby-Dick."[46] Melville, however, never published this conventional adventure quest of sailors aboard the *Pequod* in pursuit of whales; instead, he radically transformed the novel's premise with the creation of Ahab, the tragically flawed captain who operates as a foil for the narrator, Ishmael, as the latter contemplates his own existence.[47] The novel that we know today—published in August 1851—stretches the first-person narrator to exist between two extremes: both providing a standardized account of events and people on the *Pequod* and cultivating a personal voice through metaphysical speculations and discursive information.

In *The Waves*, Stella captured the split nature of Ishmael's existence by layering motifs that are divided between convention and individuality. Evoking convention, the artist appropriated illustrations for ornamental rain gutters that he found in a turn-of-the-century catalogue of cast-iron manufacturers near Glasgow, Scotland.[48] Additionally, he borrowed Chinese folk designs for window lattices that he discovered among the more than twelve hundred examples catalogued by Daniel Sheets Dye in *A Grammar of Chinese Lattice* (1937) (**figure 8**).[49] In terms of individuality, Stella modified the wave shape that he had invented for his *Had Gadya* prints, debuting the wave-whale form that became the most ubiquitous, and arguably most important, motif across media in his enterprise for *Moby Dick* (**figure 9**). For each of the thirteen prints in *The Waves*, the artist combined these three motifs, often in ways that correspond to each element's innate existence as standardized unit or autographic flair. In *The Counterpane* (**plate 19**), for example, the rectangular lattice that nearly covers the print's surface in hexagons and triangles, along with the black-and-white sketch of a rain gutter at the work's center, holds the composition together in a way that makes it akin to scaffolding—scaffolding that then supports the mercurial posturing of the wave-whale form, repeated twice but in asymmetrical fashion.

44. Stella, cited in Wallace 2000, 245.

45. Olson 1997.

46. Olson 1997, 35–37. Olson cites a letter that Melville wrote to Richard Henry Dana on May 1, 1850, about "the whaling voyage": "It will be a strange sort of a book, I fear; blubber is blubber you know; tho you may get oil out of it, the poetry turns as hard as sap from a frozen maple tree;-& to cook the thing up, one must needs throw in a little fancy, which from the nature of the thing, must be ungainly as the gambols of the whales themselves. Yet I mean to give the truth of the thing, spite of this."

47. Olson 1997, 38–39. Olson claims that Melville rewrote his novel based two major influences: his reading of Shakespeare's plays (of which he received a compendium in 1849) and his introduction to the author Nathaniel Hawthorne.

48. Leider 1990, 176.

49. Dye 1937.

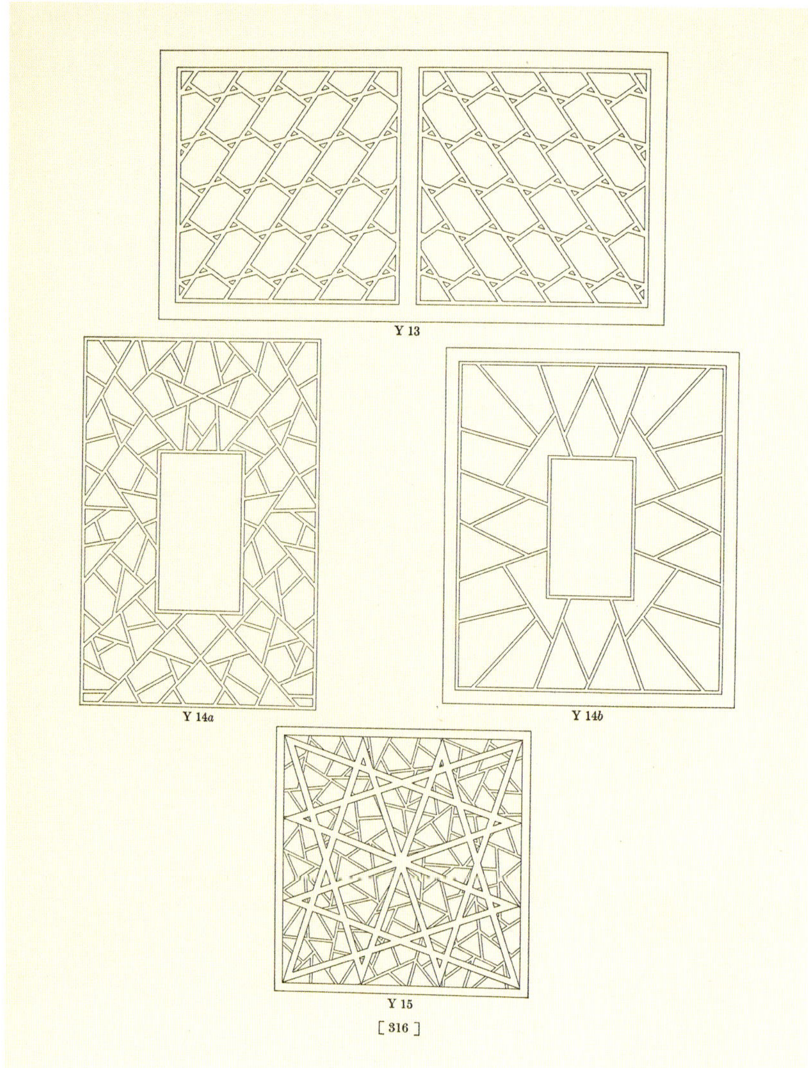

Stella's use of a visual template to anchor aberrant expression echoes various instances in *Moby-Dick* in which Ishmael applies this technique to make sense of what he does not know. For example, Ishmael compulsively gathers information about whales to establish a taxonomy that is deliberately open-ended and able to accommodate deviations. After enumerating various species in the chapter "Cetology" (the science of whales), he writes:

> *If any of the following [uncertain, fugitive, half-fabulous] whales shall hereafter be caught and marked, then he can readily be incorporated into this System . . . I now leave my Cetological System standing thus unfinished . . . This whole book is but a draught—nay, but the draught of a draught.*[50]

50. Melville 2003, 123. "Even as the great Cathedral of Cologne was left, with the crane still standing upon the top of the un-completed tower . . . God keep me from ever completing anything. This whole book is but a draught—nay, but the draught of a draught."

Figure 8 Illustration from Daniel Sheets Dye, *A Grammar of Chinese Lattice*, 1937. Marquand Library of Art and Archaeology, Princeton University

In this chapter, Melville enacts a subtle shift in the point of view of his first-person narrator: from Ishmael the young sailor (embedded in the sequential unfolding of this story) to Ishmael the writer (aware of being the force behind the structuring of this story).[51] This notion of one person, divided, surfaces with greater magnitude in relation to Ishmael's strained efforts to speak on behalf of others. Melville's invention of the "wicked" Ahab for the book's second, published version undoubtedly increased the narrative burden that Ishmael carried. As Olson remarked: "[Ishmael] cries forth the glory of the crew's humanity. Ishmael tells *their* story and *their* tragedy as well as Ahab's, and thus creates the *Moby-Dick* universe in which the Ahab-world is, by the necessity of life—or the Declaration of Independence—*included*."[52] In this interpretation, Ishmael's

51. Bezanson 1953. Bezanson gives the first exhaustive account of the many sides of Ishmael's persona, or selves, throughout the novel.

52. Olson 1997, 58 (italics in original).

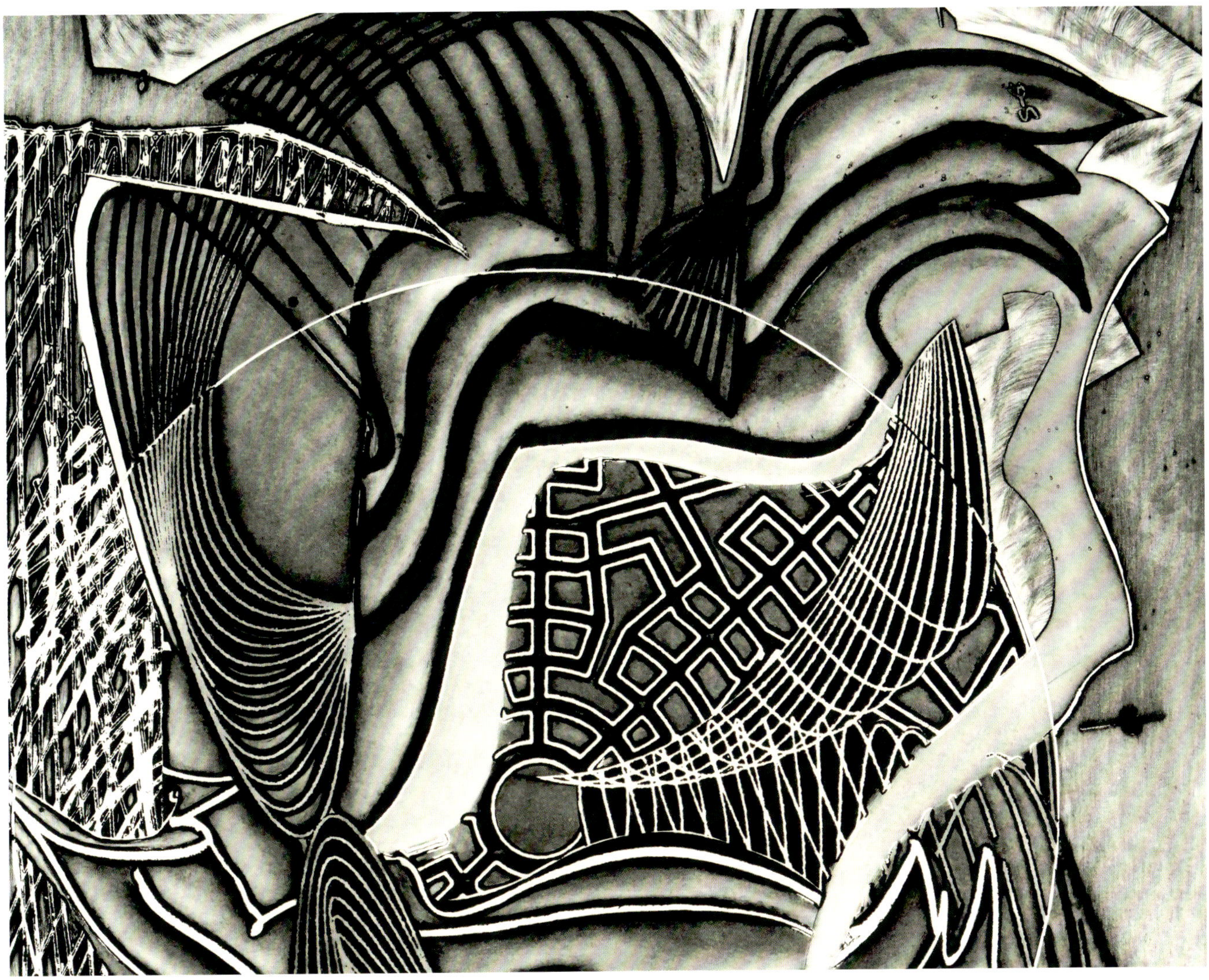

Figure 9 Detail of plate 21, *The Funeral*

burden is also his ticket to freedom, suggesting that the anachronistic survival of Ishmael in literature—the relevancy of his first-person narrative to this day—pivots on its exceptional admission of humanity at its best and worst, "all of her space, the malice, the root."[53]

In his nimble movement from one character's voice to another and finally to his own, Ishmael exists on the theoretical cusp of self-dissolution. This mode of kaleidoscopic activity is also essential to the working methods of an abstract artist—a prejudice articulated by Stella in his Norton Lectures, given in the period just before which he linked his artistic output with *Moby-Dick*. In praise of one of the progenitors of abstraction, Vassily Kandinsky, Stella described this category of artist:

> *[Kandinsky] saw that by simply ignoring the stationary pose of the artist at work, the fixed point of view, he could set the orientation of his own point of view completely free. Instead of using his easel to prop up a window on the world, Kandinsky used it to support a windshield moving through the universe. We see Kandinsky in front of his easel at the controls, confidently aware that both he and his painting are in motion.*[54]

With his series *Moby Dick Deckle Edges* (1993), Stella explored the fullest expression of the artist—himself—"at the controls" by establishing collage, and navigating its spatial incongruities, as a requisite step in the creation of his prints.

Through his preliminary collages for this series, the artist generated a more advanced sensibility for weaving intersecting planes—"putting it down, tucking it under, folding it, and pushing and struggling with it until it conforms to that magical shape in his mind," described Ken Tyler, the master printmaker behind most of Stella's prints produced by Tyler Graphics. Whereas earlier series of prints for *Moby Dick* "had taken large chunks and put them together," *Moby Dick Deckle Edges* responded to an actual collage and the necessity of producing its "folded-over version" in print.[55] These nine large-scale works are the most visually compressed of Stella's prints for *Moby Dick*. Together, the prints comprise a dizzying array of shapes and patterns in contrasting palettes that cannot be contained within illusory rectangular frames; their pictorial spillage is an artificial counterpart to the uneven "deckle edges" that result from traditional papermaking processes.

Due to the general tenor of excess found in such prints as *The Monkey Rope* (***plate 26***), with its sweeping horizontal proportions, the artist's later production of abstract art has been characterized as "maximalist"—a pronounced distinction from his prevalent association with Minimal art during the first decade of his career.[56] In fact, Stella had unintentionally authored one of the cornerstones of Minimalism with his 1964 statement "What you see is what you see"—deployed then, and still today, by those who believe that art's meaning

53. Olson 1997, 15. Also, Melville wrote to the author Nathaniel Hawthorne: "That is the Ahab-world, and it is wicked." Cited in Olson 1997, 54.

54. Stella 1986, 89.

55. Ken Tyler, cited in Wallace 2000, 221.

56. Barber 1998, 4. Barber notes in the introduction to her interview: "[Stella's] work since the mid-1960s has been increasingly complicated, colorful, mannerist, extravagant, so that his friends teasingly call him 'FATHER OF MINIMALISM—MOTHER OF MAXIMALISM.'"

is wholly present to the viewer: instantaneously available to his or her sight with nothing deferred or obscured.[57] This interpretive conceit falters with the metaphoric intimation of occupied interior space in Stella's prints for *Moby Dick Domes* (1992). The artist here tested the physical boundaries of what his flat prints comprising the *Moby Dick Engravings* could withstand when pushed toward three-dimensionality.[58]

For *The Cabin. Ahab and Starbuck (Dome)* (*plate 22*), Stella, working with Tyler Graphics, recycled the rectangular plate from the *Moby Dick Engraving* bearing the same title but replaced the flat, circular section at center with a dome-shaped plate, causing the paper to protrude six inches from the large picture plane of approximately six feet by four feet (*figures 10–13*). For each sequence of engraving and dome, he repeated this innovative process of shaping a single sheet of paper—without tearing it or adding collaged elements—and substituted the engraving's tonal gray scale with dynamic colors for the domes. This combination of spherical depth and explosive palette brings volumetric life to the tangible surface of each dome print, repeatedly referred to by both artist and printmaker as "pregnant."[59] In *The Cabin. Ahab and Starbuck (Dome)*, several motifs, like the white wave-whale form, exist on both the flat and curved planes, traversing the juncture between them and giving the impression of paper actively swelling. The viewer's sensation of these dome prints as precariously withholding information—as if on the brink of bursting and releasing what lies beneath—extends to the corpus of works in Stella's *Moby Dick*.

Any individual's experience of Stella's *Moby Dick* is "necessarily incomplete," remarks the art historian Robert Wallace, who penned an entire book on Stella's relationship to this novel but has yet to see all of the extant works after a decadelong pursuit.[60] This notion of the viewer never grasping *Moby Dick* in its entirety correlates to the fact that the artist lacked a controlling vision of this enterprise from its inception. Even Stella's preliminary decision to title works after chapters neither limited his production to the novel's structure (he far surpassed the model of one work per chapter) nor determined the iconography of individual pieces (he retroactively assigned titles with no intention of mirroring literary content in visual form). Ultimately, the artist's self-conception as protagonist—to "keep [*Moby Dick*] going"—is suitably ambiguous for this classic literary narrative and the elusive presence of its first-person narrator. "There is no staying in any one place; for at one and the same time everything has to be done everywhere," states Ishmael. "It is much the same with him who endeavors the description of the scene."[61] Or, in the case of Stella, it is much the same with the abstract artist who innovatively pursues the spirit of a lost human figure in pictorial space.[62]

57. Stella, cited in Glaser 1995.

58. For more on this series, see p. 25 in this volume.

59. Wallace 2000, 151.

60. Wallace, cited in Dimock 2014, 156. Dimock remarks that Wallace, the quintessential viewer, has seen "only 129 of the 135 chapter titles, and only 177 of the existing 300 artworks. The others are in private collections and not available."

61. Melville 2003, 260.

62. Stella 2000a, 65. "That's what it takes to make most people believe that a painting looks real," the artist wrote in his treatise on perception, "Grimm's Ecstacy" (1991). "It's hard for us to admit, but we believe abstraction must inhabit the same pictorial space that makes figuration convincing."

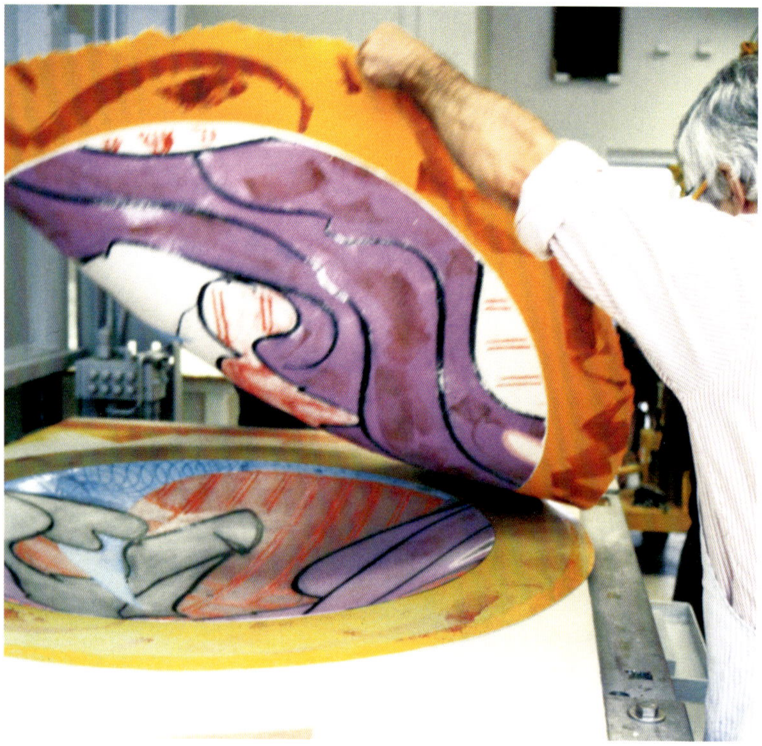

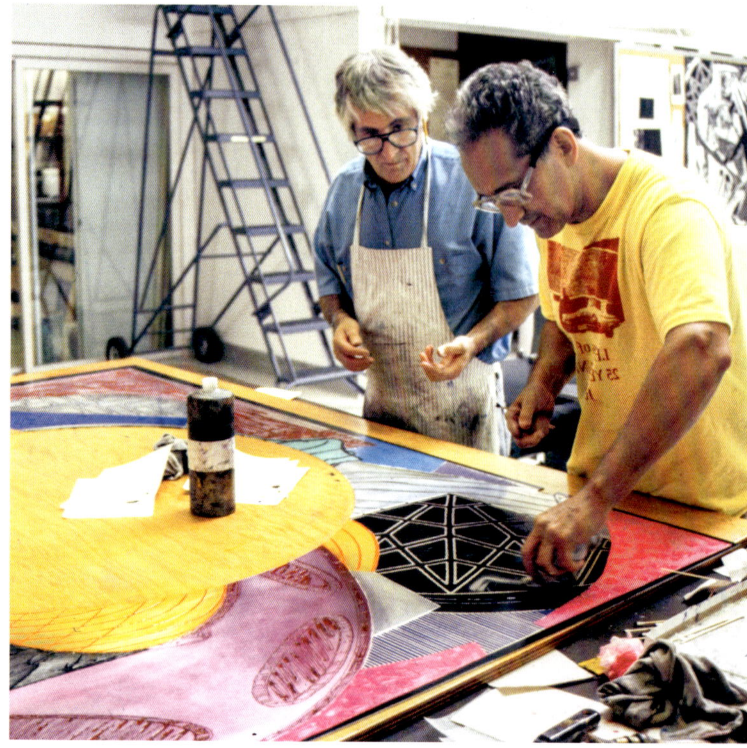

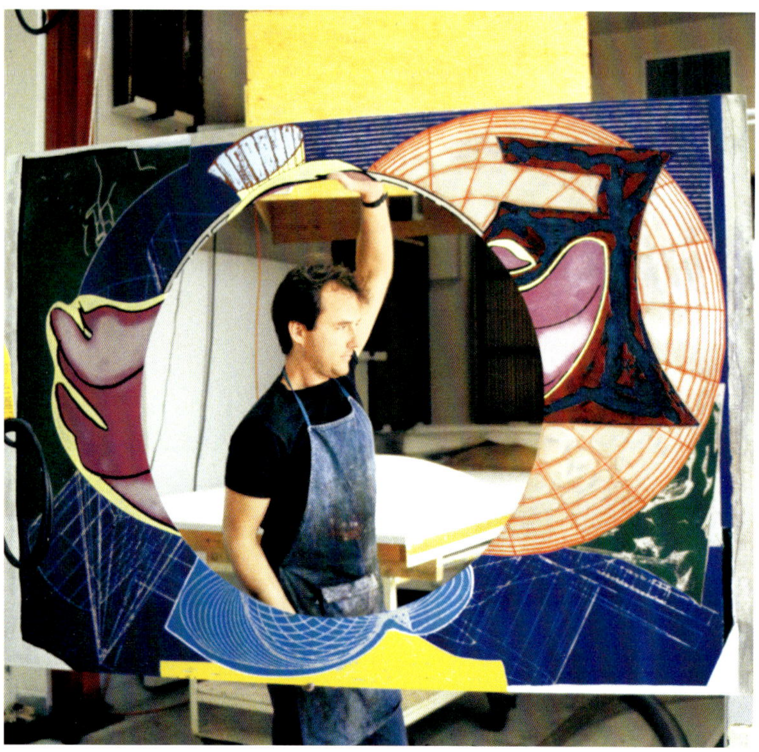

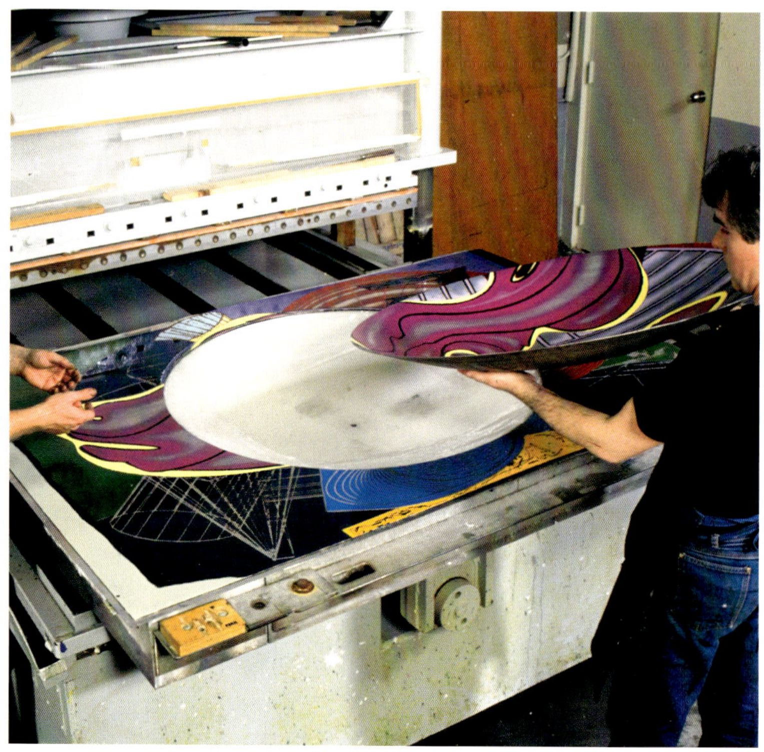

Figures 10–13 Kenneth Tyler, Frank Stella, and printmakers at Tyler Graphics at work on *Moby Dick Domes*, Mount Kisco, New York, 1988–91. National Gallery of Australia, Canberra. Gift of Kenneth Tyler, 2002

The Relief of Shaping Surfaces: Imaginary Places plates 27–41

Through his rigorous engagement with Melville's *Moby-Dick*, Stella circuitously reconnected with the artistic vanguard of his youth, the Abstract Expressionists, who had used this novel as "one of the few acceptable legacies of the American past."[63] In similar style, Stella was now, from the 1980s onward, treating Abstract Expressionism as one of the few acceptable progenitors of his illustrious career, despite his fraught relationship with this movement during his formative years.[64] Stella's descriptive passage on the webbed skeins of the artist Jackson Pollock, taken from the Norton Lectures, aligned the gestural abstraction of this artist with the dramatic narrative space of Caravaggio:

> *The question of where the paint skeins are in relation to the painting's surface is an important one because it seeks to define the working space of abstract painting. The fact that this working space is defined by a contradiction which allows the paint skeins to be* in two places at the same time *should give us pause.*[65]

Stella's decisive qualification of "working space" therefore hinges upon inexplicable surface activity—a tension between materiality and illusion—that renders motion in a static medium. He further substantiated these thoughts in the late 1980s and 1990s through recurring citations of Pollock and other Abstract Expressionists, claiming that their brushwork—the skeins, strokes, swipes, and other painterly excesses—forged a "kind of abstract naturalism by supplying a representation of motion apparently caught in the medium of paint."[66]

Stella conspicuously adopted this "abstract naturalism" from 1994 to 1999, when producing prints whose titles came from fictional locations catalogued in *The Dictionary of Imaginary Places*. This body of work—three print series and seven individual prints—stands at a high-water mark of the artist's exploration of printmaking techniques that conflate surface as shape, and vice versa. For *Juam* (***plate 38***), named for the fictional island in Melville's novel *Mardi* (1849), Stella deployed a wooden base embedded with nearly 150 metal plates of varying shapes and sizes to pull a single impression.[67] This type of "relief printing," according to the artist, translates the "apprehended gesture of motion into a stamped-out immediate impression," which, in turn, self-reflexively reveals that "the immediate action of creating the image truly mimics the image."[68]

Stella's "frozen gesture" thus enlivens the pictorial fantasy of Abstract Expressionism—that the viewer bears witness to action within a static medium—by impregnating the support itself with a sense of motion. Similar to Tyler Graphics' innovation of a type of handmade paper to withstand spherical stretching for *Moby Dick Domes*, Stella's primary printmaking studio once again experimented with topographical permutations of its handmade paper for *Juam*,

63. Motherwell, cited in Schultz 1995, 126.

64. Tomkins 1984, 63. Tomkins noted that Stella's Black Paintings of 1958–60 had been perceived as "a rebuke to the 'painterly' excesses of Abstract Expressionism."

65. Stella 1986, 84 (emphasis mine).

66. Stella, 2000b.

67. For *Juam*, Stella started with a working collage, which had become his customary first step since *Moby Dick Deckle Edges*; over the course of two years, he reworked and translated this preparatory collage into 40 aluminum plates and 102 irregularly shaped metal elements; he then embedded these within a single woodblock base to create a one-hit impression. For further details, see p. 28 in this volume.

68. Stella 2000b, 87.

accommodating the heavily embossed impression from this poured-metal relief plate. The studio also invented for this series a vacuum-forming relief technique that shaped paper molds and printing elements for such prints as *Perinthia* (*plate 35*), named after Calvino's imaginary city in his novel *Le città invisibili* (Invisible Cities, 1972). *Perinthia*'s complex paper structure — accentuated by the print's monumental scale of nearly two and a half feet in diameter — conjures the fantastical effect of motion for the viewer, who seems to be imagining a landscape with a dynamic surface that undulates across valleys, plains, and mountains.

Around the period during which he produced prints of *Imaginary Places*, Stella, in his lectures, interviews, and writing, firmly placed his relief printing within the lineage of painting via Abstract Expressionism. The artist's discursive maneuvers to disassociate his works from specific artistic movements seem to belatedly answer prevalent critical inquiries regarding the ontological status of his works during the 1960s.[69] "Frank Stella says that he is doing paintings, and his work could be considered as painting," observed the Minimal artist Donald Judd in 1964 before asserting his contrarian view: "Most of the works, though, suggest slabs, since they project more than usual."[70] Judd thus proposed that Stella's earliest works, with their unusually thick sides, not be read as *paintings*, but rather as three-dimensional *objects* and as progenitors to Minimalism, the 1960s movement most known for simplified geometric forms made of industrial materials.

Situating Stella's oeuvre within the lineage of sculpture, however, deafens the revolutionary impact of his shaped surfaces as reinvigorating *pictorial* space — and therefore explains why the artist eschewed associations of his works with postwar sculpture.[71] Stella remained steadfast in his commitment to proving the historical existence and future viability of relief within the pictorial field. "From the beginning, say the caves at Lascaux, painting has accommodated, if not sought, a variety of surfaces and shapes," argued the artist during a lecture in 1995:

> *Our idea of a painting convention, the flat pictorial rectangle, usually a version of a view out the window, is really not the norm we generally think it is in the history of Western art. Painting in the ancient world covered a great variety of surfaces — the insides and outsides of buildings, the insides of tombs and the outsides of the funerary vessels.*[72]

For Stella, the future livelihood of painting depended on excavation of the medium's past.

69. Leider 1970, 47. "It is precisely Stella's ambivalence about the literalist implications of his own paintings that is fundamental to what he is all about," wrote Leider, before describing how easily the artist's early work had been instrumentalized by various camps and their distinct periodization of art history. By the 1980s it could no longer be said that Stella was ambivalent, given his extensive verbal commentary on both his work and art history at large.

70. Judd 1975, 153.

71. See De Duve 1990, 305n50. The author argues that "Stella always rejected this interpretation, saying that he does not consider the stretcher's thickness as a function of the painting's module and that, for him, the shadow cast by the stretcher on the wall . . . far from turning the painting into an object, was meant to emphasize its two-dimensionality." Another dominant argument against reading Stella's painting as "object" came from the art critic Michael Fried, also a longtime ally of Stella, who elaborated on why three-dimensional art failed to meet the standards of Greenbergian modernism in his seminal essay "Art and Objecthood" (1967); he stated that immersion in the artwork's formal composition — its shape, material, and color — would lift the viewer out of everyday temporality and validate his or her existence as a unified subject within an idealistic order. Fried's urge to claim a higher purpose for medium-driven qualifications arose from concerns that without such qualifications painting would be subject to literalist interpretations, becoming nothing more than a conventional "object." He famously motioned toward art's higher

Conclusion: Rewriting Abstraction

Stella claimed in the early 1980s that his work was "determined by the fact that [he] was born in 1936," obliquely eulogizing his own oeuvre for capturing the zeitgeist of twentieth-century art history: to celebrate and interrogate abstraction in turns.[73] Even a literal reading of this statement invites a desirable correlation between Stella's biography and America's earliest story of abstraction writ large: Barr's 1936 exhibition *Cubism and Abstract Art*. As part of the first generation of American artists to develop professionally within an environment dominated by abstract art, Stella felt an emboldened sense of responsibility to both sustain its relevancy within a larger narrative of art history and to be a participant in its stylistic progression.[74]

Although Stella courted the critical discourse of formalism during his early years of production, this discourse evolved in a manner that constrained, rather than broadened, the scope of abstraction.[75] By the early 1980s, the artist sought to reintegrate characteristics that had been identified as bêtes noires by the ideological apparatus of art critics, curators, art historians, and artists behind formalism — these characteristics included pictorial illusionism, metaphorical content, and shaped surfaces. For Stella, coupling abstract art with literary narratives and printmaking techniques proved to be ideal for manifesting these undervalued characteristics.

purpose in the essay's concluding sentence: "Presentness is grace." See Fried 1998.

72. Stella 2000b, 89.

73. Stella, cited in Tomkins 1984, 57. Although Tomkins does not provide the source for this quote, the artist expressed a similar sentiment around the time of this *New Yorker* profile; he tied his birth year to the project of abstraction, stating, "access to abstraction to anyone born after 1936 is direct and unencumbered" (Stella 1986, 164).

74. Stella 1986, 155–58. Stella explained: "It was not enough to worry that in the pursuit of art one might fail to catch up to it; in addition, one had to worry about doing part of the job to keep it running. The change from student to participant changed my position as an observer of art making and art history."

75. Stella, cited in Hobbs 2011, 26. "The popular denigration of formalism lasting from the 1970s to the 1990s probably wouldn't have been so consequential if it had been limited to critical and academic discourse," wrote Stella in 1999. "Unfortunately it spread to the practicing art world and made painting the target and foil for all the newer art activities which saw themselves as the successors of painting."

Illustrations after
El Lissitzky's Had Gadya
1984

Between 1917 and 1919, the Russian artist El Lissitzky created two sets of gouache illustrations for a title page and the ten verses of *Had Gadya*, a concatenated children's song traditionally sung at the end of the Passover Seder. In the first, the artist worked in a folk-art–inspired style; however, as he returned to the subjects, Lissitzky transformed the letters and figures of each scene into flat geometric shapes arranged in interlocking planes, thus marking the artist's transition from depicting subjects of Jewish cultural heritage to practicing avant-garde abstraction. The later set — published in 1919 as a book of color lithographs in an edition of seventy-five copies — captures the influences of Futurism and Russian Supremativism, as well as the dynamic optimism of the Bolshevik Revolution. The illustrations' formal integration of image and text is considered a milestone in twentieth-century book design.

plate 1 *Had Gadya: Front Cover*, 1984

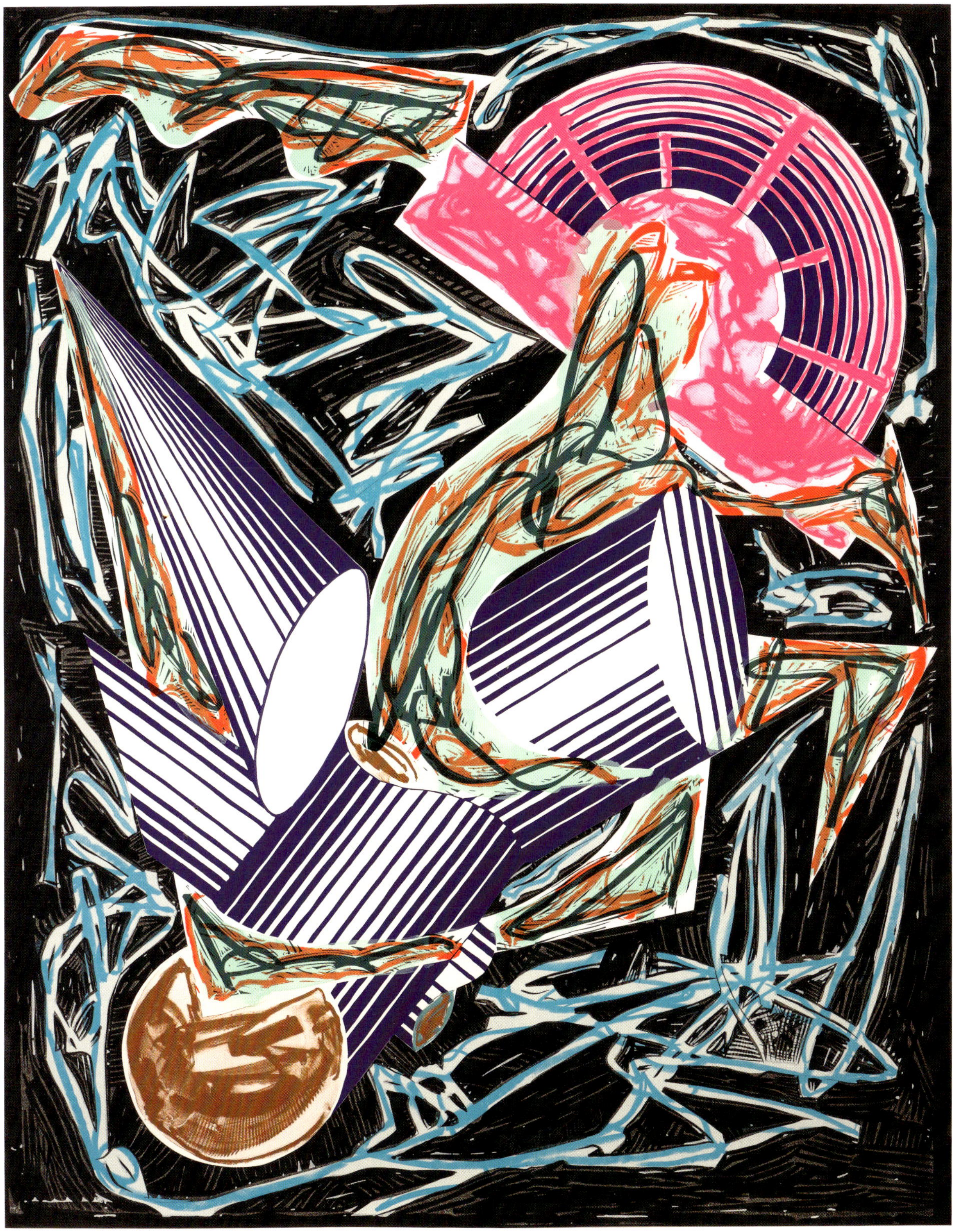

plate 2 *One Small Goat Papa Bought for Two Zuzim*, 1984

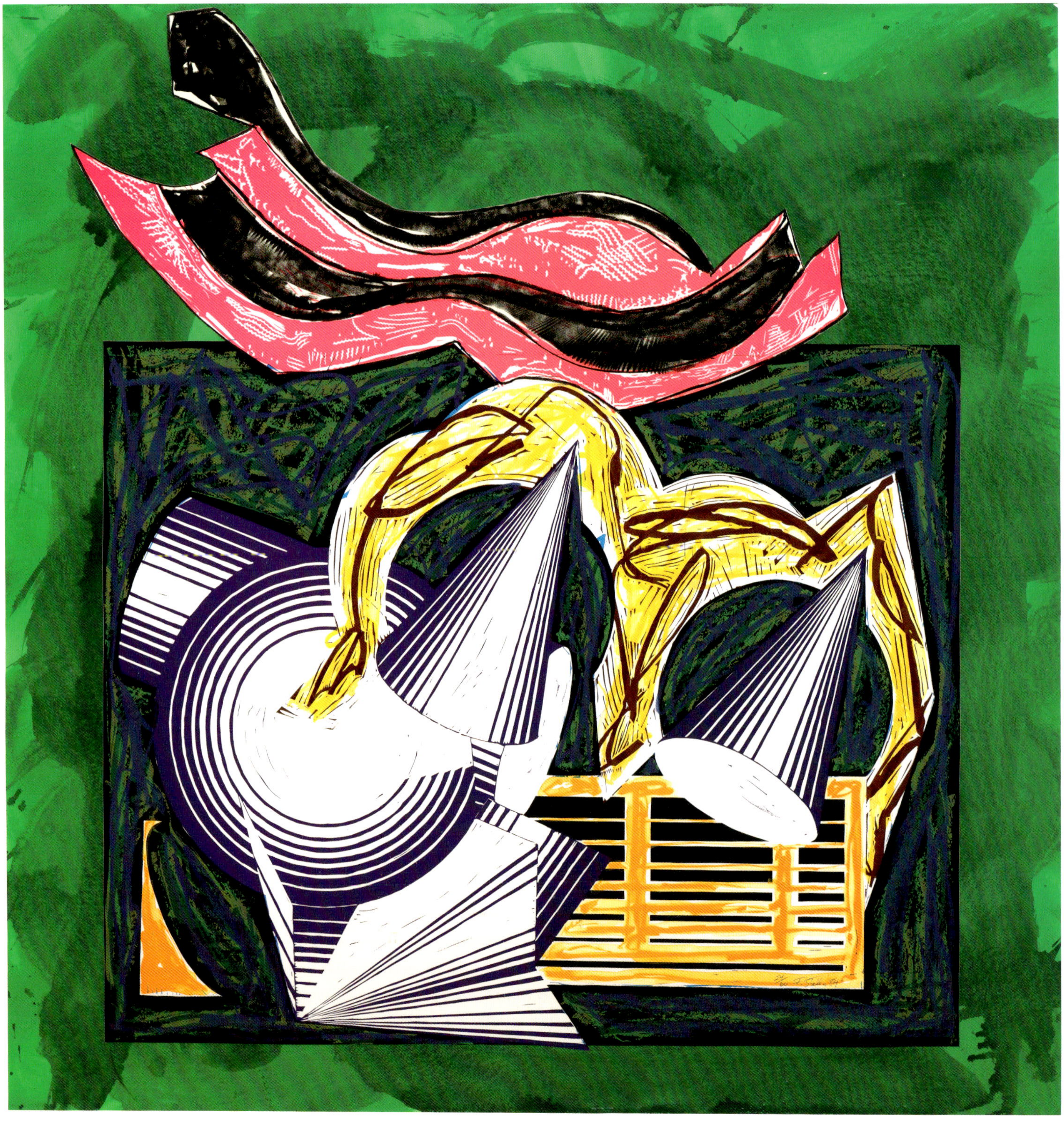

plate 3 *A Hungry Cat Ate up the Goat*, 1984

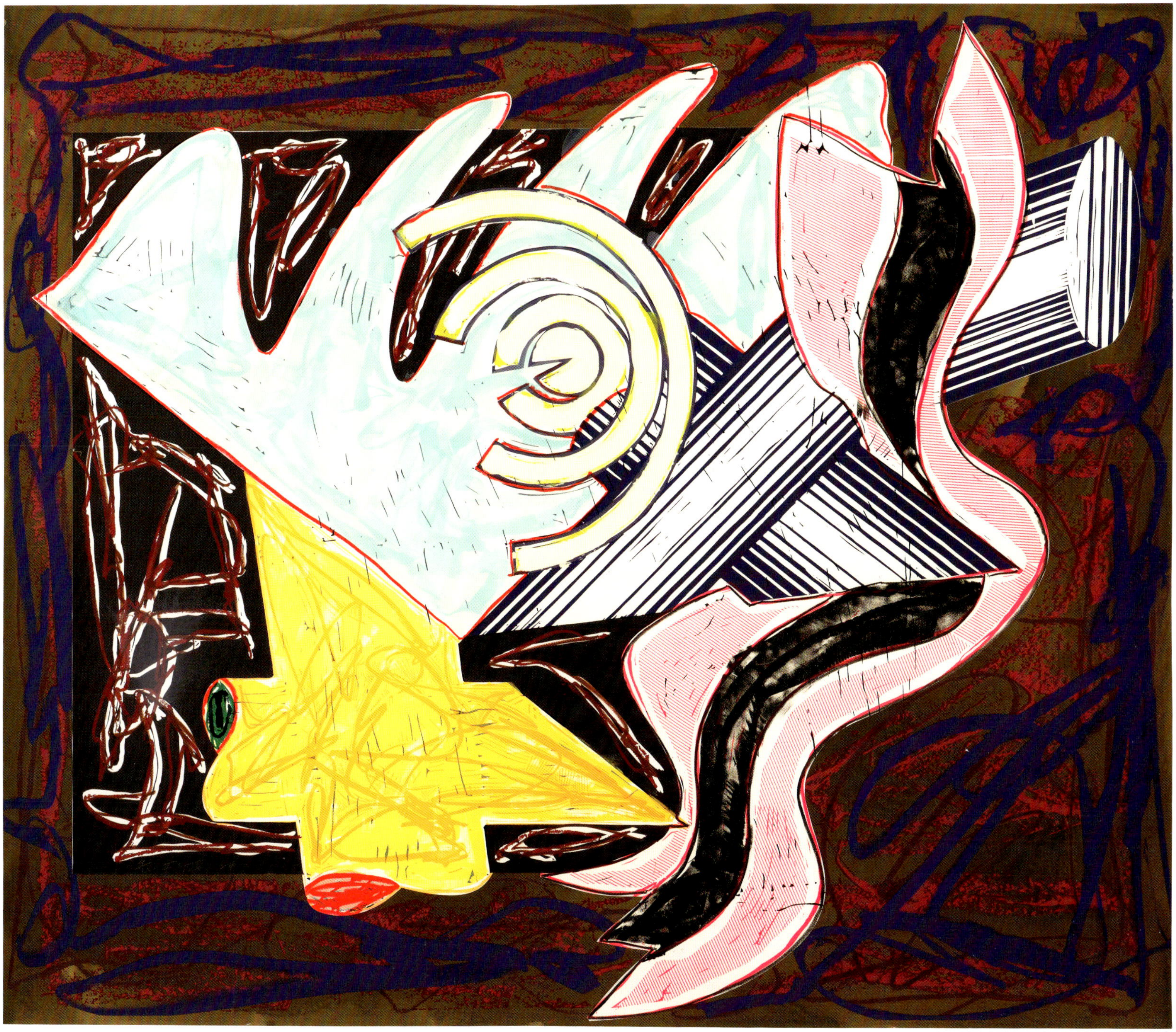

plate 4 *Then Came a Dog and Bit the Cat*, 1984

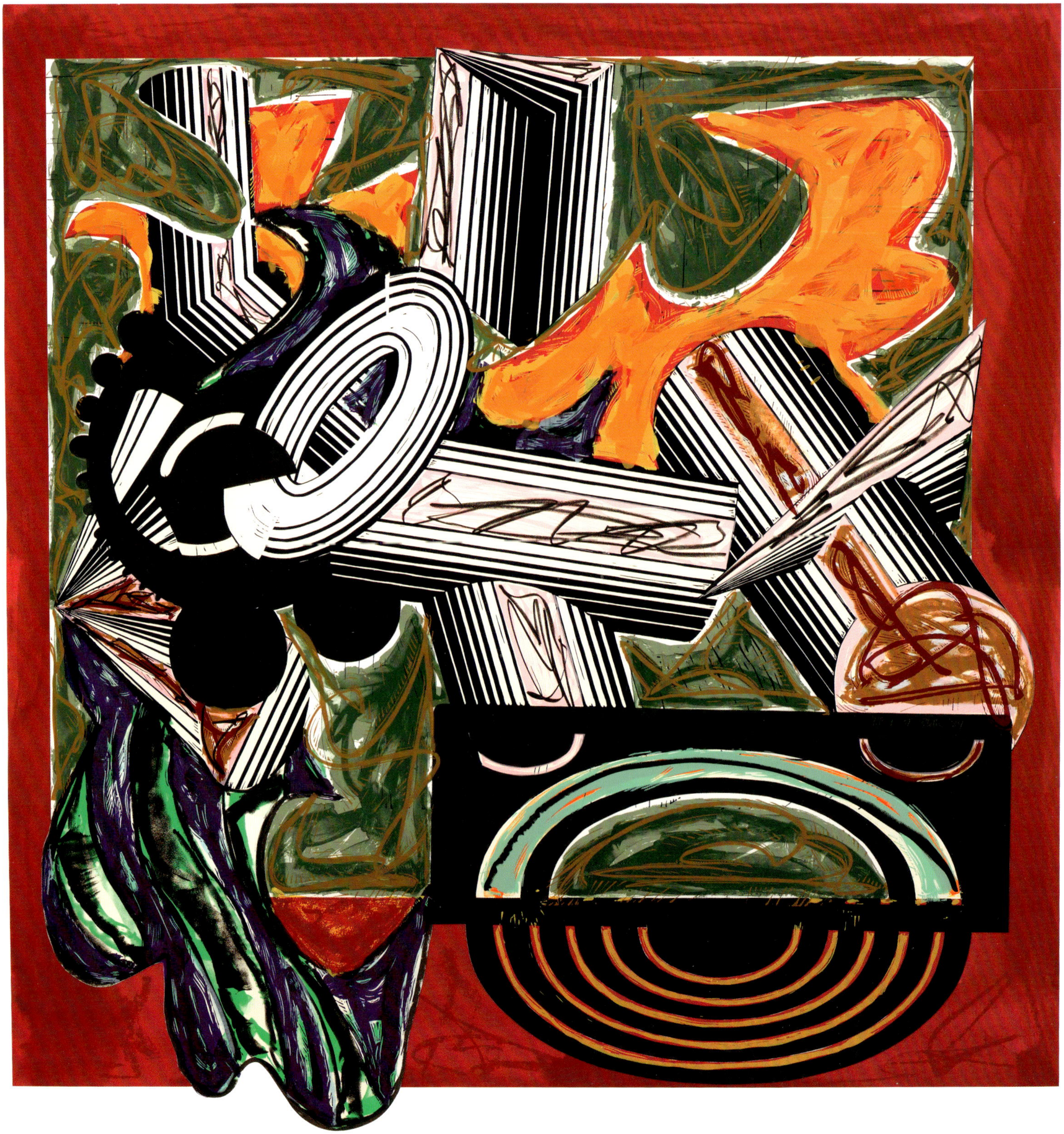

plate 5 *Then Came a Stick and Beat the Dog*, 1984

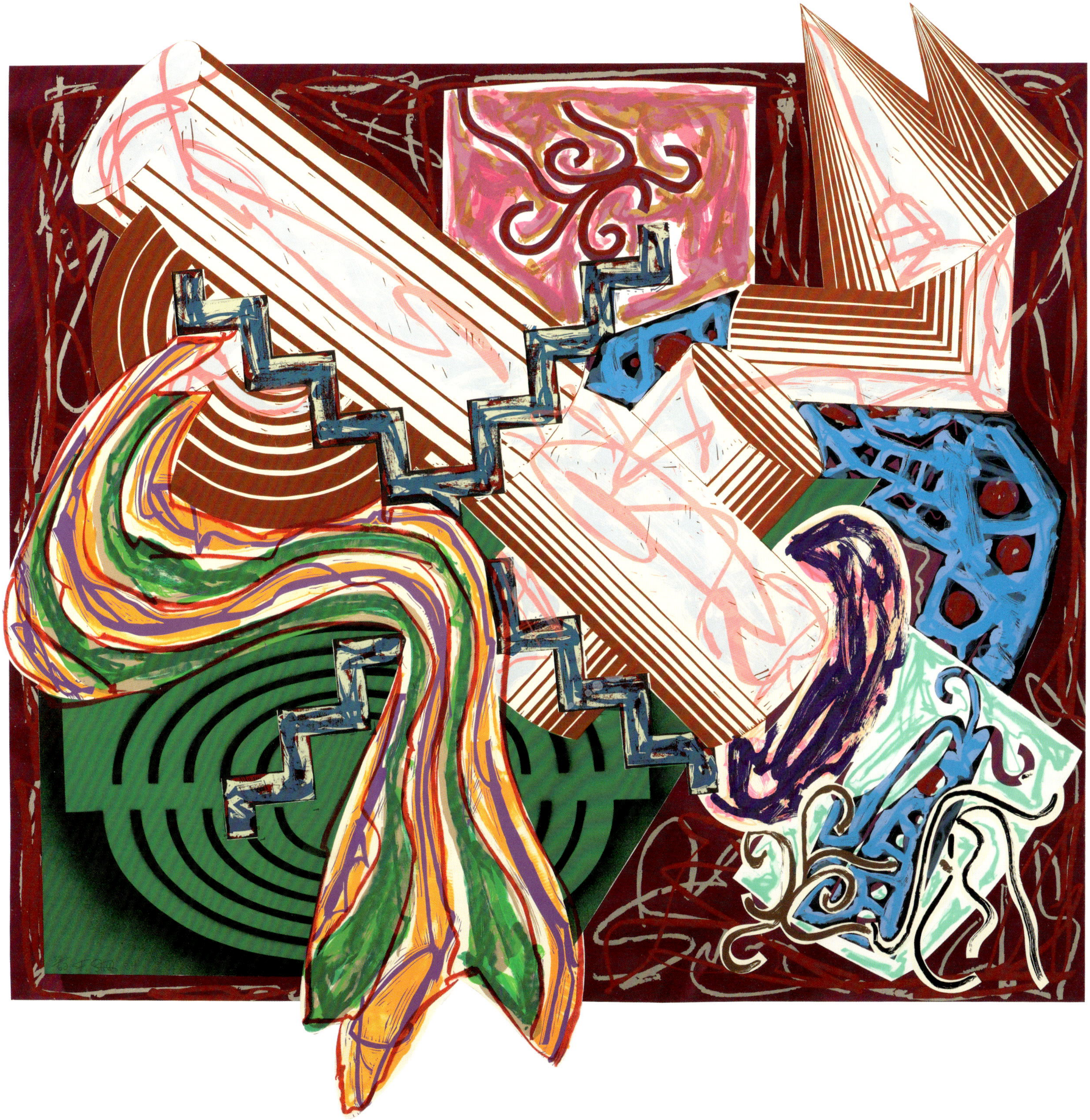

plate 6 *Then Came a Fire and Burnt the Stick*, 1984

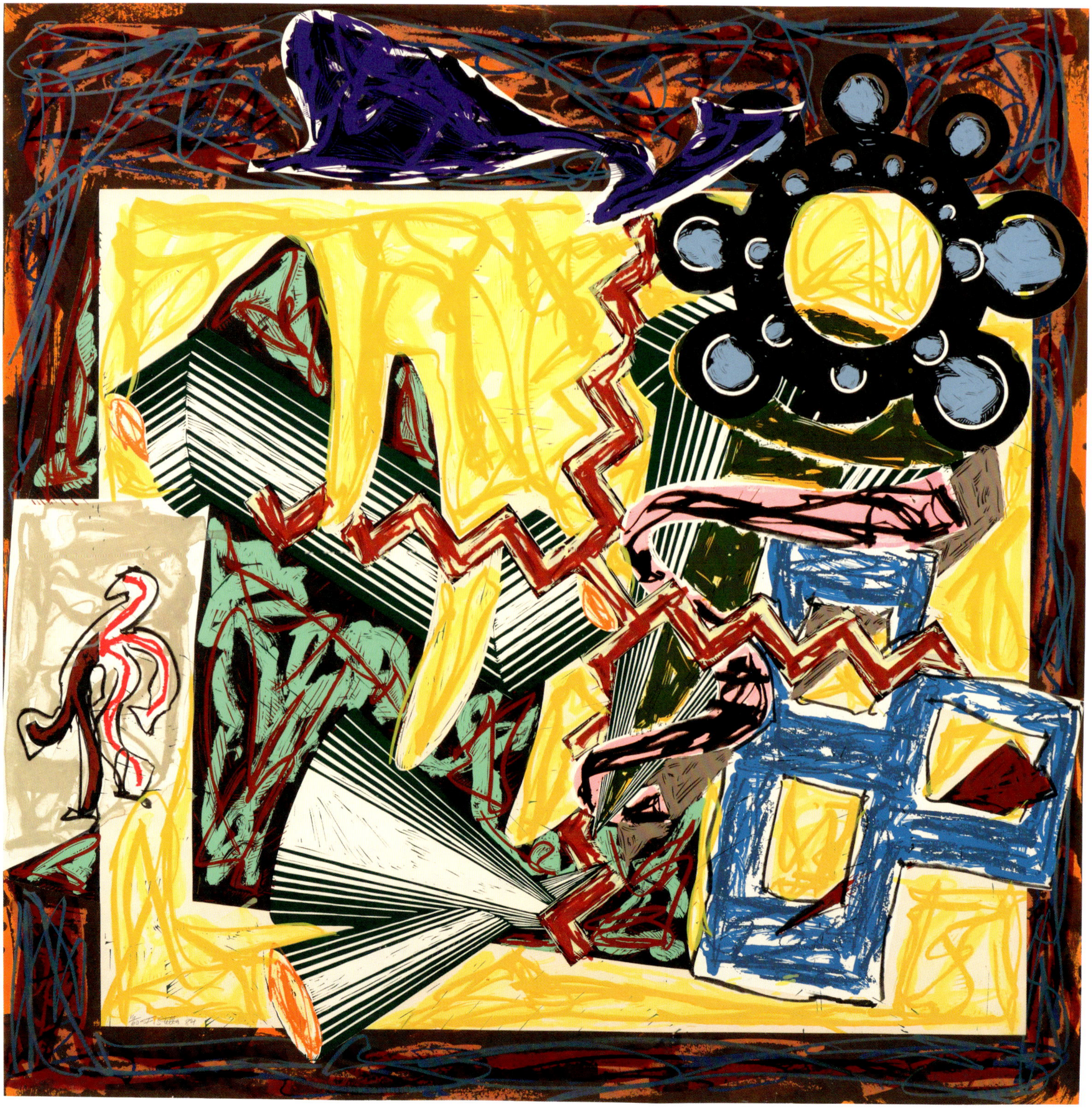

plate 7 *Then Water Came and Quenched the Fire*, 1984

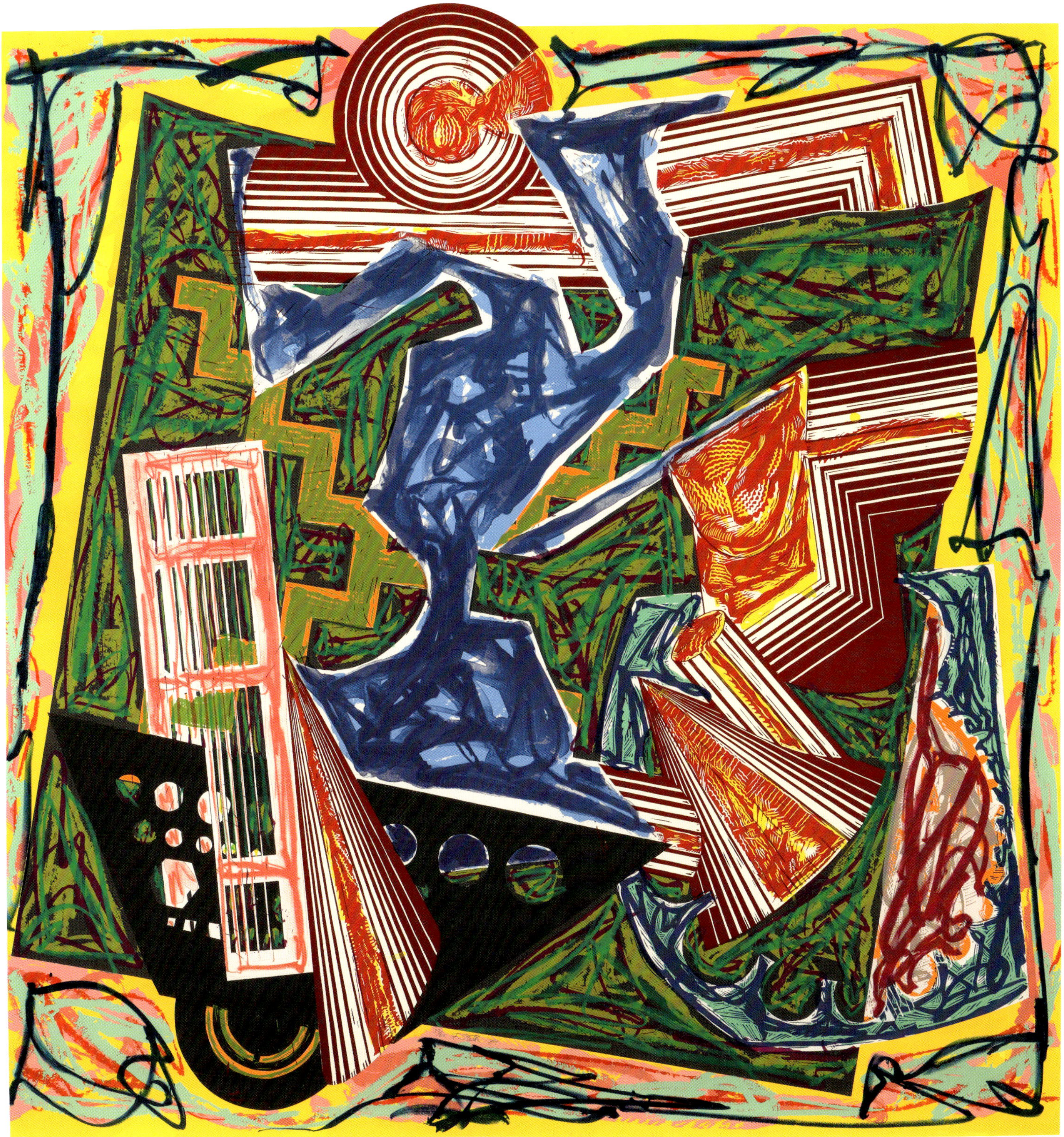

plate 8 *Then Came an Ox and Drank the Water*, 1984

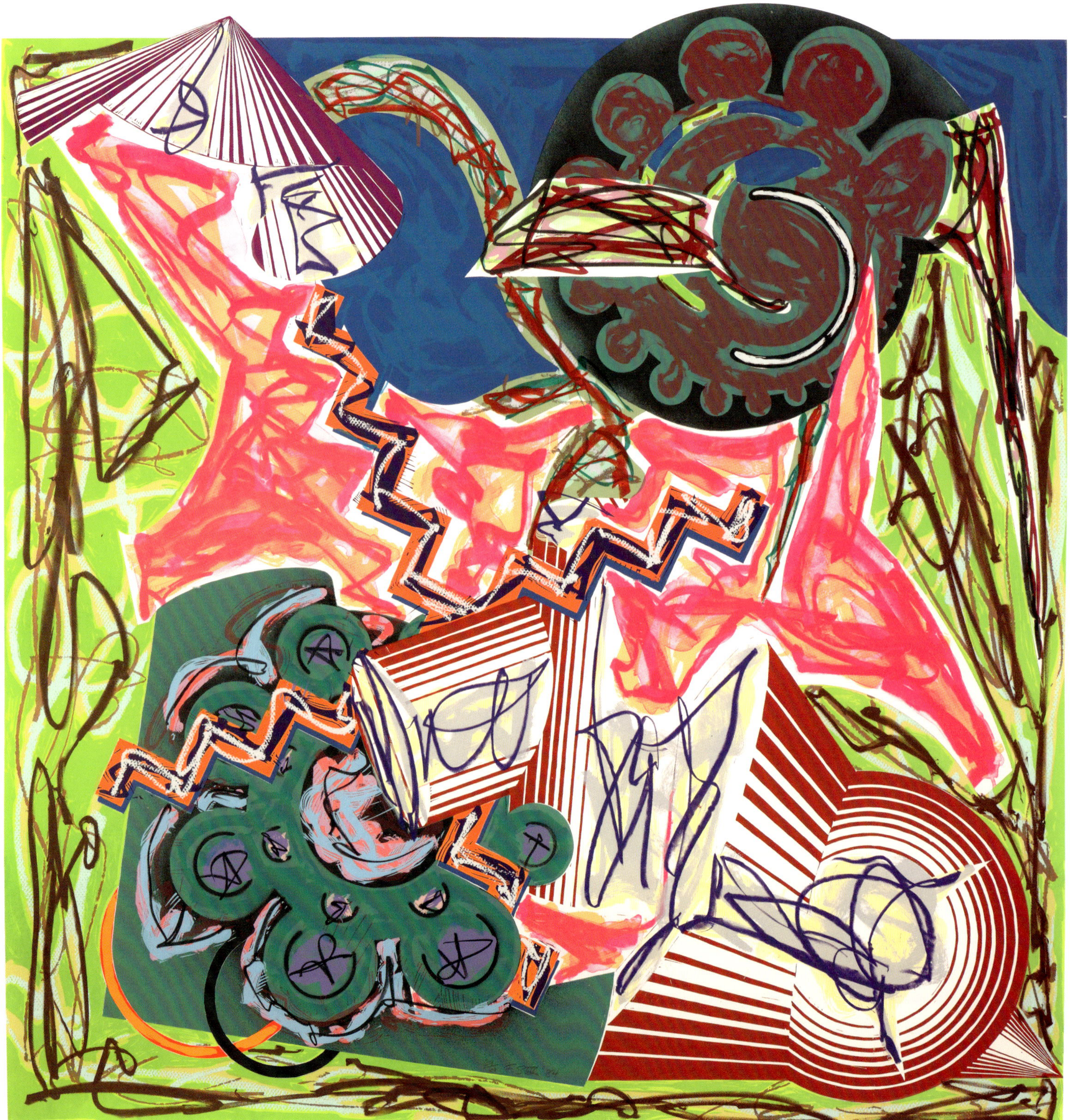

plate 9 *The Butcher Came and Slew the Ox*, 1984

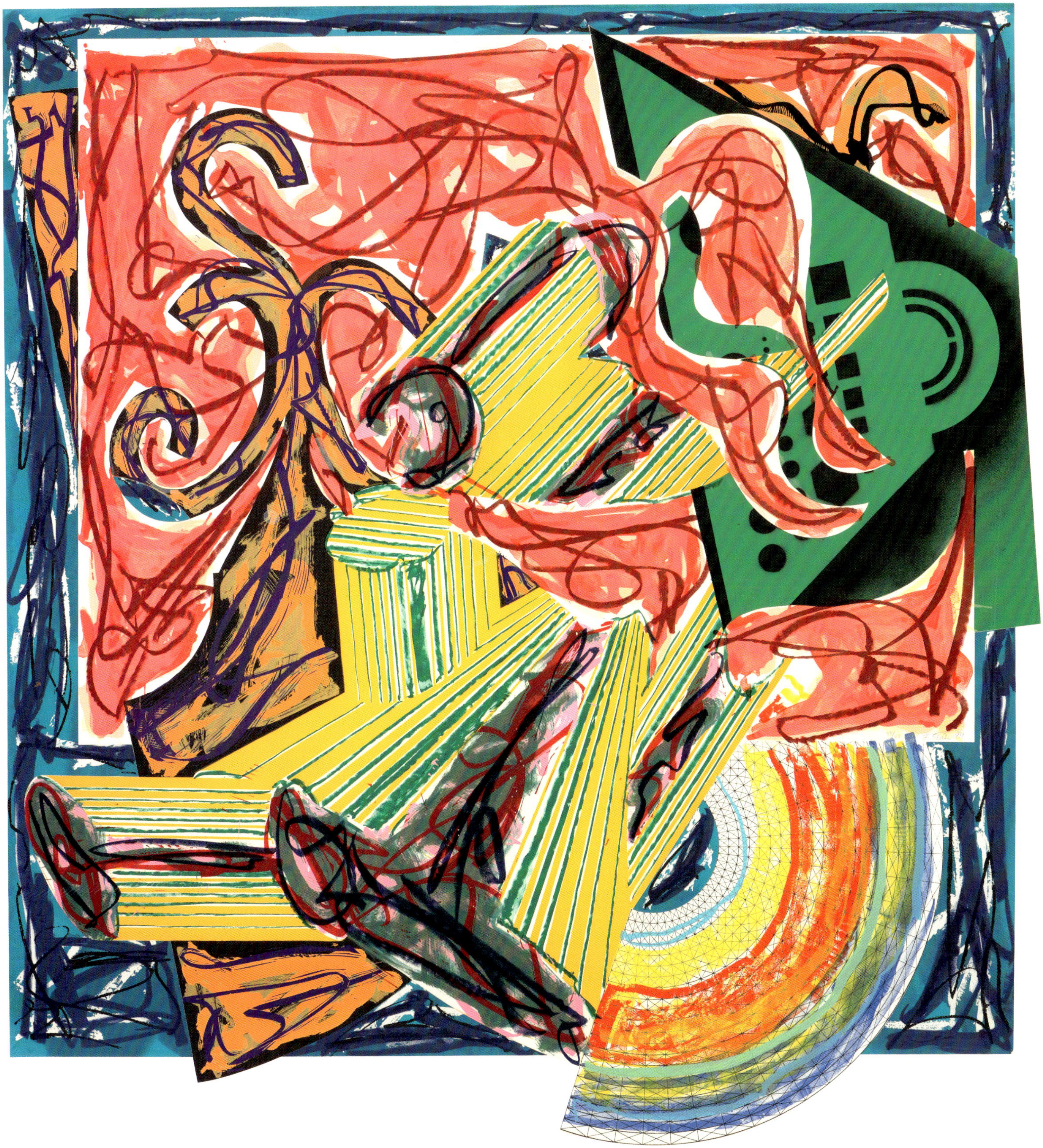

plate 10 *Then Came Death and Took the Butcher*, 1984

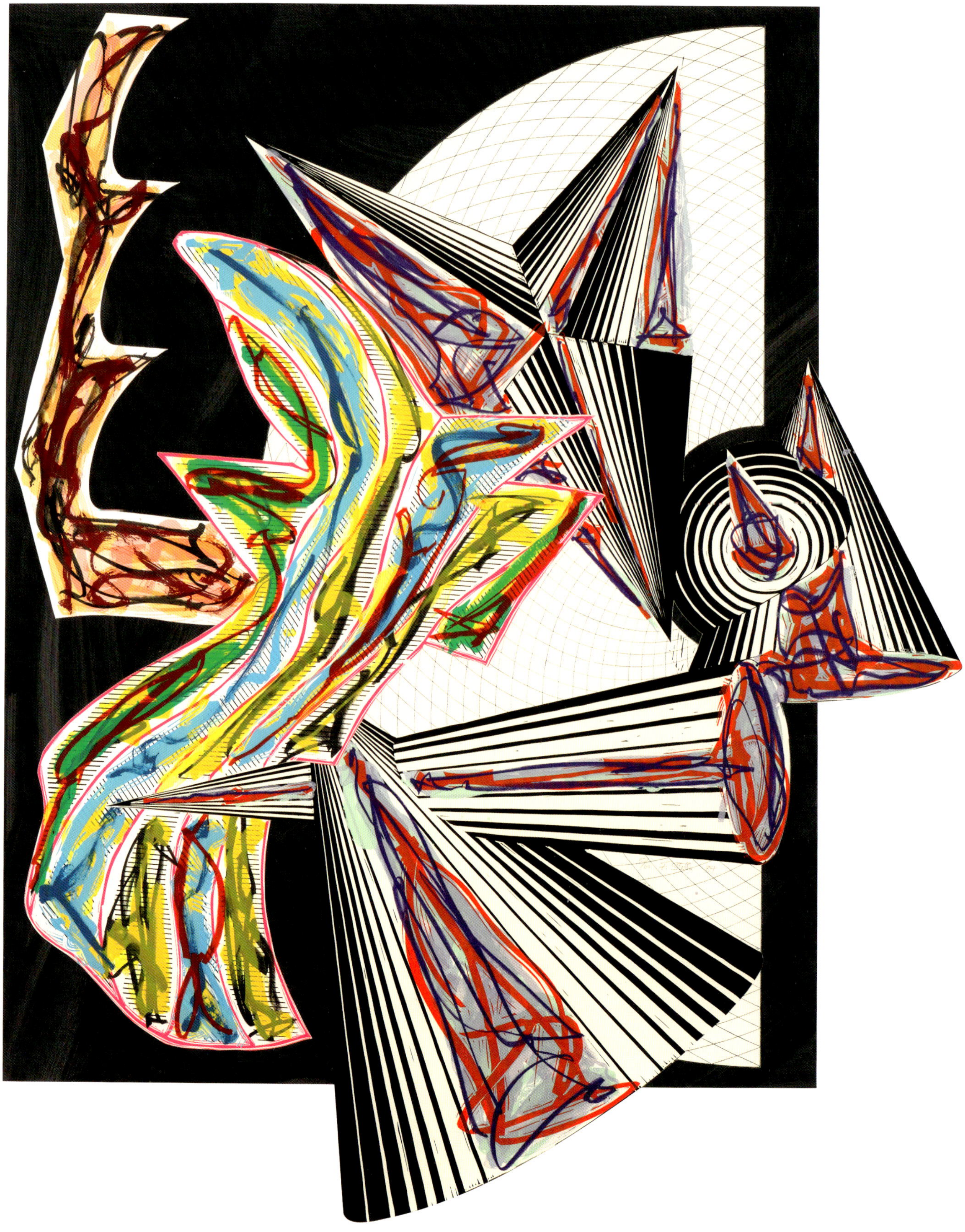

plate 11 *And the Holy One, Blessed Be He, Came and Smote the Angel of Death*, 1984

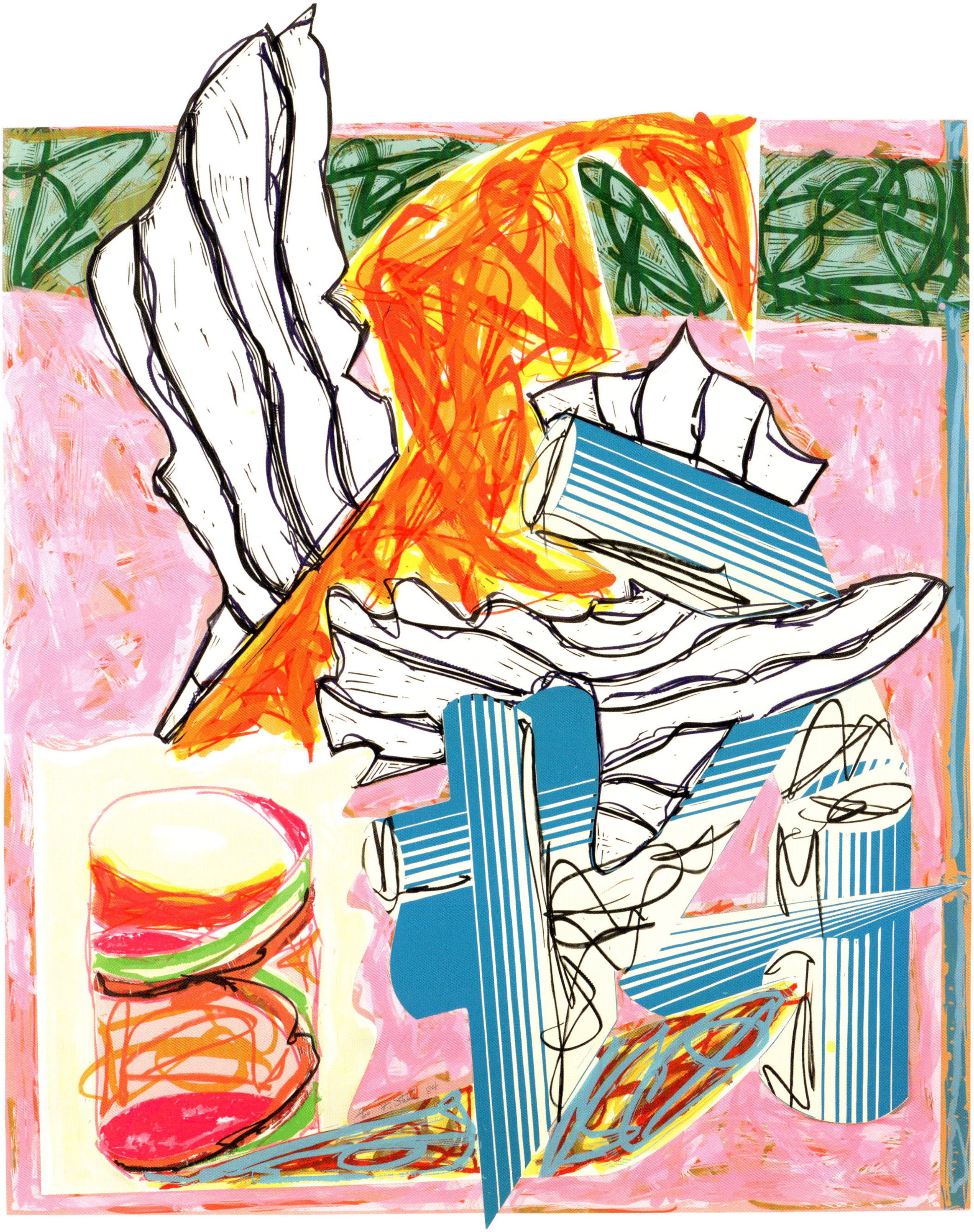

plate 12 *Had Gadya: Back Cover*, 1984

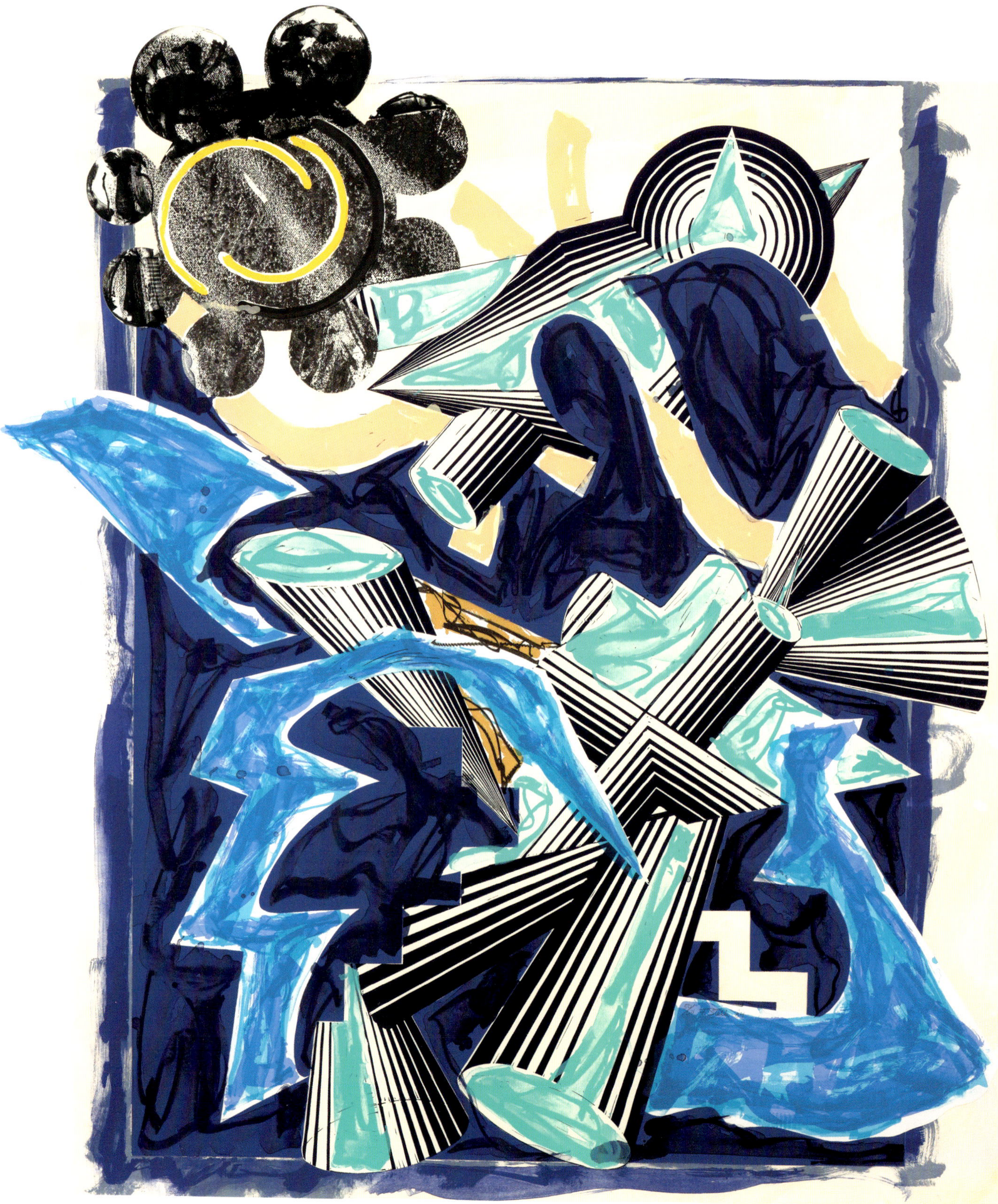

Frank Stella

The Cones and Pillars have a blunt, primitive quality to them as paintings . . . They have very much the spirit of a well-told folk tale. They are very active, they're very fantasy-like, and they are very simple. I had the feeling that with a little bit of mental jockeying their forms could represent things. It wasn't hard to imagine them being a cat or a person.

Italian Folktales
1988–89

In compiling a collection of two hundred Italian folktales, first published in 1956, Italo Calvino created the first comprehensive Italian-language anthology of this genre. As an author, Calvino is known for his use of allegory and fantasy; for this collection, he undertook extensive research of nineteenth-century European folklore, assembled tales from the various dialects and regions of Italy, translated them into standard Italian, and revised the language and symbolism to privilege Italian cultural references and to ensure that the stories would be accessible to and engaging for a popular audience. The complete work was translated into English in 1980, from which point it became the standard collection in English of Italian tales.

plate 13 *Bene come il sale, State I* (As Dear as Salt, State I), 1989

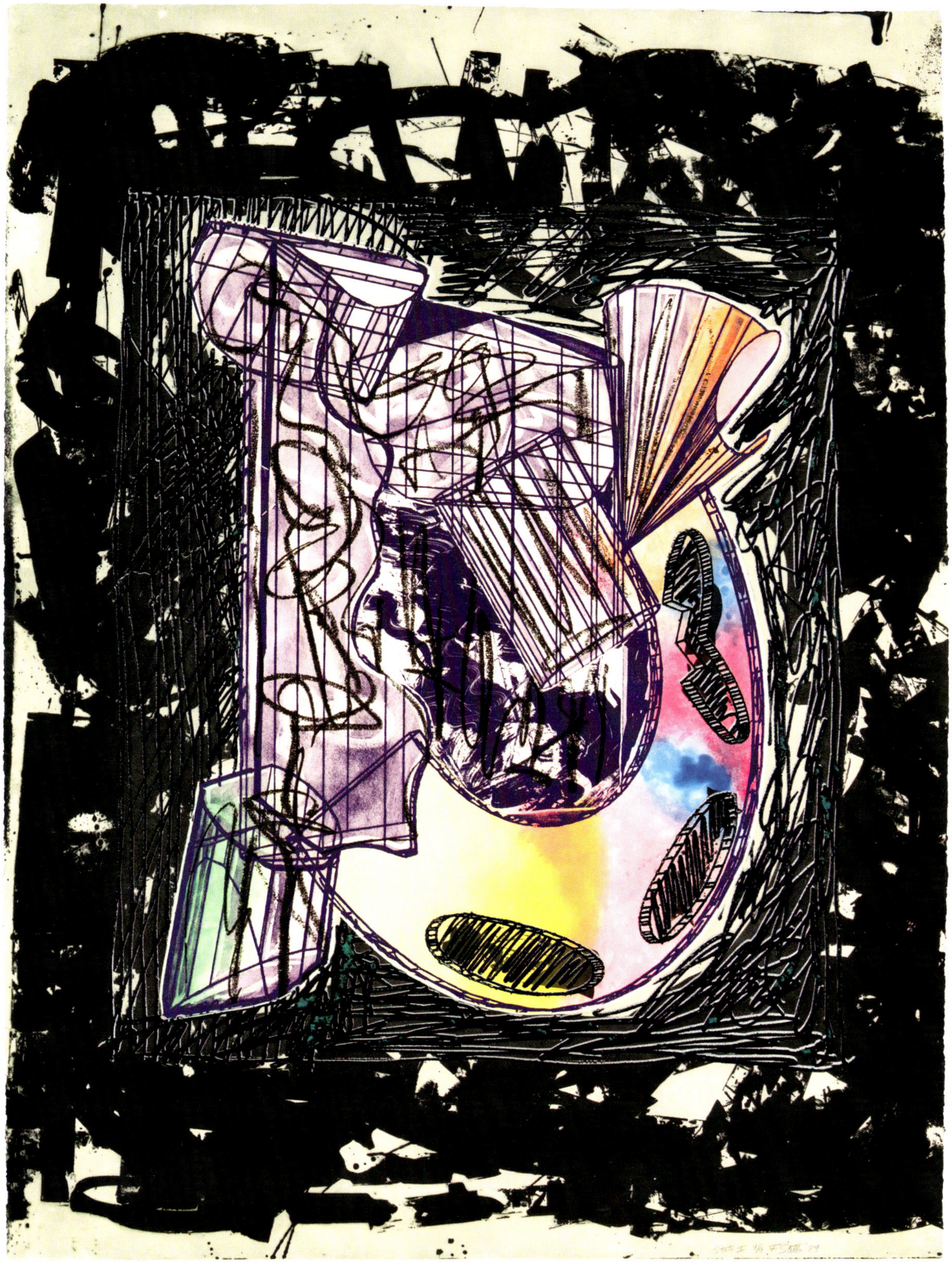

plate 14 *Bene come il sale, State III* (As Dear as Salt, State III), 1989

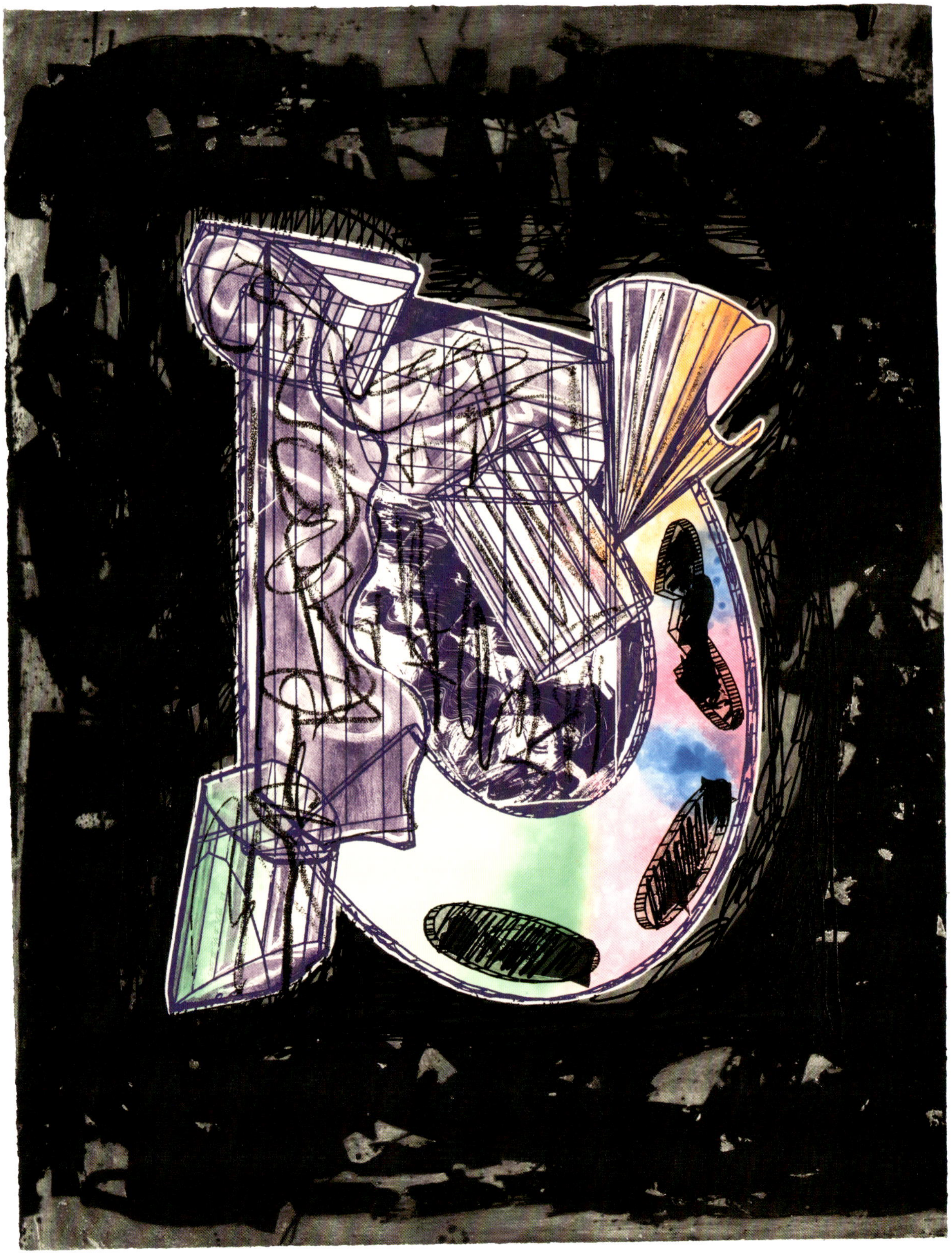

plate 15 *Bene come il sale, State IV* (As Dear as Salt, State IV), 1989

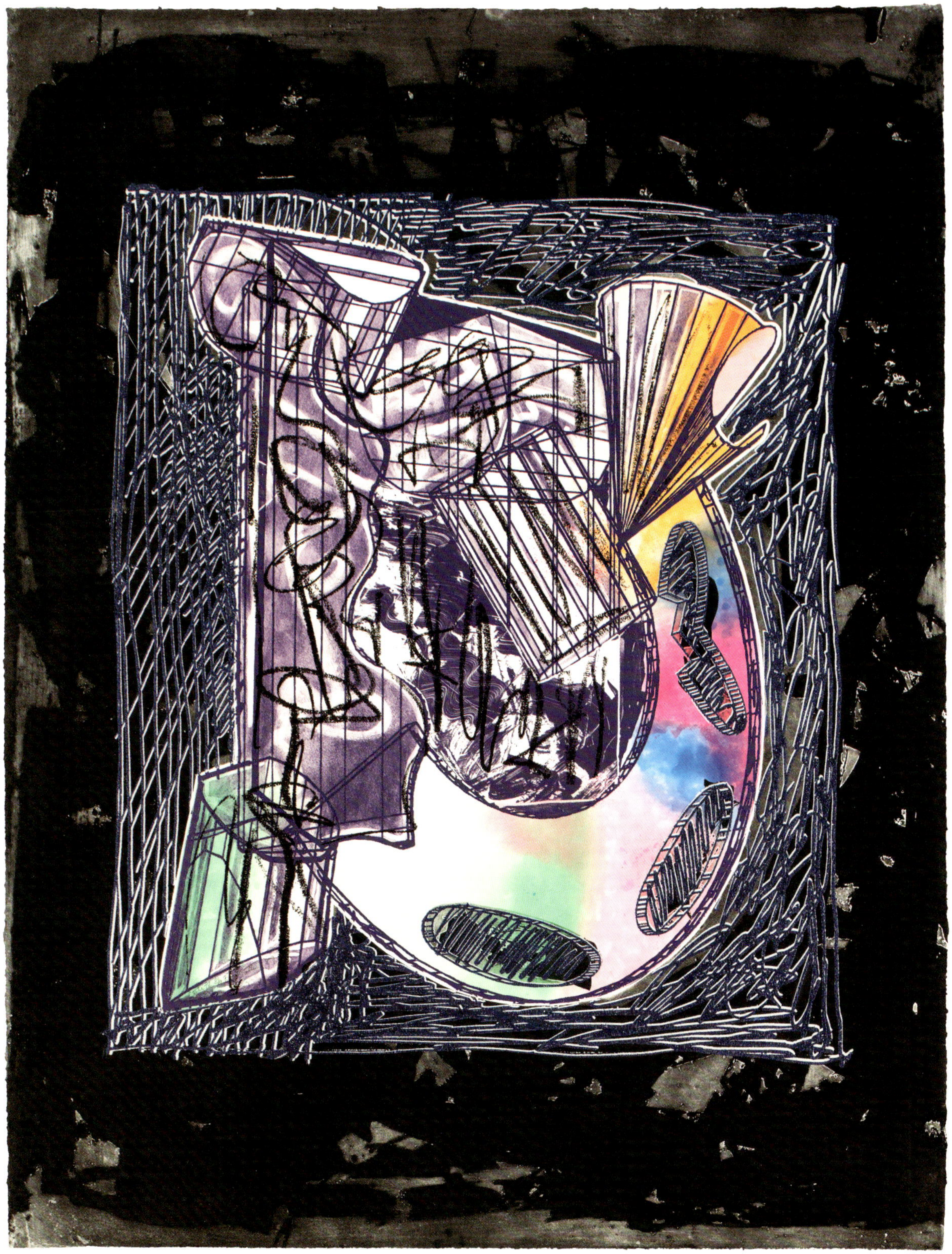

plate 16 *Bene come il sale* (As Dear as Salt), 1989

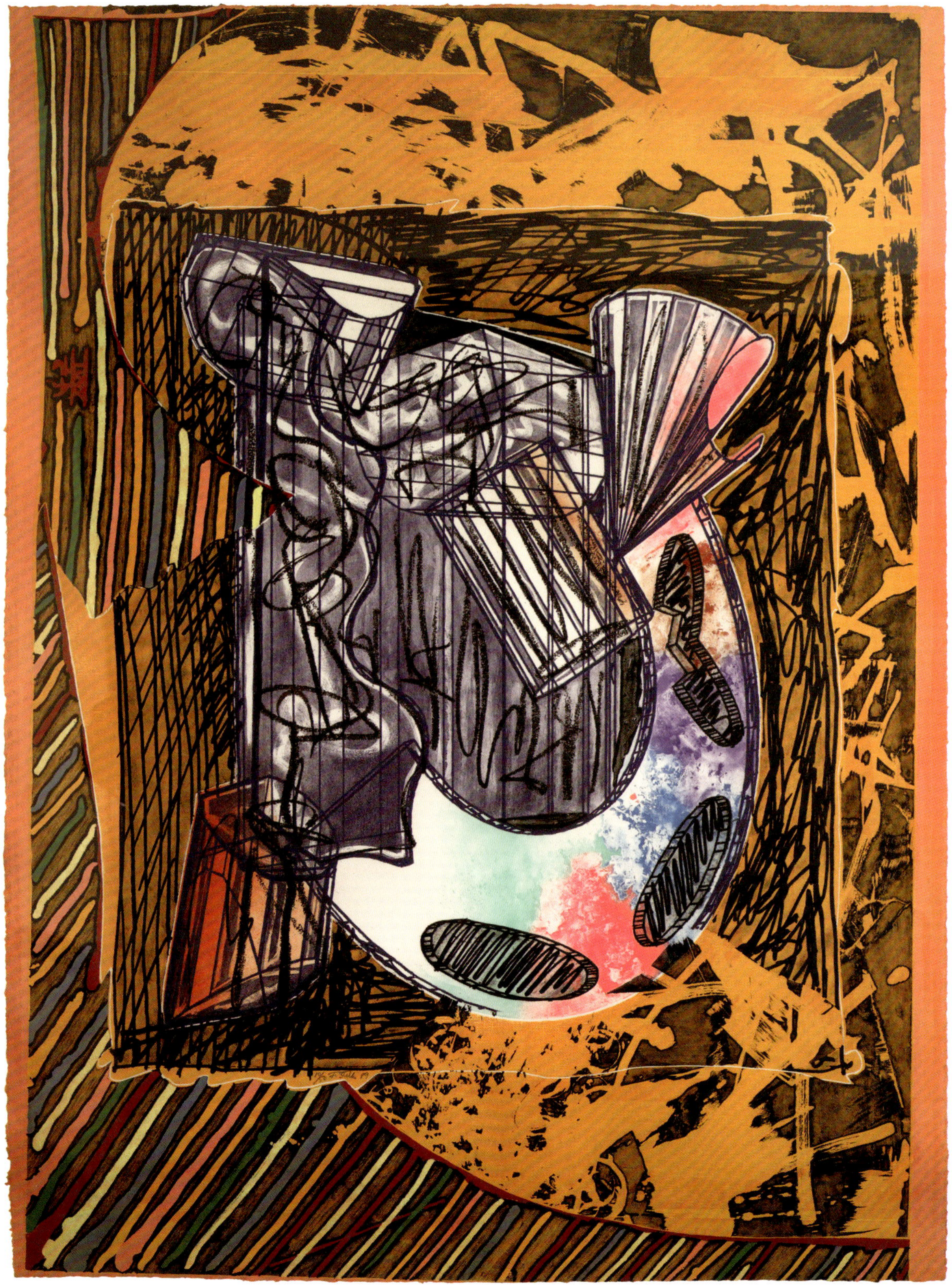

plate 17 *Giufà e la berretta rossa* (Giufà and the Red Cap), 1989

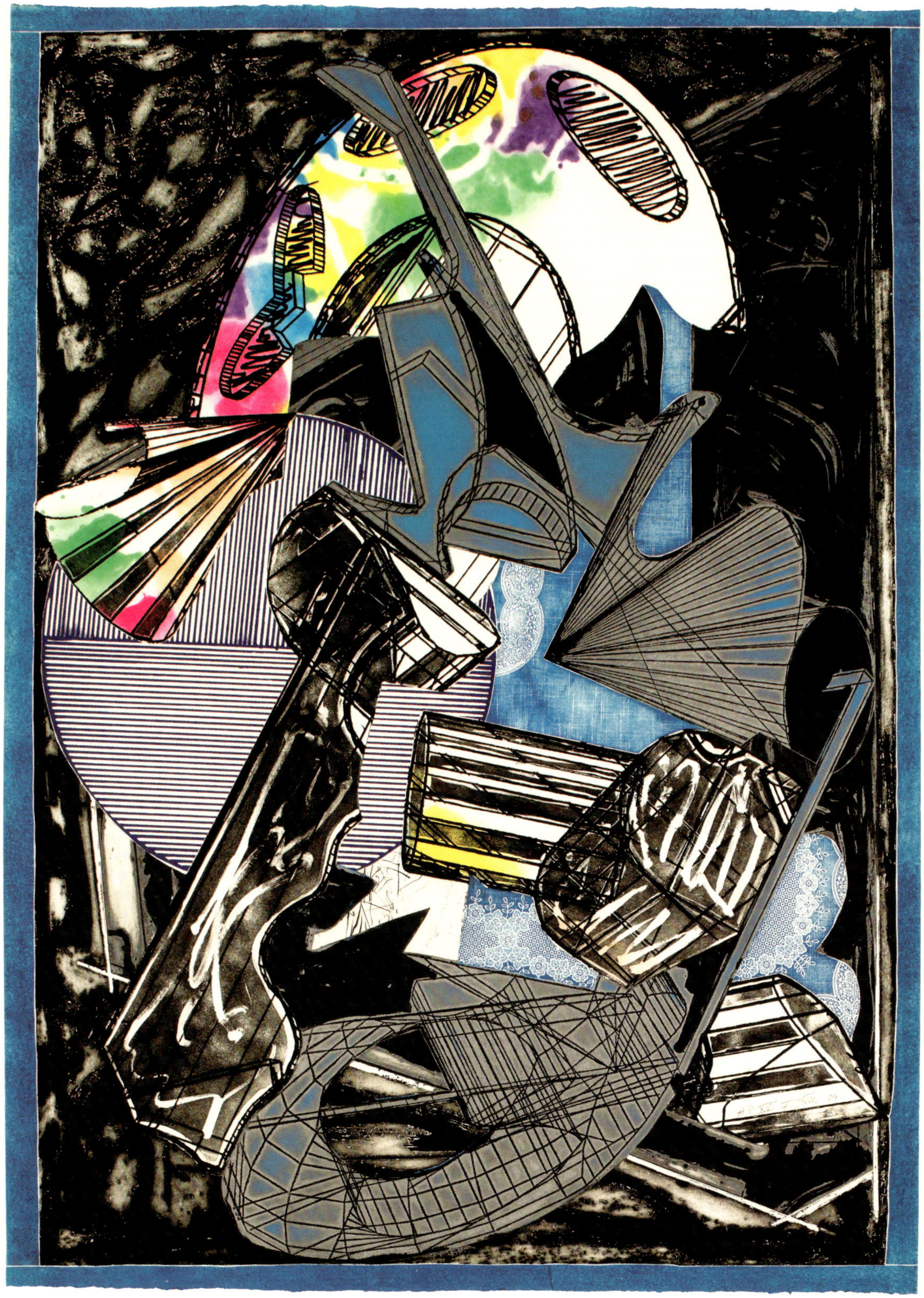

The Moby Dick Prints
1989–93

Herman Melville's epic novel entwines a detailed treatise on nineteenth-century American whaling with the metaphysical tale of Captain Ahab and his tragic obsession with revenge on a gargantuan white whale named Moby-Dick, leading to the destruction of the ship *Pequod* and all but one of her crew. First published in 1851 to modest commercial success, *Moby-Dick* was out of print by the time of Melville's death in 1891. By the 1920s, however, the author's significance had been firmly established, and *Moby-Dick* became recognized as a towering masterpiece of American literature.

In 1930, Lakeside Press commissioned Rockwell Kent to design and illustrate the novel in a deluxe three-volume set that was simultaneously issued by Random House in a single-volume trade edition that remains in print.

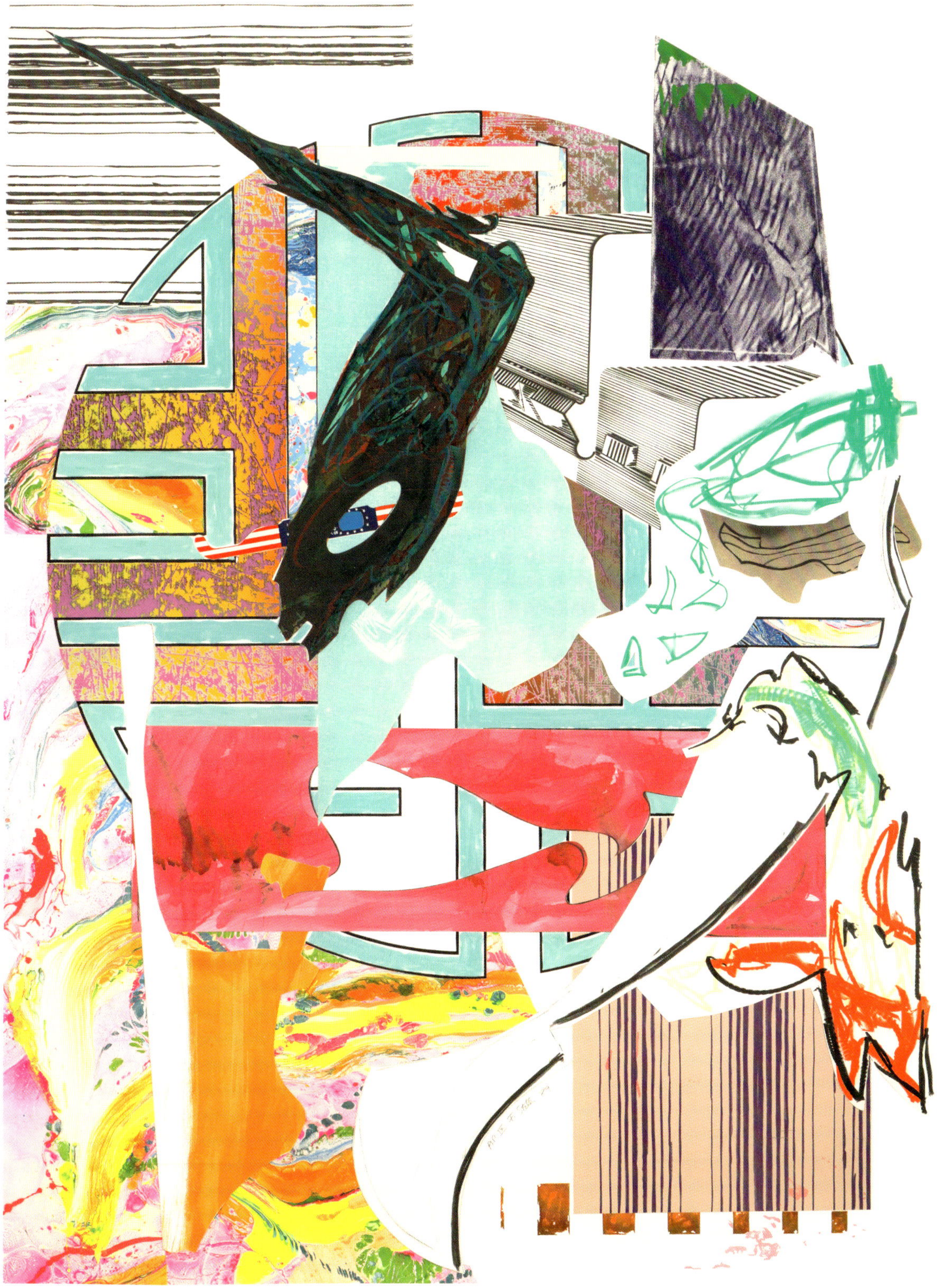

Frank Stella

The idea of the wave and its various permutations is what drives this new series. Once I started on the wave shape, I saw it began to look like a whale—a combination of waves and whales. I got the idea for the shapes at the aquarium, particularly from watching the way the Beluga whales move. The idea of the whale reminded me of *Moby Dick*, so I decided to go back and read the novel and the more I got into it, the more I thought it would be great to use the chapter headings of the novel for the titles of the pieces.

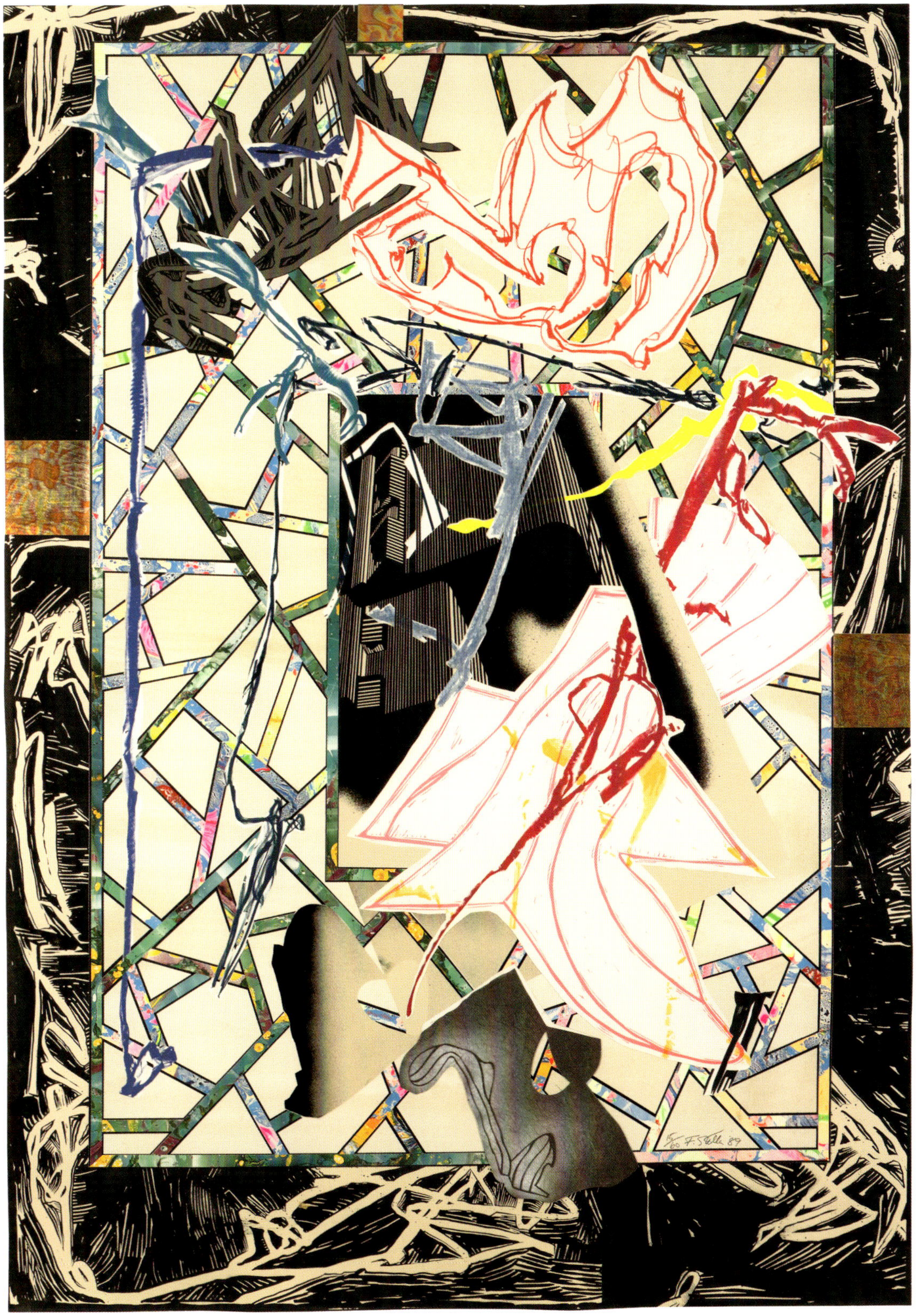

plate 20 *Stubb and Flask Kill a Right Whale*, 1991

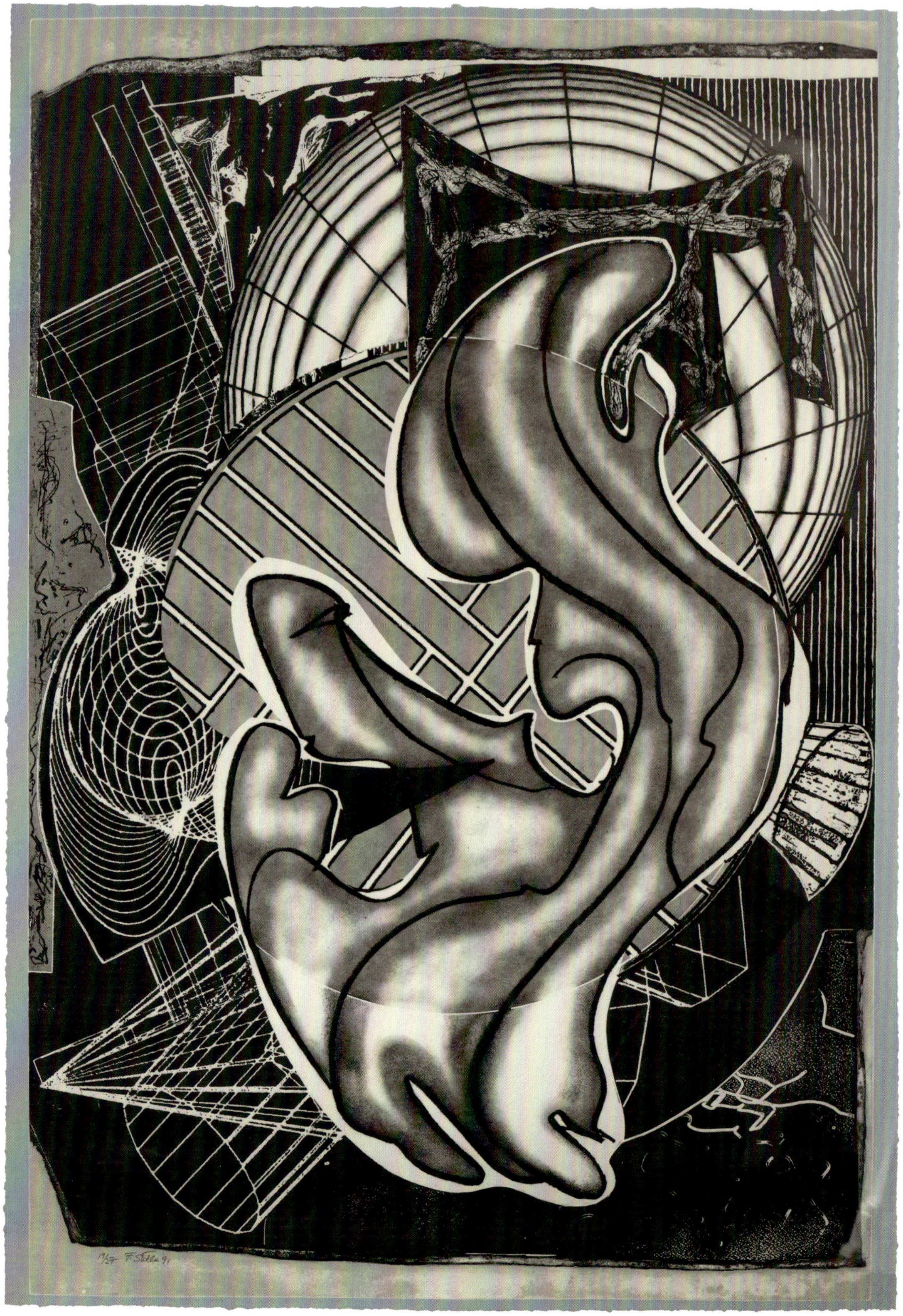

plate 21 *The Funeral*, 1991

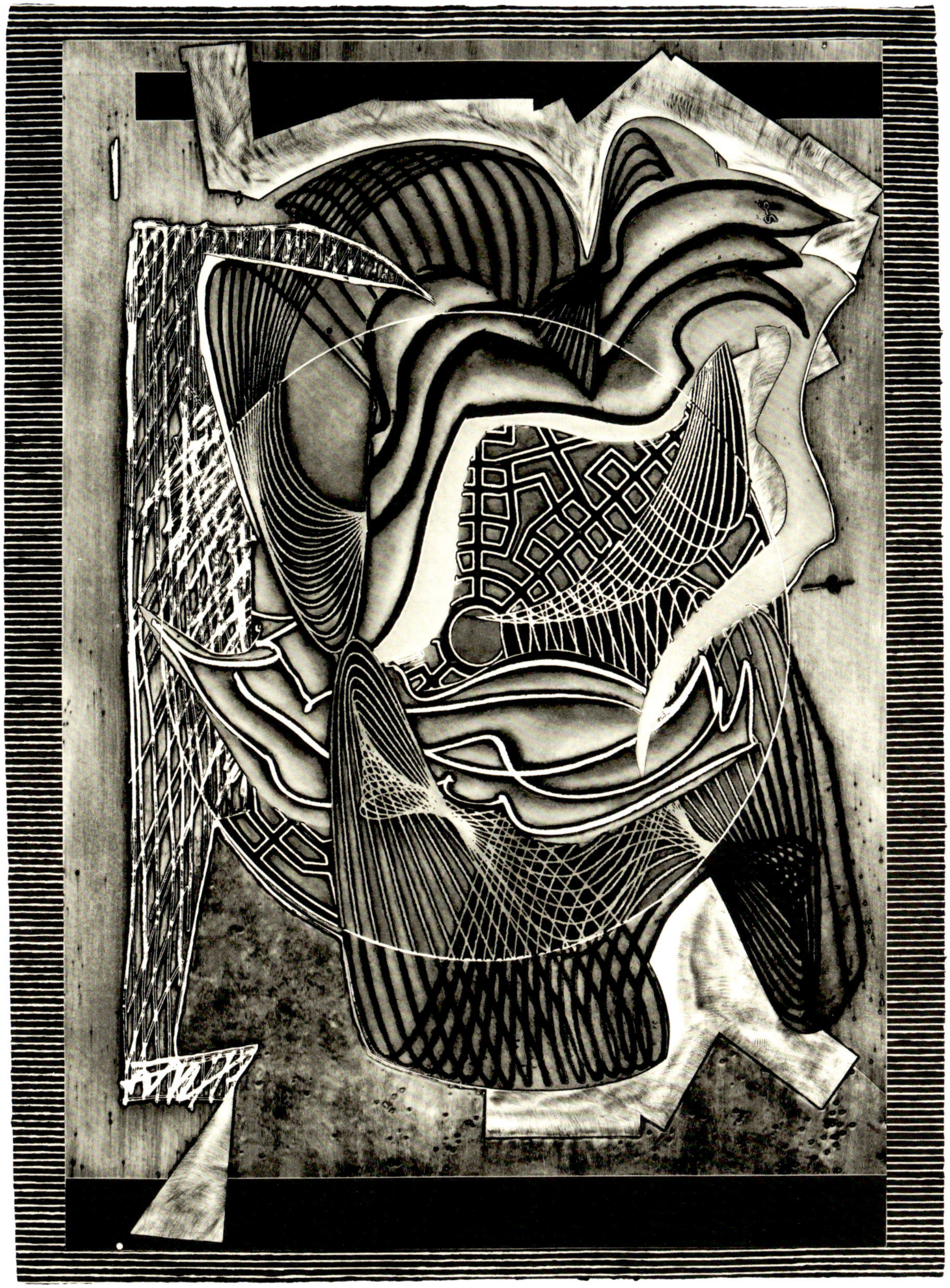

plate 22 *The Cabin. Ahab and Starbuck (Dome)*, 1992

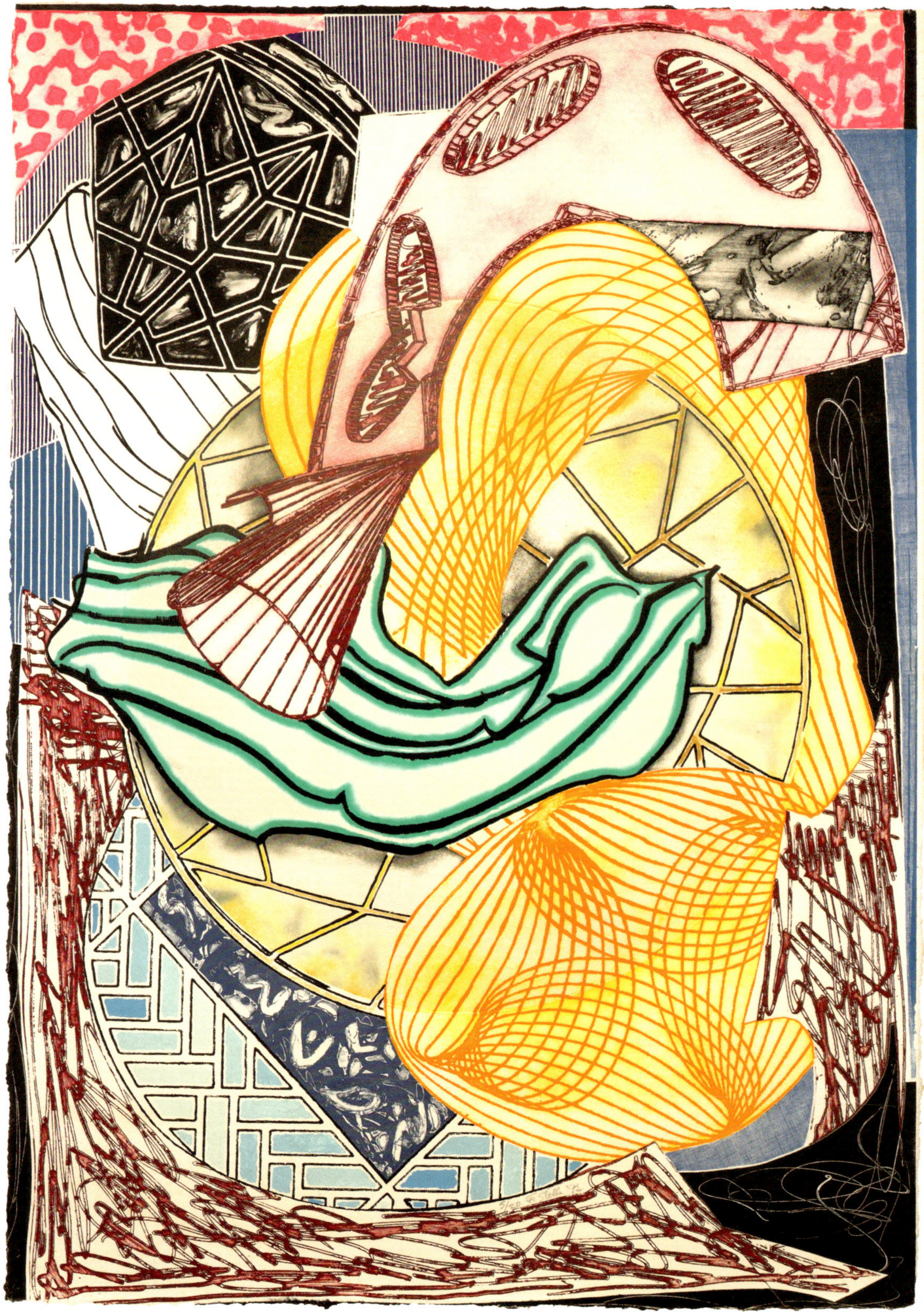

plate 23 *Jonah Historically Regarded (Dome)*, 1992

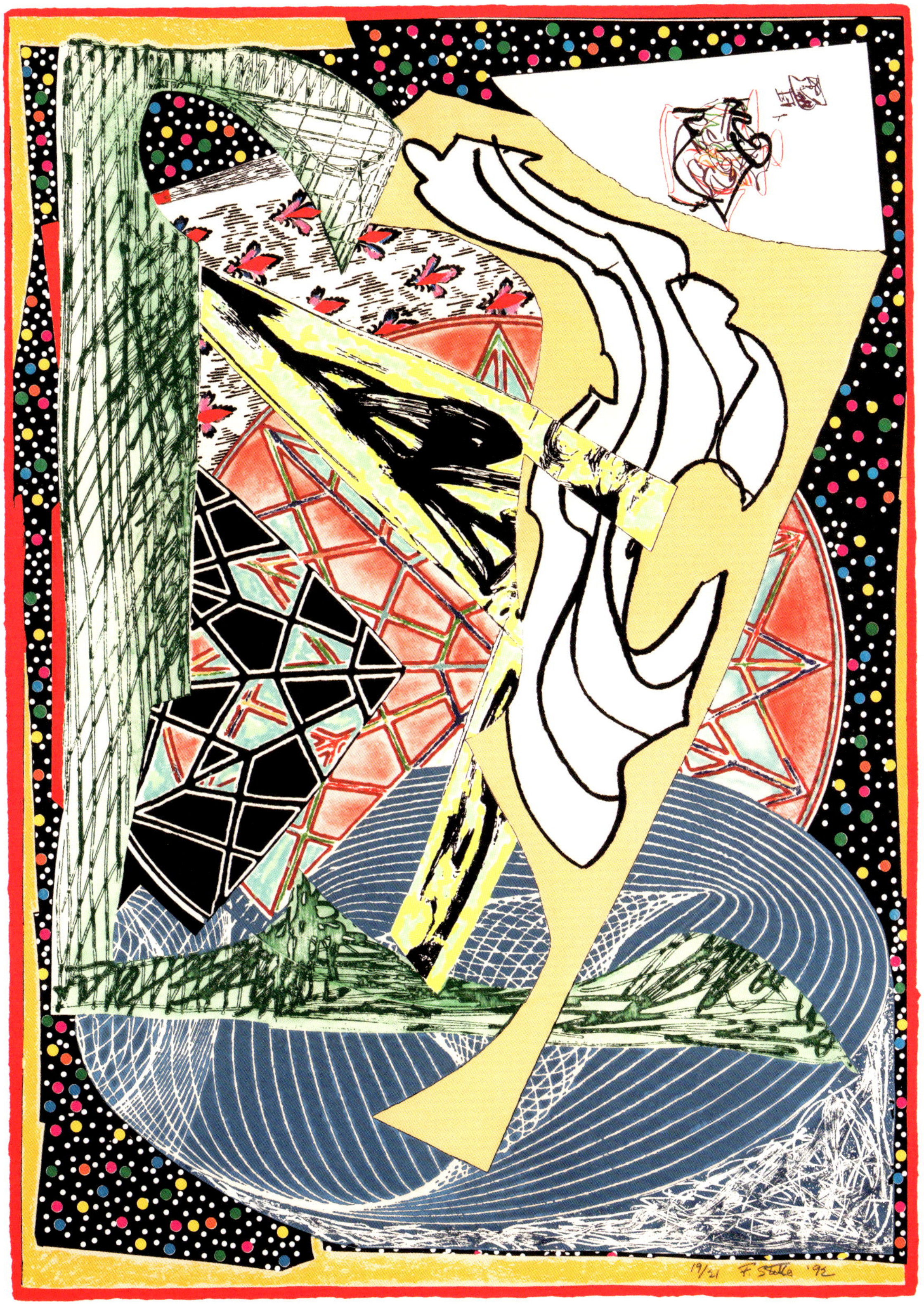

plate 24 *The Battering Ram*, 1993

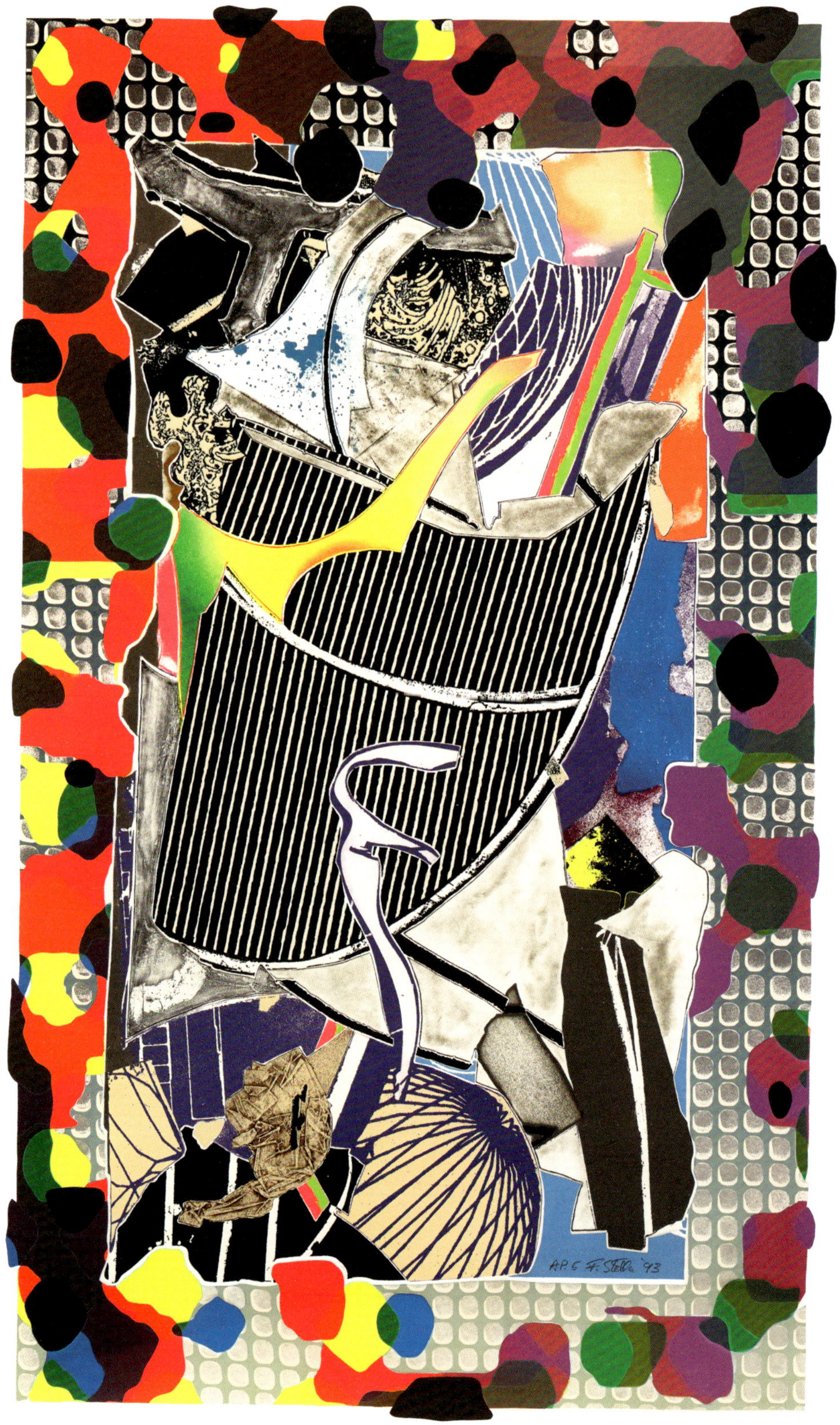

plate 25 *The Affidavit*, 1993

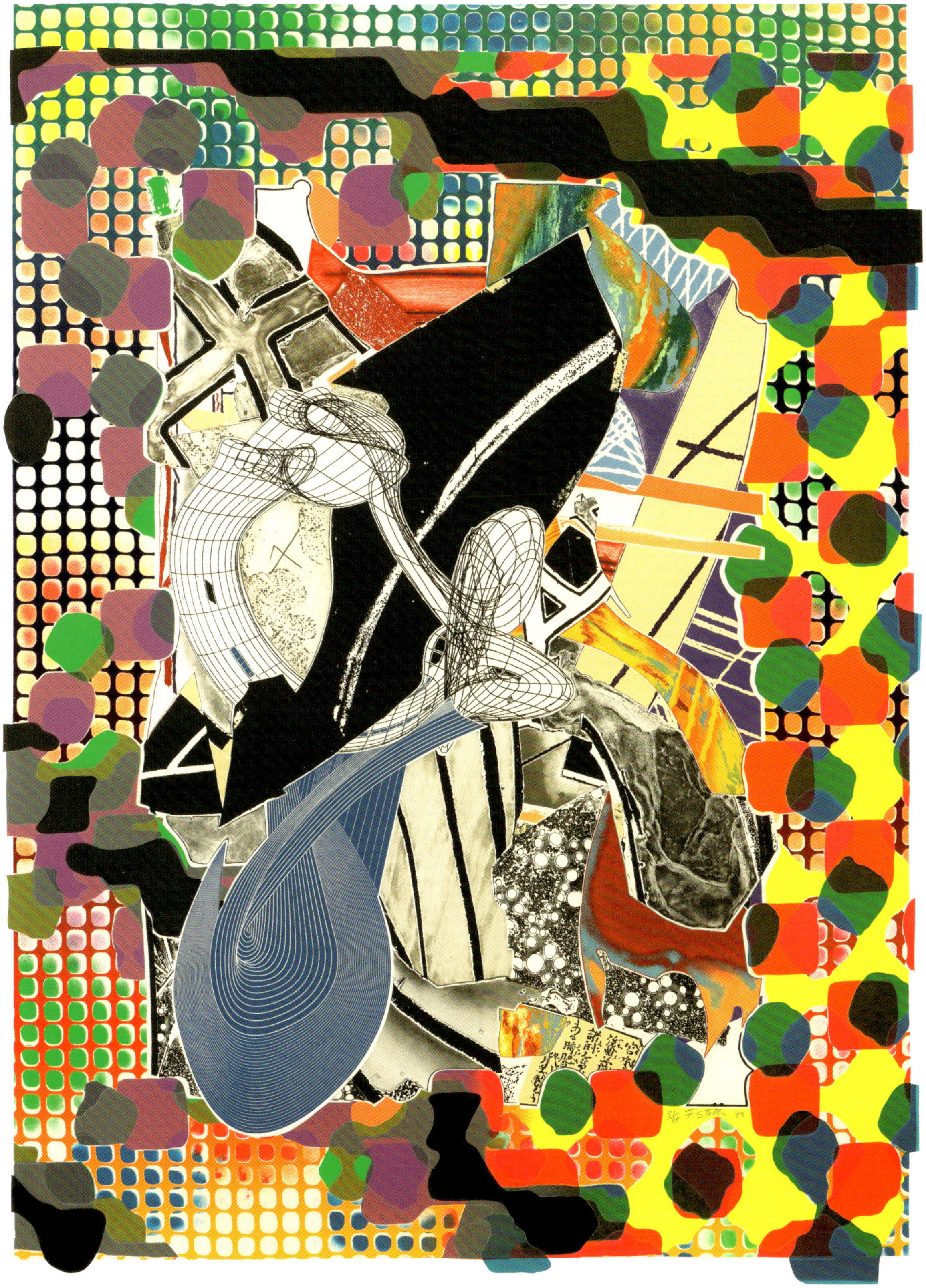

plate 26 *The Monkey Rope*, 1993

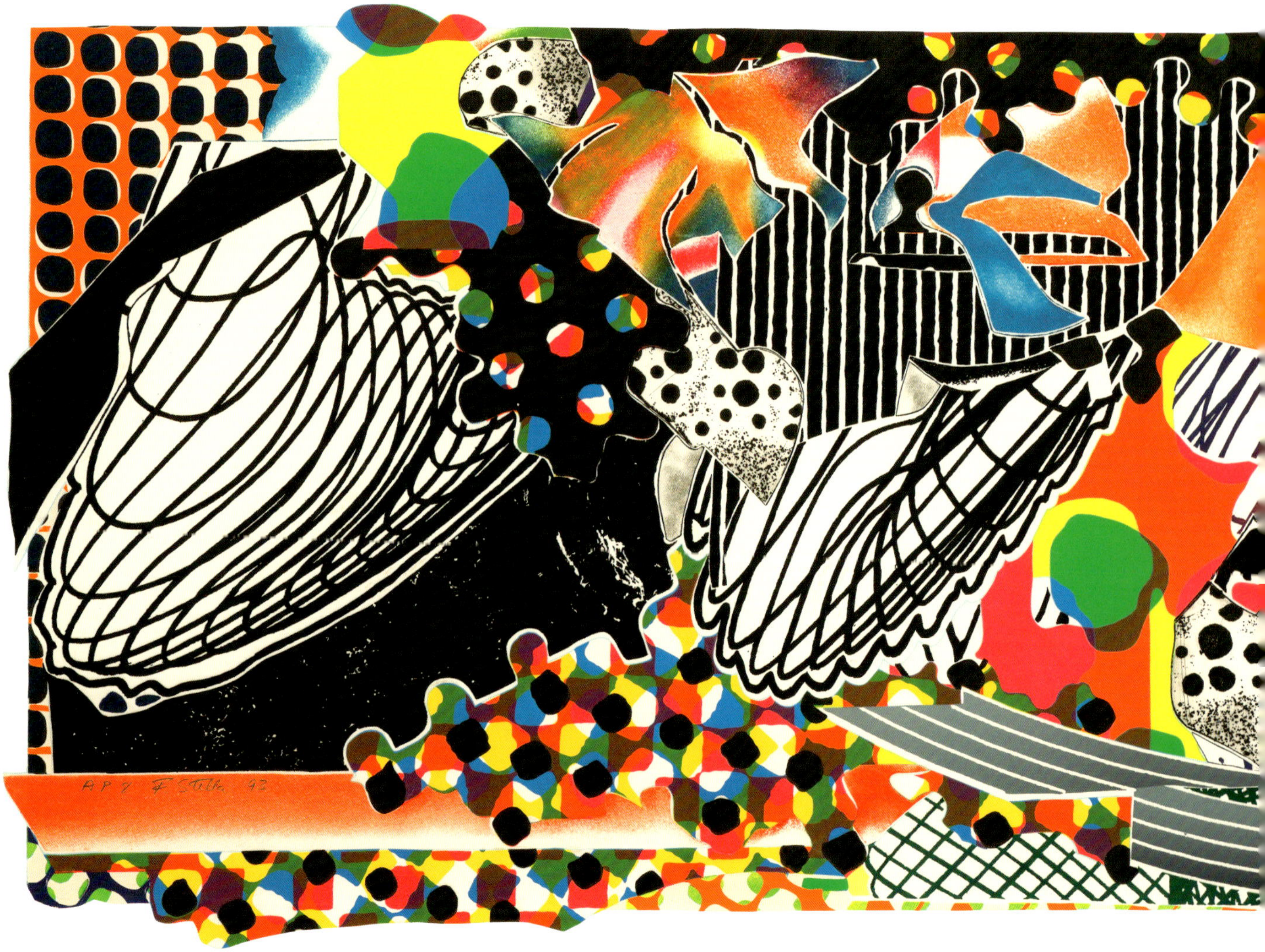

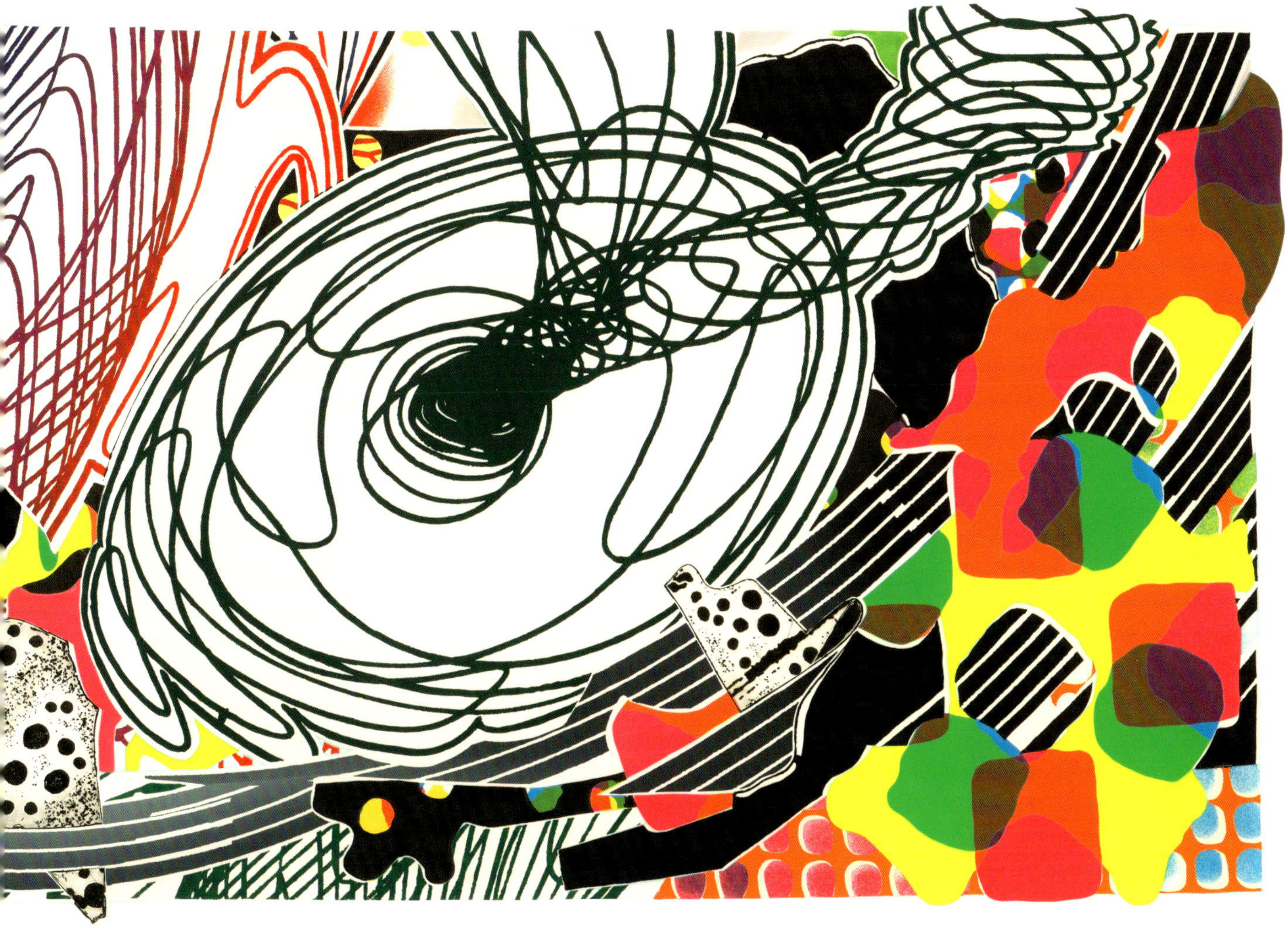

Imaginary Places
1994–99

Suspended between the genres of atlas, encyclopedia, and nineteenth-century guide for the armchair traveler, Alberto Manguel and Gianni Guadalupi's *The Dictionary of Imaginary Places* catalogues twelve hundred fictional lands, cities, seas, and other places in world literature. Drawing from writers throughout history — from Homer to J. R. R. Tolkien — the authors focus on fantastical locales described as existing on earth, excluding heavens, hells, and locations of the future; the encyclopedia also details one place invented by each author. The book includes a number of illustrations by Graham Greenfield, as well as maps and charts by James Cook, that provide visual interpretations of the associated entries.

plate 27 *Swoonarie*, 1995

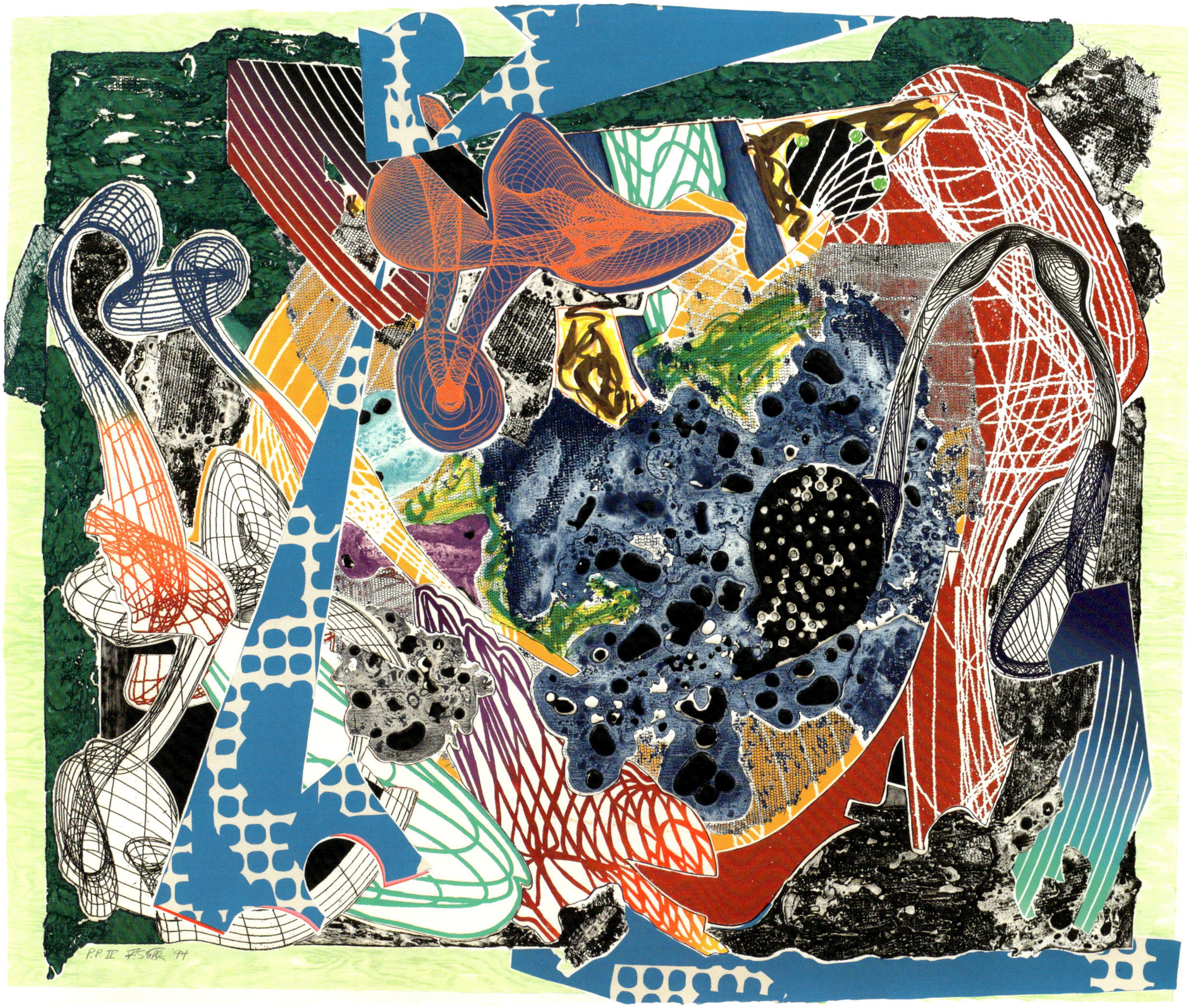

plate 28 *Feneralia*, 1995

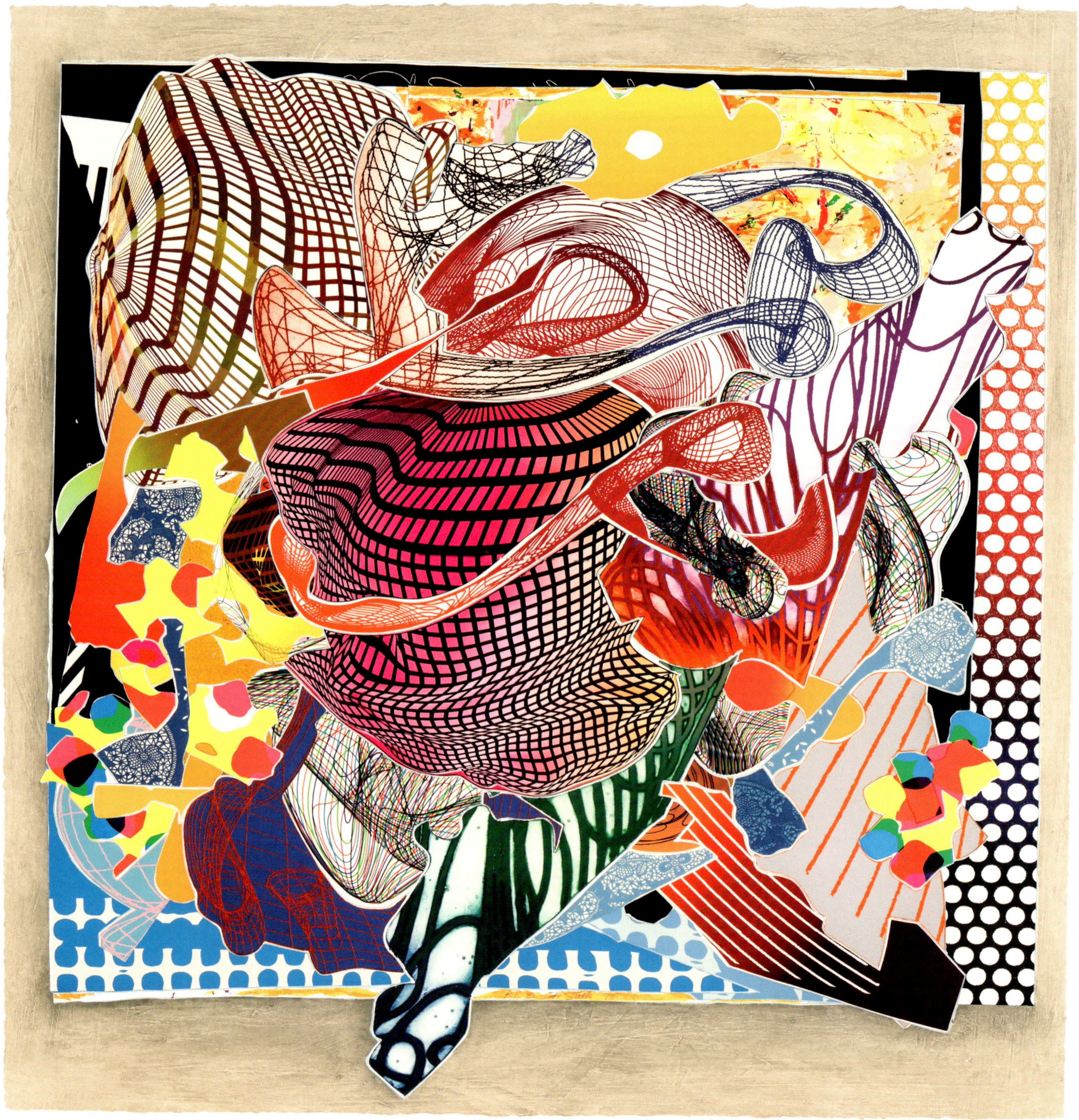

plate 29 *Fanattia*, 1995

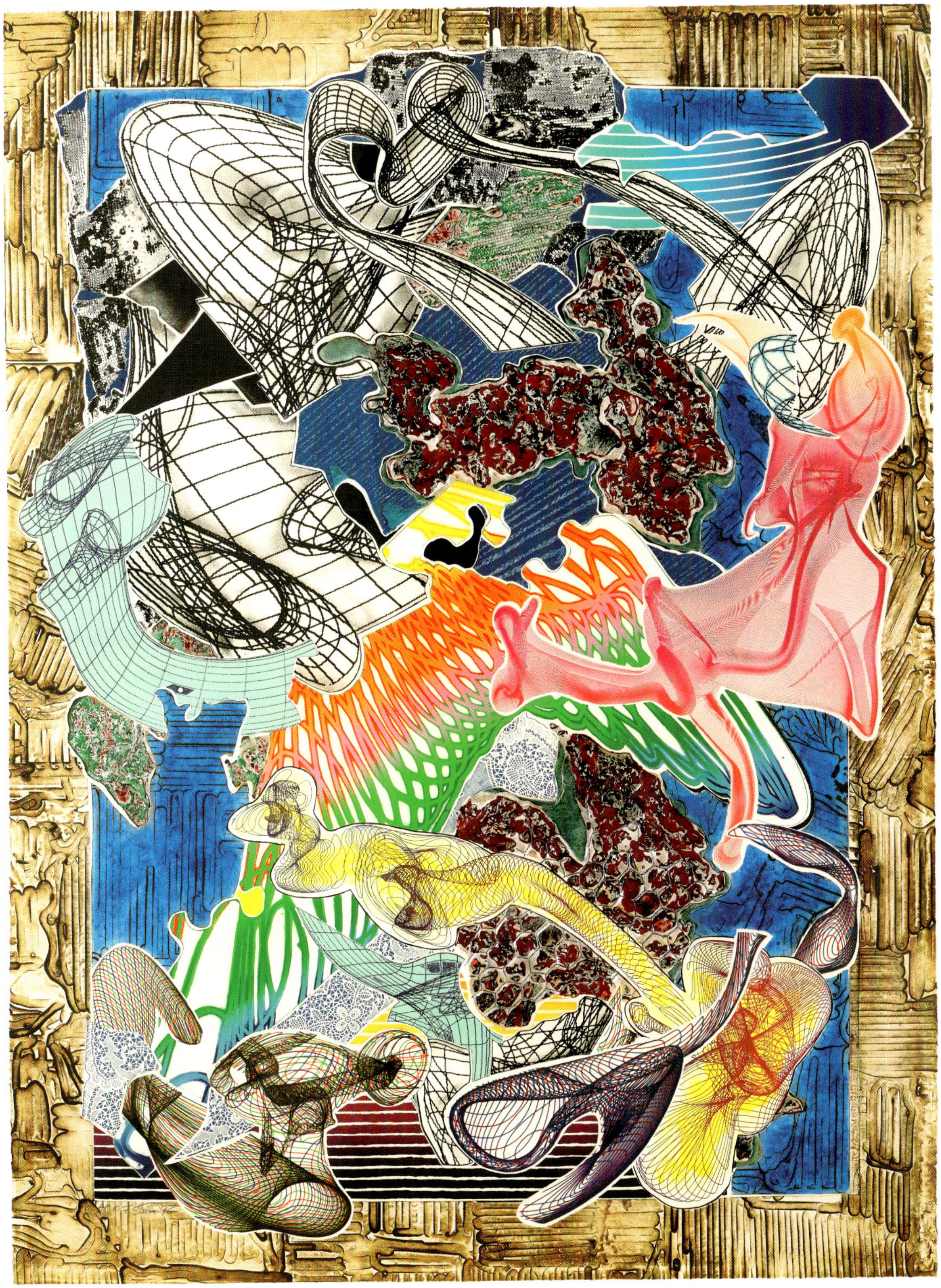

plate 30 *Despairia*, 1995

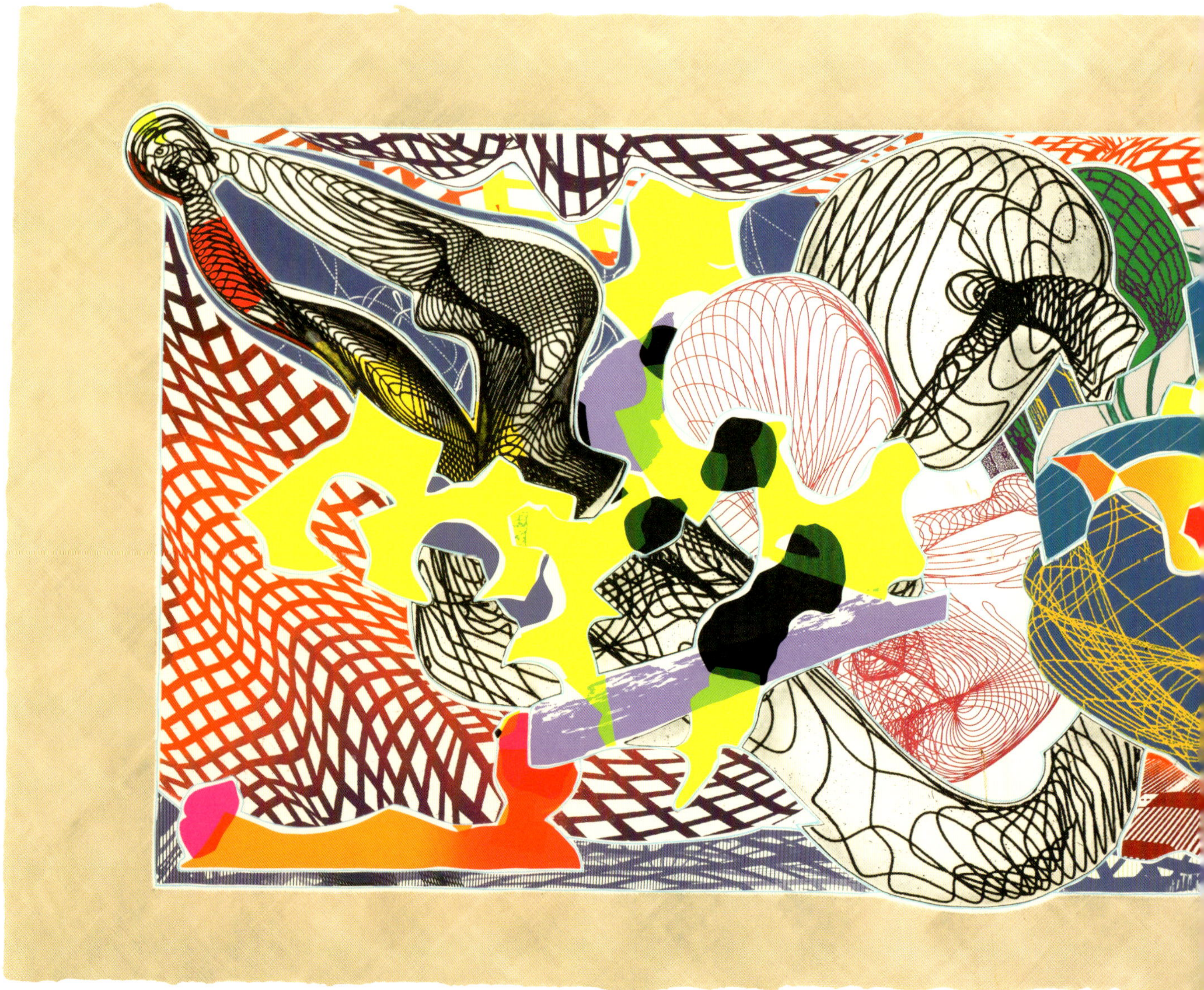

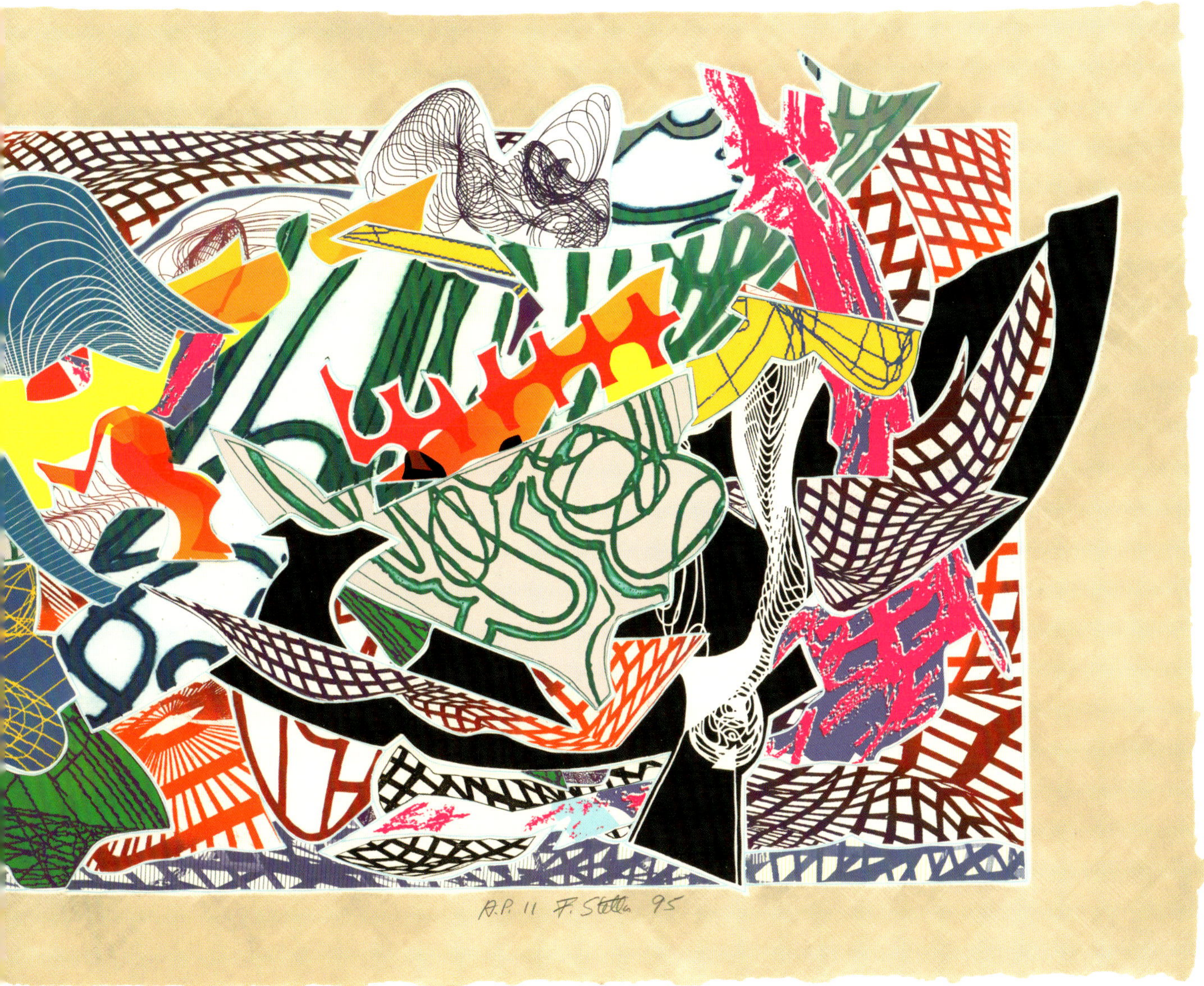

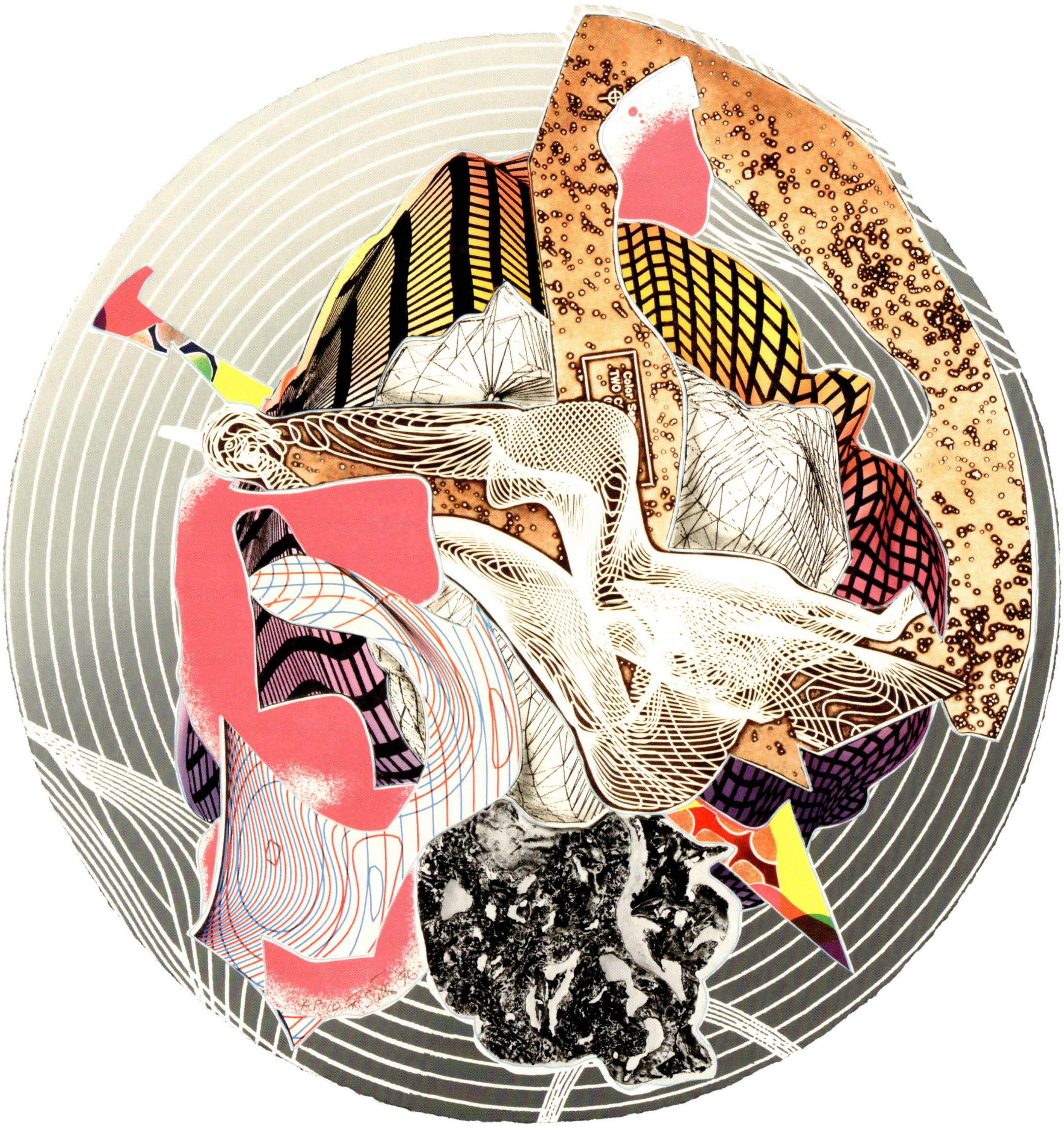

plate 32 *Dubiaxo*, 1996

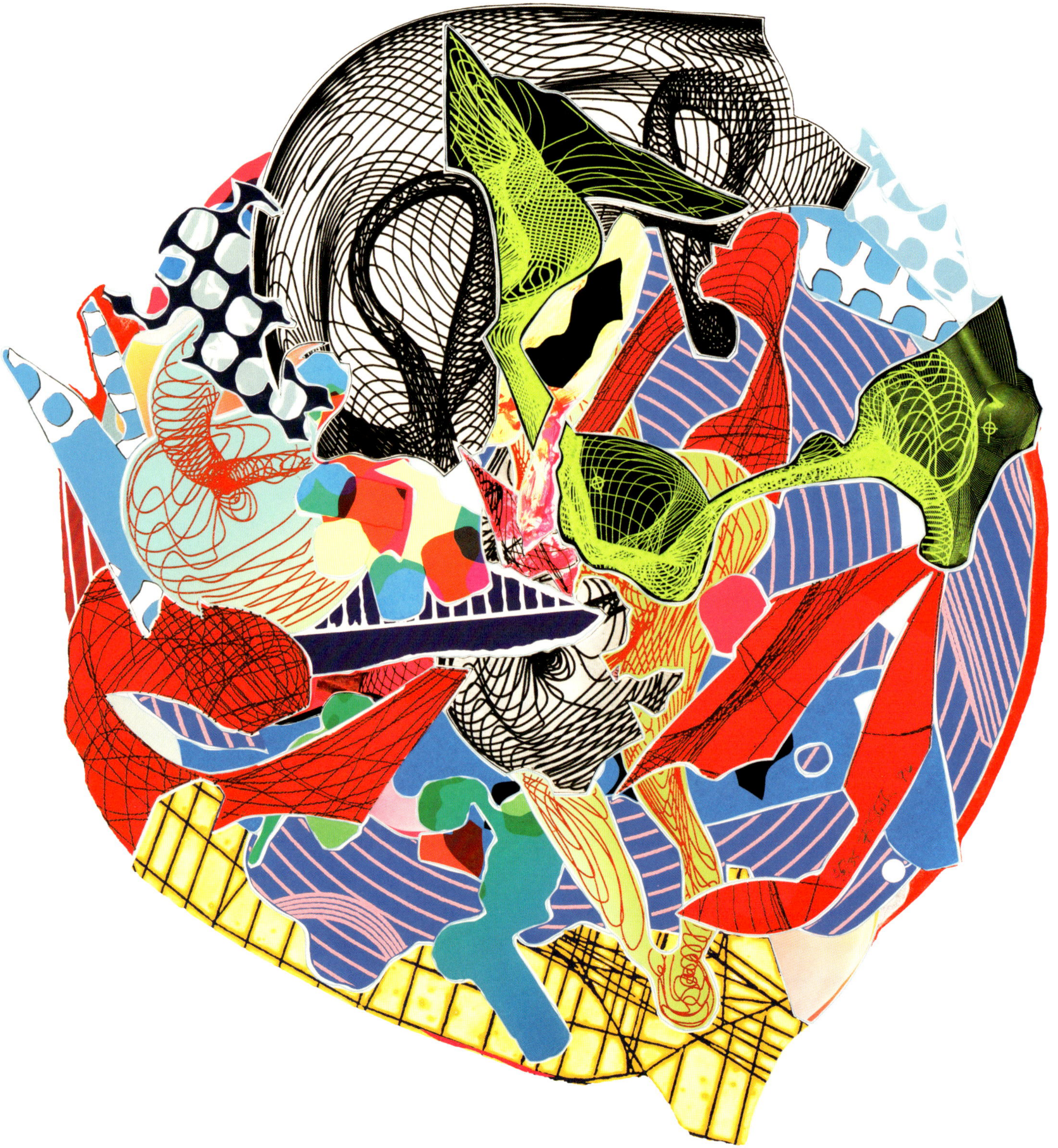

plate 33 *Fattiburg*, 1996

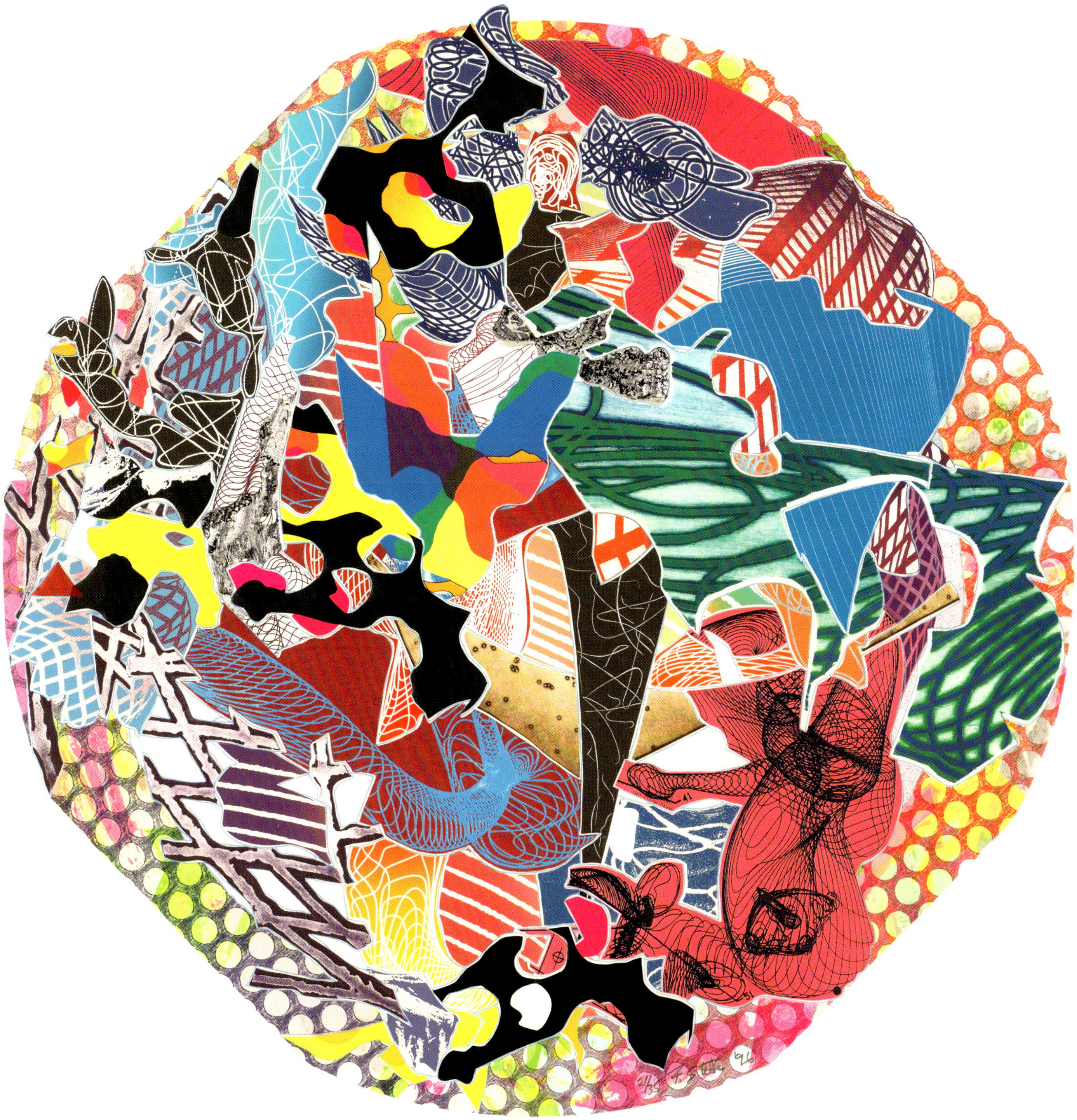

plate 34 *Fattipuff*, 1996

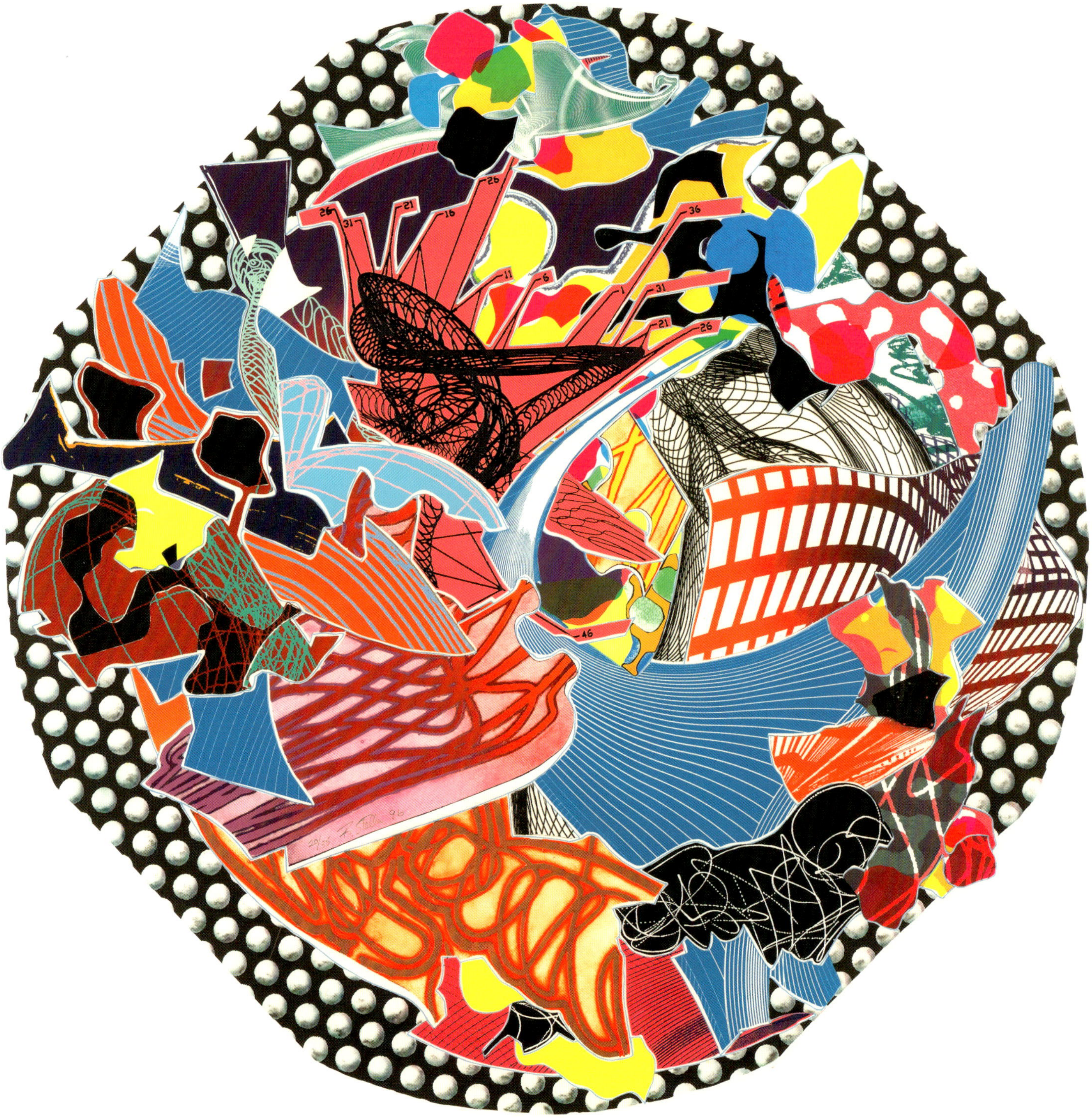

plate 35 *Perinthia*, 1996

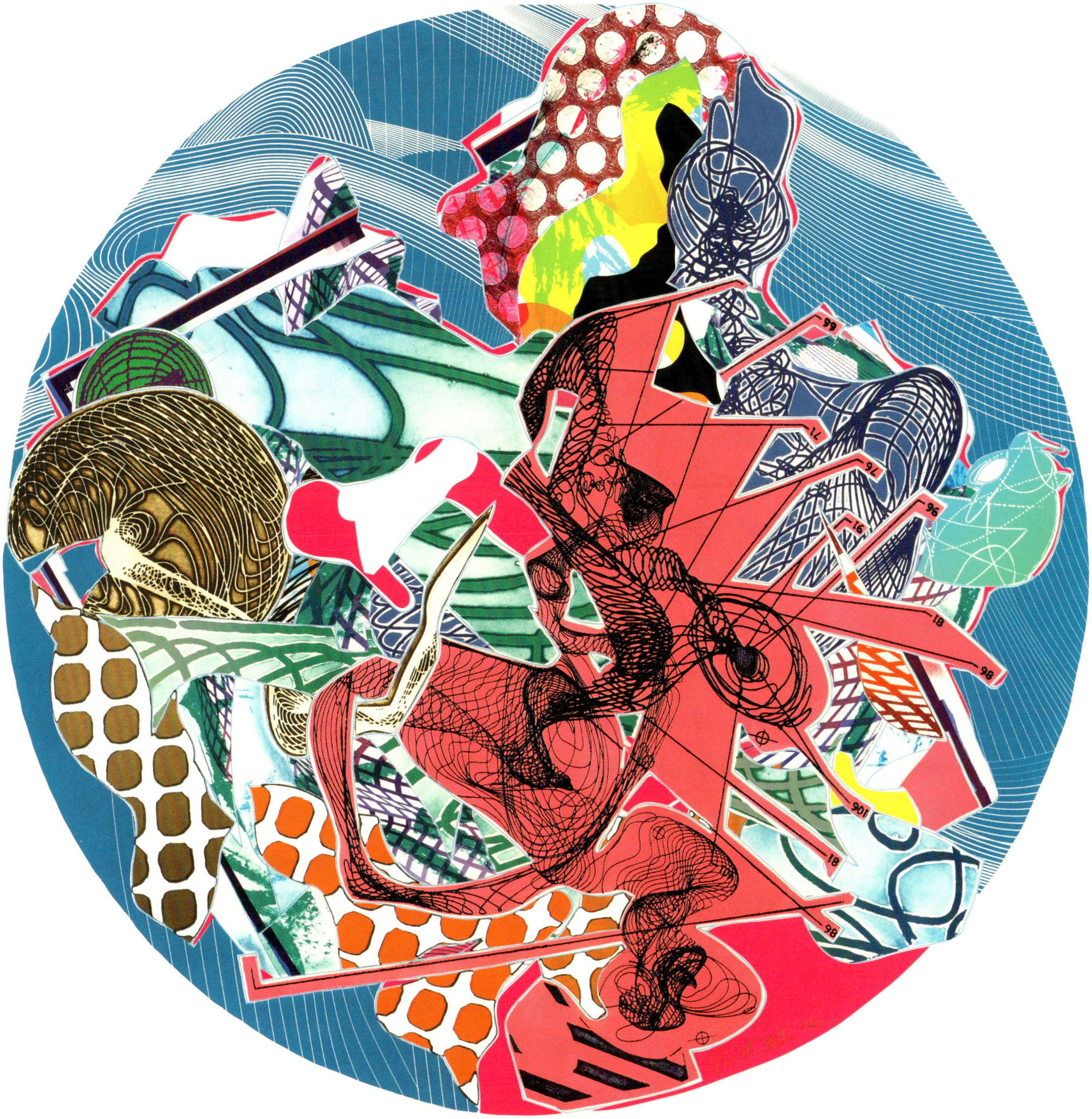

plate 36 *Sanor*, 1996

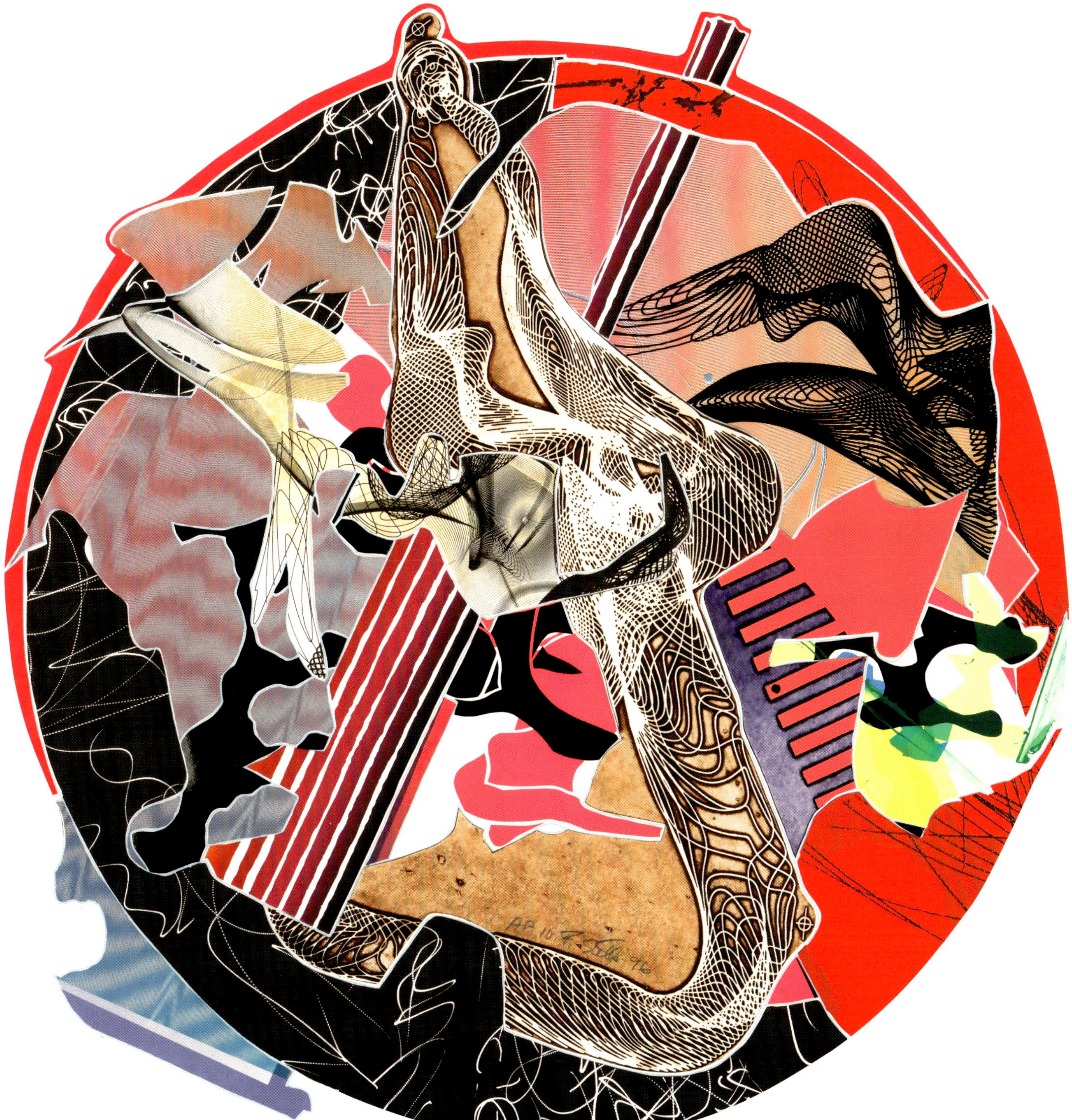

plate 37 *Juam, State I*, 1997

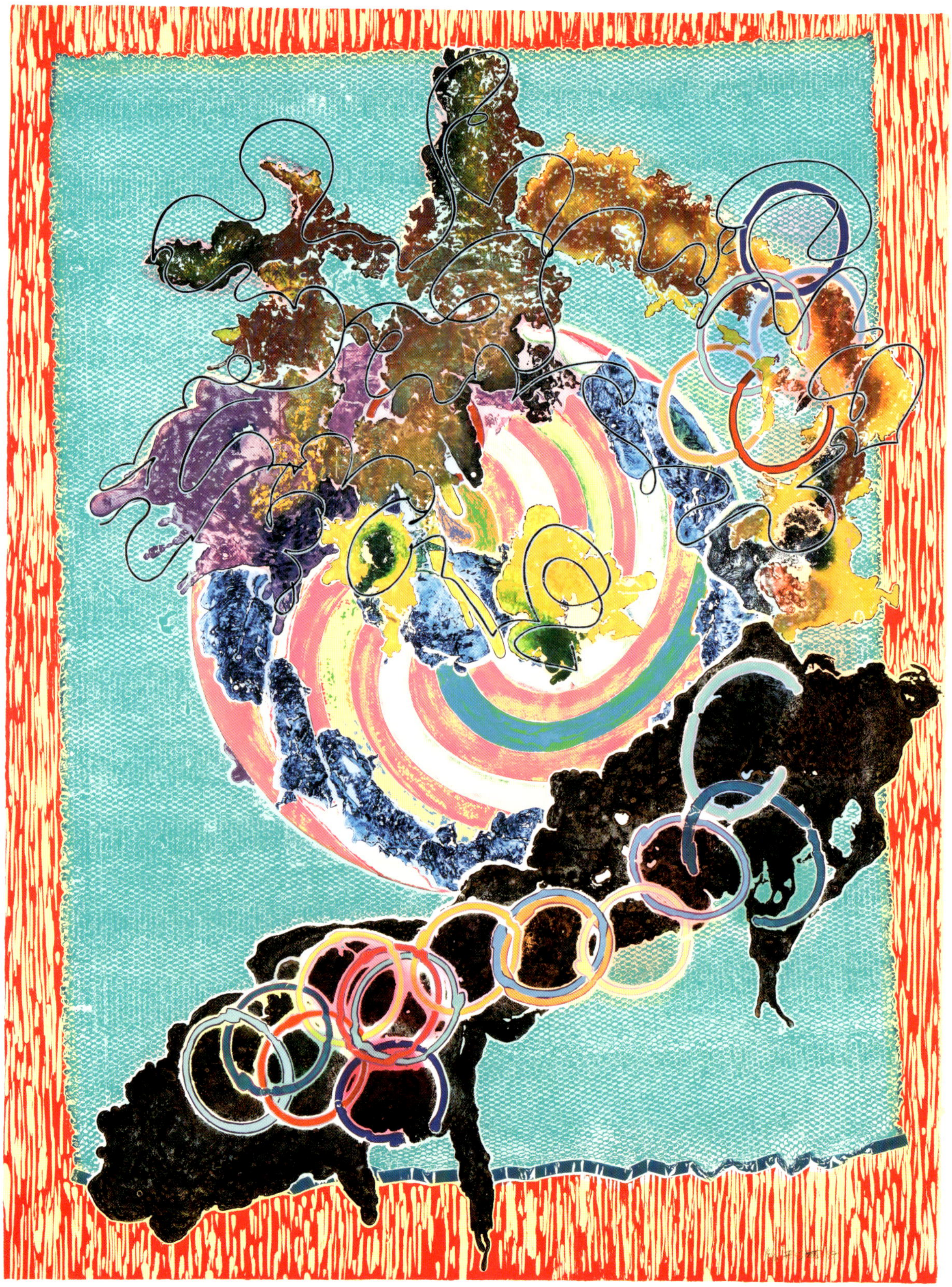

plate 38 *Juam*, 1997

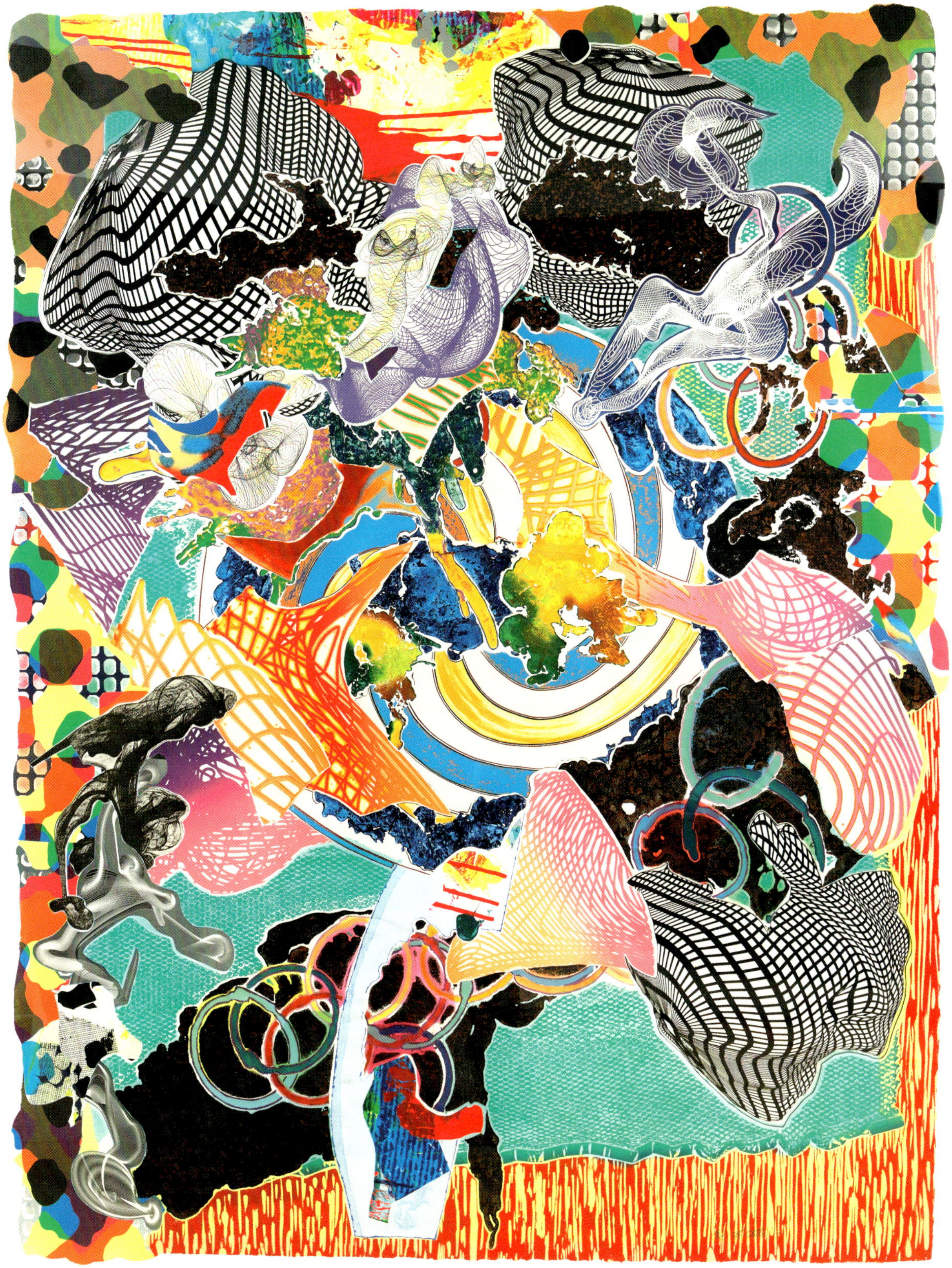

plate 39 *Coxuria, State I*, 1997

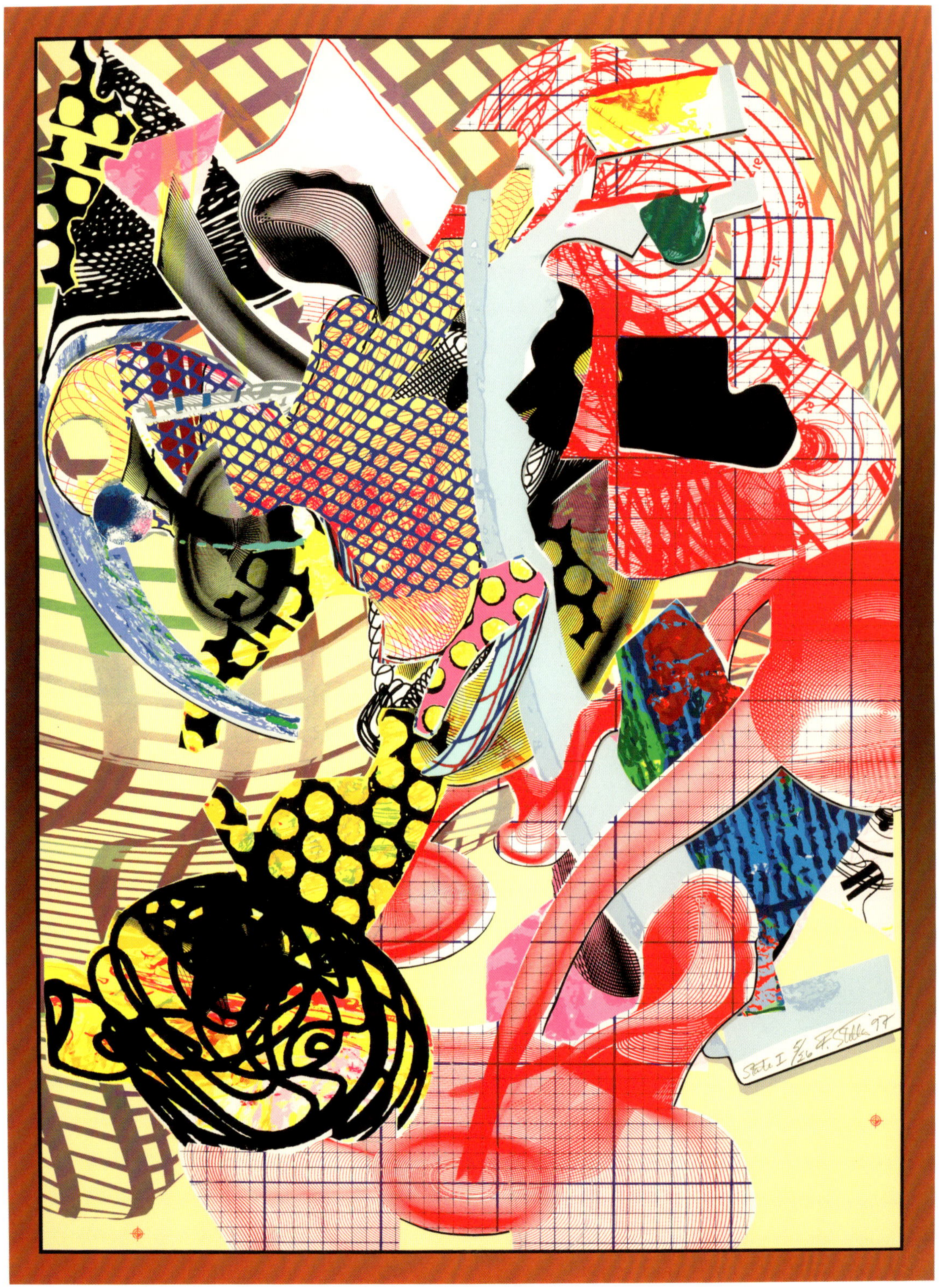

plate 40 *Cantahar*, 1998

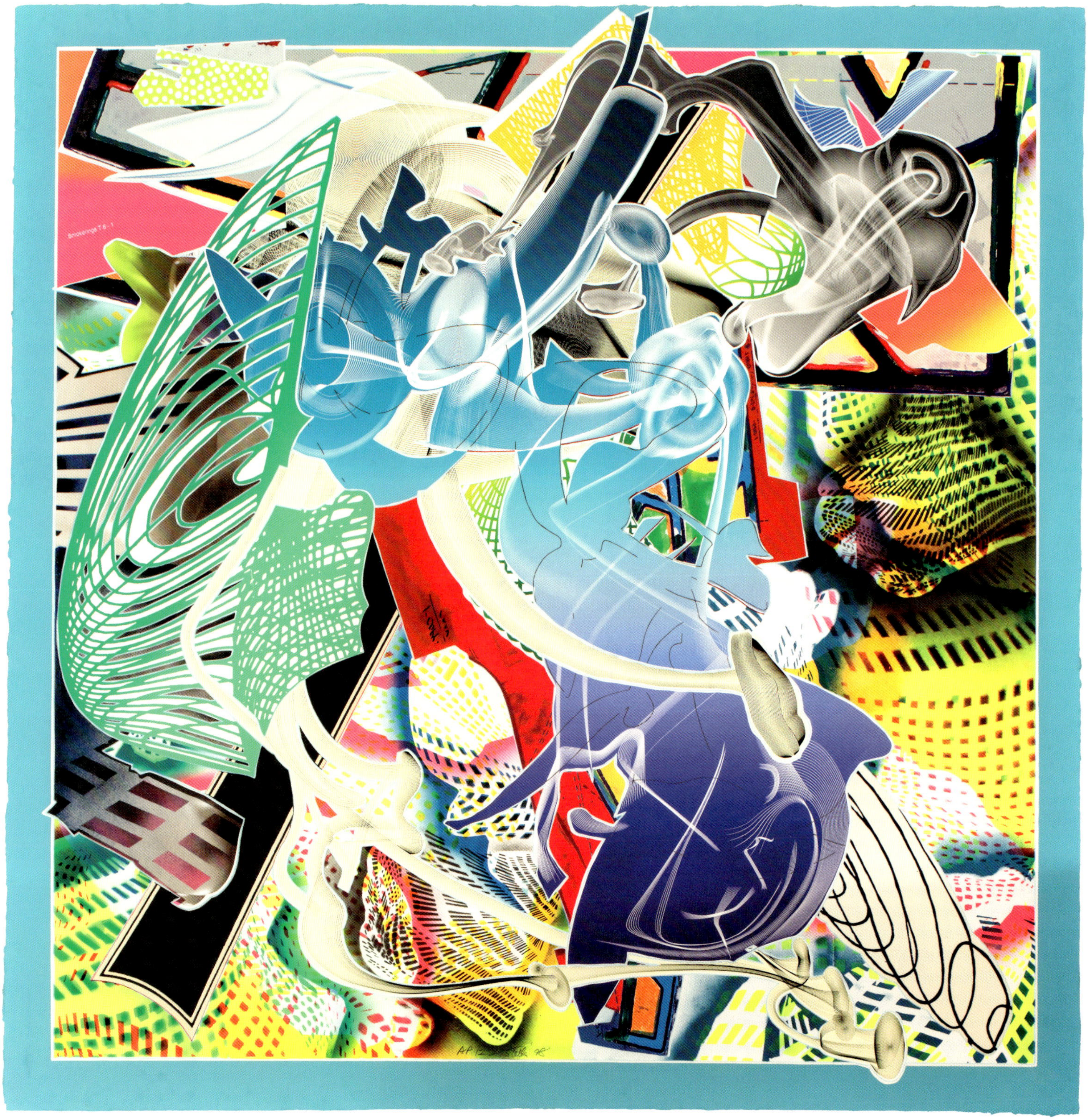

Frank Stella

If I want to reach out and try new ideas, and still hope to come up with results that make forward-moving sense, I feel I should stick with printing. I feel as though I'm in the middle of a hot streak. There is a triumphant quality to the print work that revels in its ability to translate the captured, apprehended gesture of motion into a stamped-out immediate impression.

plate 41 *Stranz*, 1999

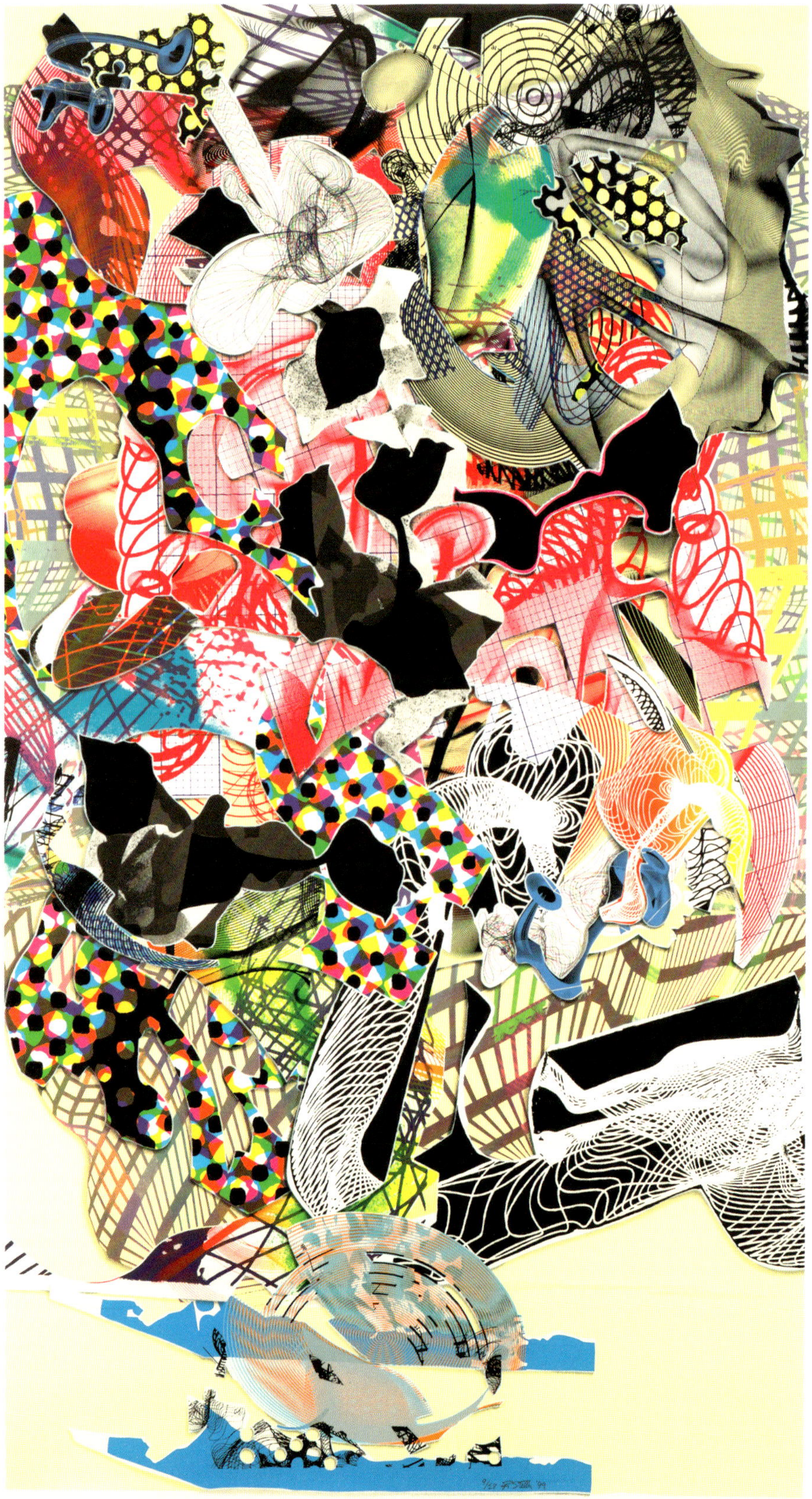

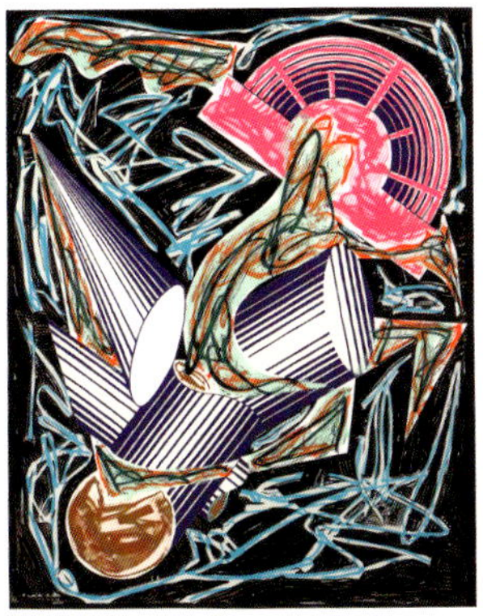

plate 1

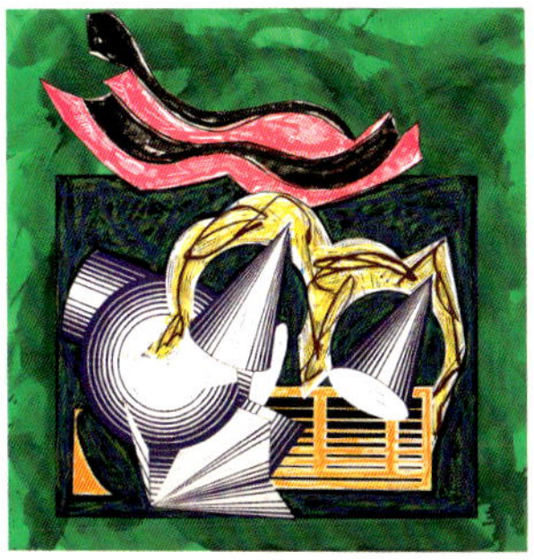

plate 2

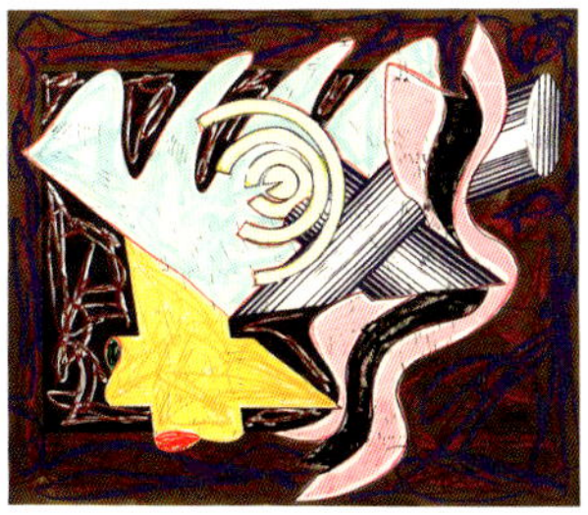

plate 3

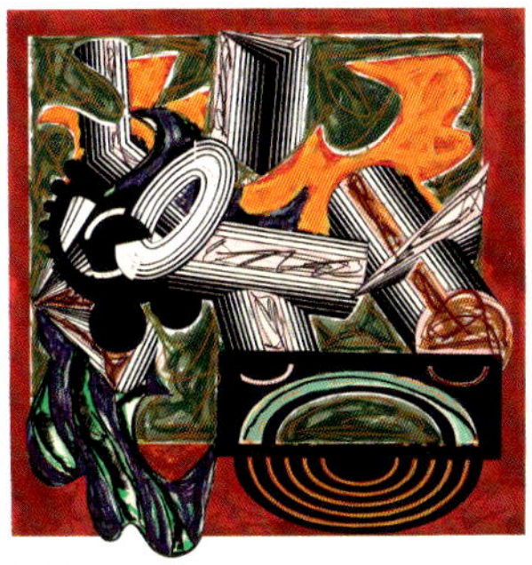

plate 4

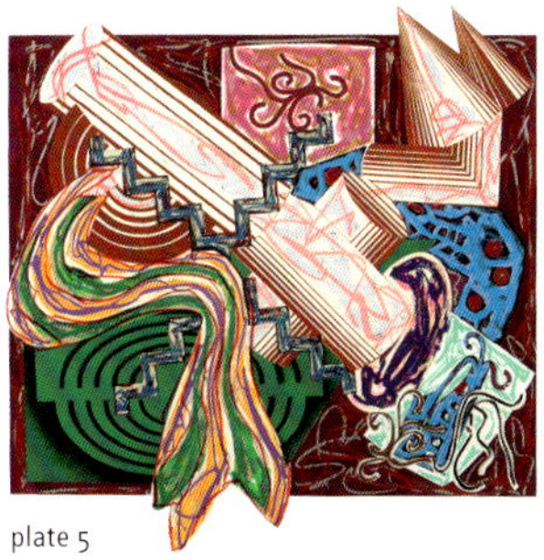

plate 5

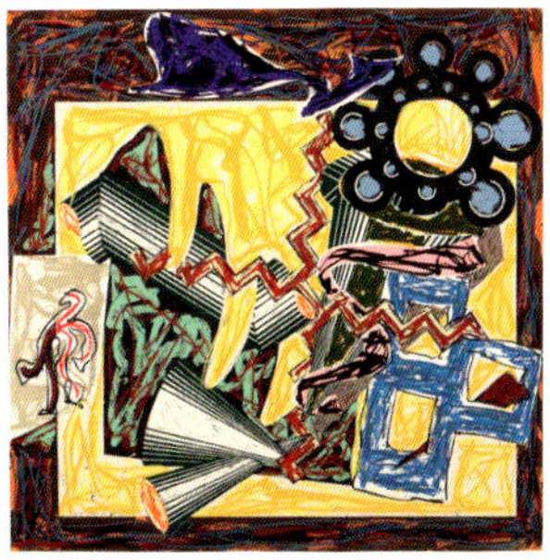

plate 6

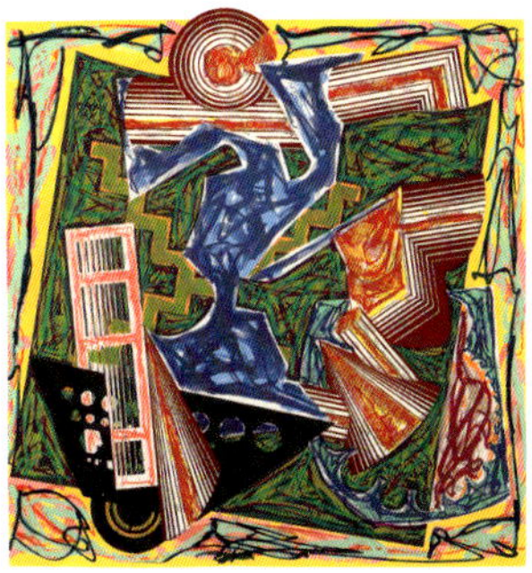

plate 7

Checklist

While many of Frank Stella's prints were developed over a period of months—in some cases years—the dates in the following checklist refer to the date of publication. The catalogue raisonné numbers refer to Axsom 2016, which details the process and press runs for each work.

Illustrations after El Lissitzky's Had Gadya, 1984

1 *Had Gadya: Front Cover*, 1984
Hand-coloring and hand-cut collage with lithograph, linocut, and screenprint, 108.0 × 86.0 cm; Publisher: Waddington Graphics, London; Axsom 170; Collection of Preston H. Haskell, Class of 1960

2 *One Small Goat Papa Bought for Two Zuzim*, 1984
Hand-coloring and hand-cut collage with lithograph, linocut, and screenprint, 133.0 × 130.2 cm; Publisher: Waddington Graphics, London; Axsom 171; Collection of Preston H. Haskell, Class of 1960

3 *A Hungry Cat Ate up the Goat*, 1984
Hand-coloring and hand-cut collage with lithograph, linocut, screenprint, and rubber relief, 115.6 × 135.9 cm; Publisher: Waddington Graphics, London; Axsom 172; Collection of Preston H. Haskell, Class of 1960

4 *Then Came a Dog and Bit the Cat*, 1984
Hand-coloring and hand-cut collage with lithograph, linocut, and screenprint, 135.9 × 131.1 cm; Publisher: Waddington Graphics, London; Axsom 173; Collection of Preston H. Haskell, Class of 1960

5 *Then Came a Stick and Beat the Dog*, 1984
Hand-coloring and hand-cut collage with lithograph, linocut, and screenprint, 134.3 × 134.0 cm; Publisher: Waddington Graphics, London; Axsom 174; Collection of Preston H. Haskell, Class of 1960

6 *Then Came a Fire and Burnt the Stick*, 1984
Hand-coloring and hand-cut collage with lithograph, linocut, and screenprint, 132.1 × 134.0 cm; Publisher: Waddington Graphics, London; Axsom 175; Collection of Preston H. Haskell, Class of 1960

7 *Then Water Came and Quenched the Fire*, 1984
Hand-coloring and hand-cut collage with lithograph, linocut, and screenprint, 137.2 × 131.1 cm; Publisher: Waddington Graphics, London; Axsom 176; Collection of Preston H. Haskell, Class of 1960

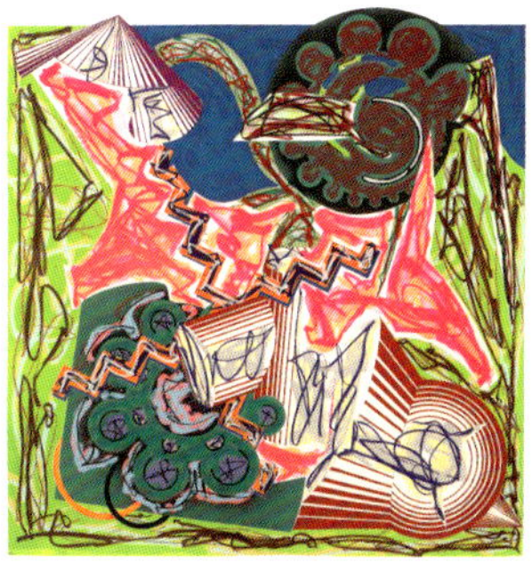

plate 8

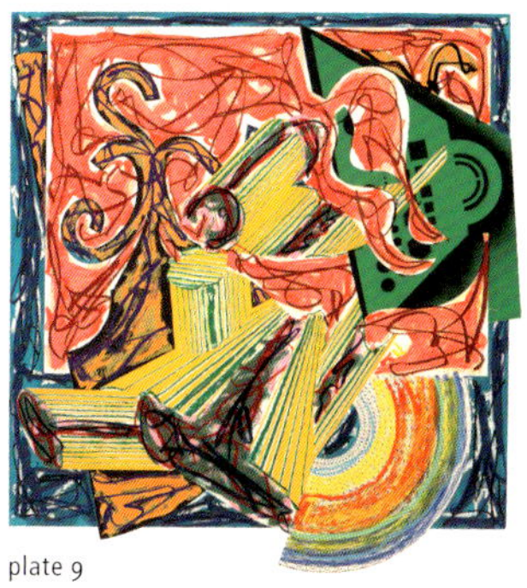

plate 9

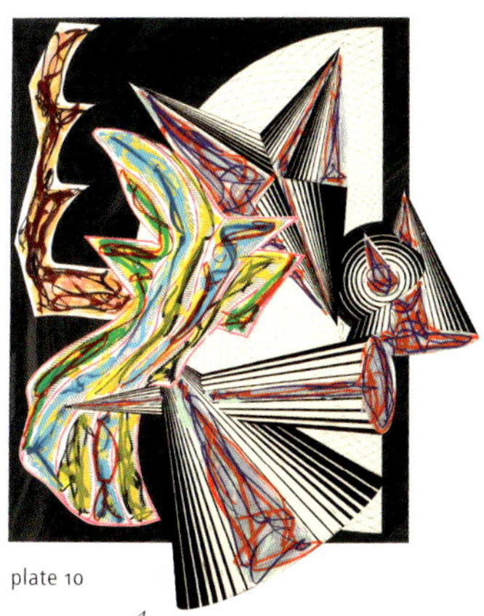

plate 10

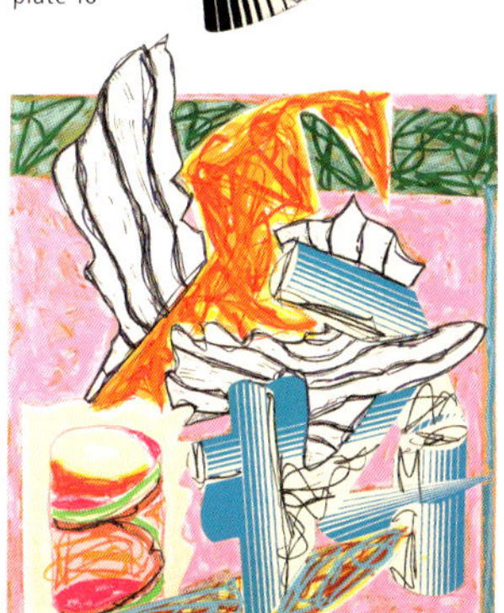

plate 11

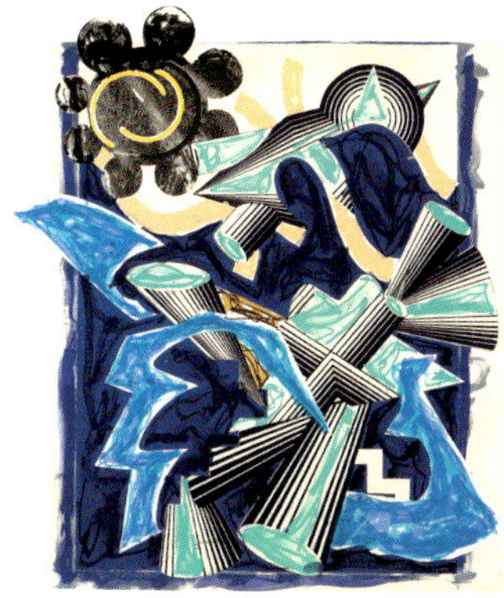

plate 12

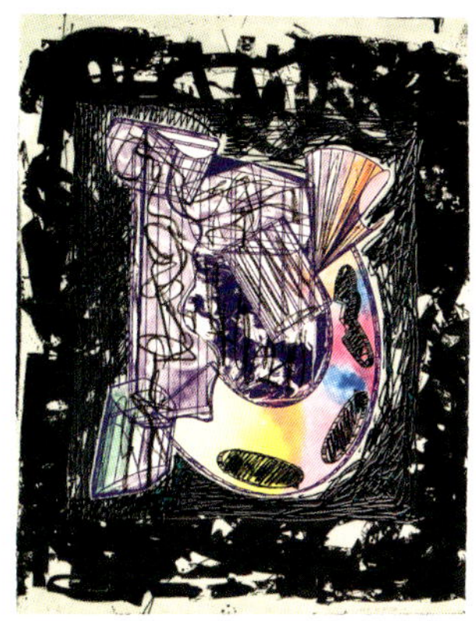

plate 13

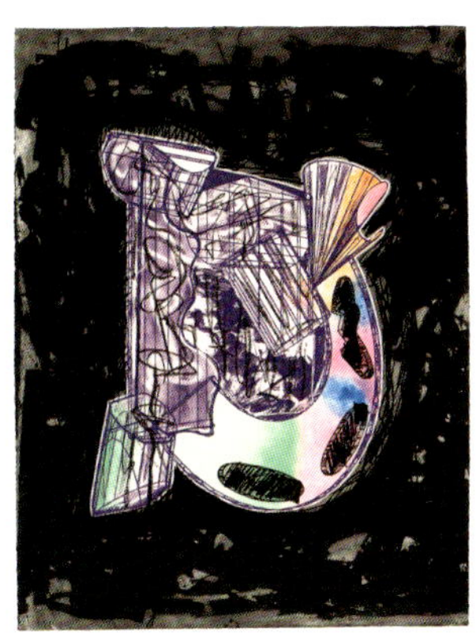

plate 14

8 *Then Came an Ox and Drank the Water*, 1984
Hand-coloring and hand-cut collage with lithograph, linocut, and screenprint, 137.2 × 133.0 cm; Publisher: Waddington Graphics, London; Axsom 177; Collection of Preston H. Haskell, Class of 1960

9 *The Butcher Came and Slew the Ox*, 1984
Hand-coloring and hand-cut collage with lithograph, linocut, and screenprint, 144.5 × 135.6 cm; Publisher: Waddington Graphics, London; Axsom 178; Collection of Preston H. Haskell, Class of 1960

10 *Then Came Death and Took the Butcher*, 1984
Hand-coloring and hand-cut collage with lithograph, linocut, screenprint, and rubber relief, 148.9 × 120.7 cm; Publisher: Waddington Graphics, London; Axsom 179; Collection of Preston H. Haskell, Class of 1960

11 *And the Holy One, Blessed Be He, Came and Smote the Angel of Death*, 1984
Hand-coloring and hand-cut collage with lithograph, linocut, and screenprint, 129.5 × 105.1 cm; Publisher: Waddington Graphics, London; Axsom 180; Collection of Preston H. Haskell, Class of 1960

12 *Had Gadya: Back Cover*, 1984
Hand-coloring and hand-cut collage with color lithograph, linocut, and screenprint, 153.0 × 134.9 cm; Publisher: Waddington Graphics, London; Axsom 181; Collection of Preston H. Haskell, Class of 1960

Italian Folktales, 1988–89

13 *Bene come il sale, State I* (As Dear as Salt, State I), 1989
Etching, aquatint, and relief on hand-dyed handmade paper, 193.0 × 149.9 cm; Publisher: Tyler Graphics, Mount Kisco, New York; Axsom 184a; Addison Gallery of American Art. Tyler Graphics Ltd. 1974–2001 Collection, given in honor of Frank Stella (2003.44.307)

14 *Bene come il sale, State III* (As Dear as Salt, State III), 1989
Etching, aquatint, and relief on hand-dyed handmade paper, 193.0 × 149.9 cm; Publisher: Tyler Graphics, Mount Kisco, New York; Axsom 184c; Addison Gallery of American Art. Tyler Graphics Ltd. 1974–2001 Collection, given in honor of Frank Stella (2003.44.308)

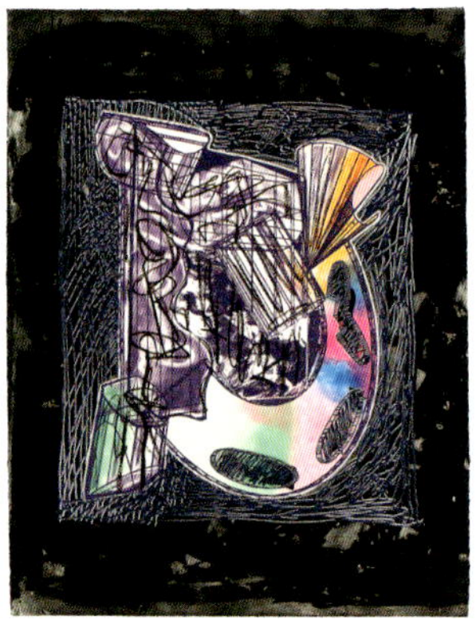
plate 15

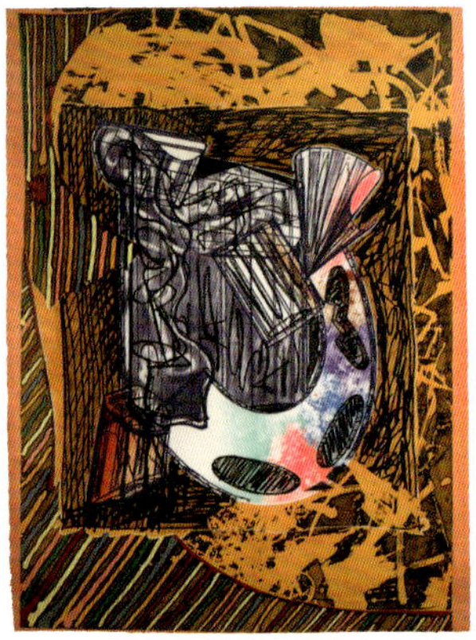
plate 16

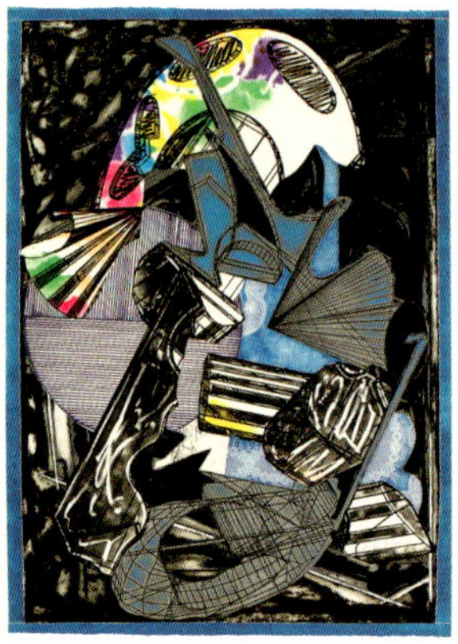
plate 17

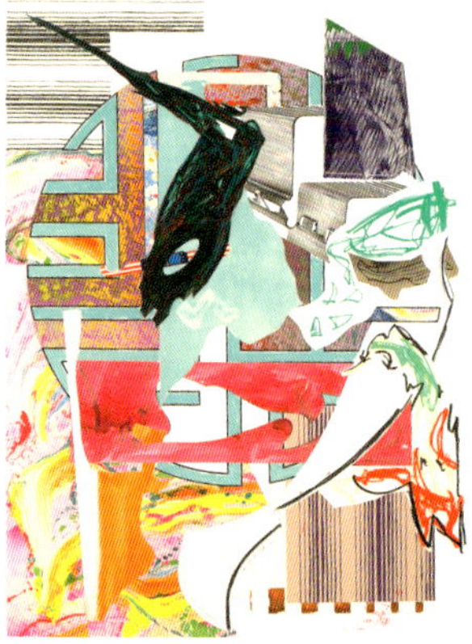
plate 18

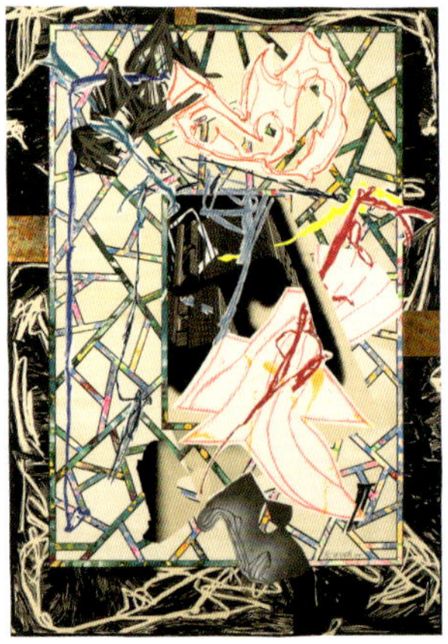
plate 19

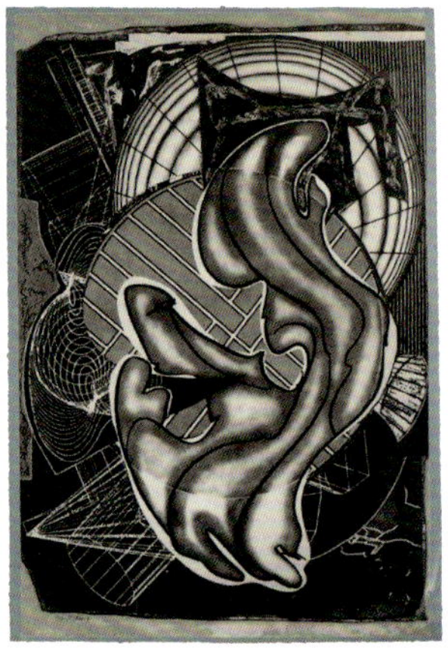
plate 20

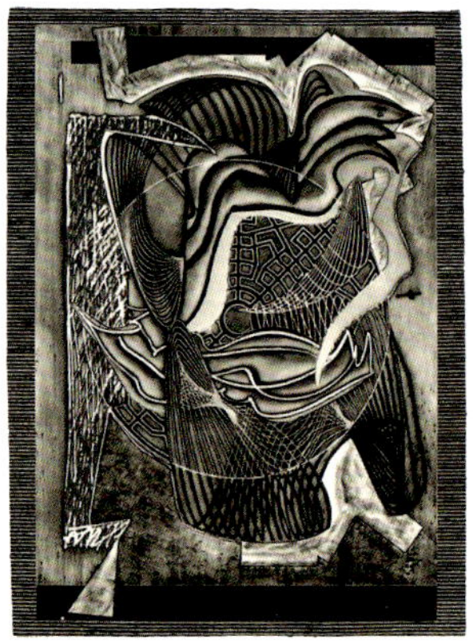
plate 21

15 *Bene come il sale, State IV* (As Dear as Salt, State IV), 1989
Etching, aquatint, and relief on hand-dyed handmade paper, 193.0 × 149.9 cm; Publisher: Tyler Graphics, Mount Kisco, New York; Axsom 184d; Addison Gallery of American Art. Tyler Graphics Ltd. 1974–2001 Collection, given in honor of Frank Stella (2003.44.309)

16 *Bene come il sale* (As Dear as Salt), 1989
Etching, aquatint, and relief on hand-dyed handmade paper, 196.9 × 149.2 cm; Publisher: Tyler Graphics, Mount Kisco, New York; Axsom 184; Collection of Rysia de Ravel d'Esclapon, Princeton

17 *Giufà e la berretta rossa* (Giufà and the Red Cap), 1989
Etching, aquatint, relief, and engraving on hand-dyed handmade paper, 197.5 × 147.3 cm; Publisher: Tyler Graphics, Mount Kisco, New York; Axsom 185; Addison Gallery of American Art. Tyler Graphics Ltd. 1974–2001 Collection, given in honor of Frank Stella (2003.44.310)

The Moby Dick Prints, 1989–93

18 *The Quarter Deck*, 1989
From the series *The Waves*
Screenprint, lithograph, and linoleum block, with hand-coloring, marbling, and hand-cut collage, 190.5 × 141.5 cm; Publisher: Waddington Graphics, London; Axsom 189; Collection of Preston H. Haskell, Class of 1960

19 *The Counterpane*, 1989
From the series *The Waves*
Screenprint, lithograph, and linoleum block, with hand-coloring, marbling, and hand-cut collage, 180.5 × 129.5 cm; Publisher: Waddington Graphics, London; Axsom 190; Collection of Preston H. Haskell, Class of 1960

20 *Stubb and Flask Kill a Right Whale*, 1991
From the series *Moby Dick Engravings*
Etching, aquatint, relief, and Carborundum on handmade paper, 193.7 × 136.5 cm; Publisher: Tyler Graphics, Mount Kisco, New York; Axsom 200; Collection of Rysia de Ravel d'Esclapon, Princeton

21 *The Funeral*, 1991
From the series *Moby Dick Engravings*
Etching, aquatint, relief, and Carborundum on handmade paper, 198.8 × 151.1 cm; Publisher: Tyler Graphics, Mount Kisco, New York; Axsom 202; Addison Gallery of American Art. Tyler Graphics Ltd. 1974–2001 Collection, given in honor of Frank Stella (2003.44.305)

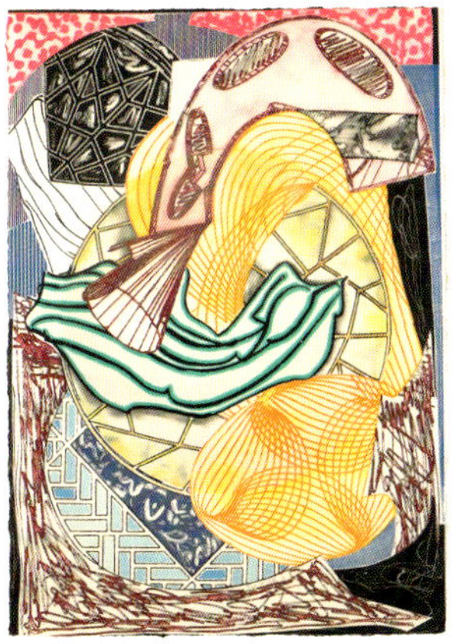

plate 22

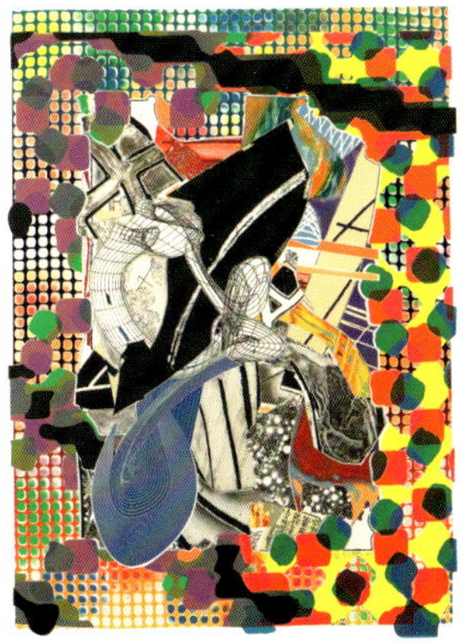

plate 25

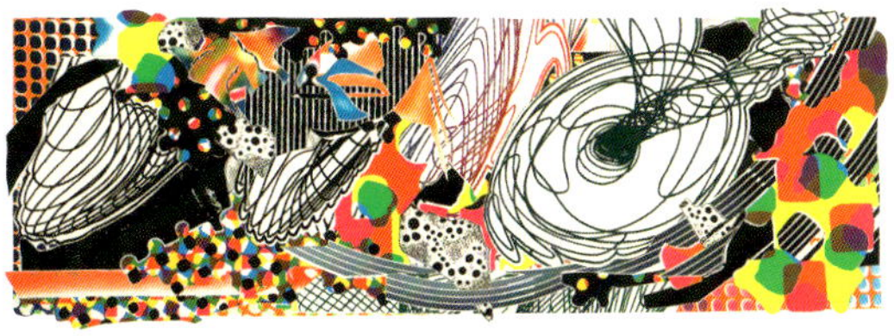

plate 26

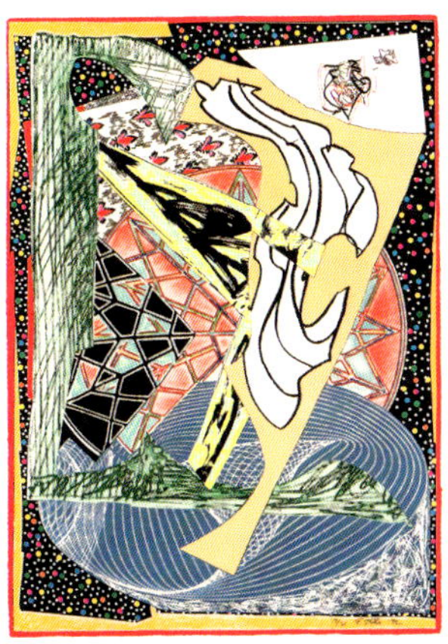

plate 23

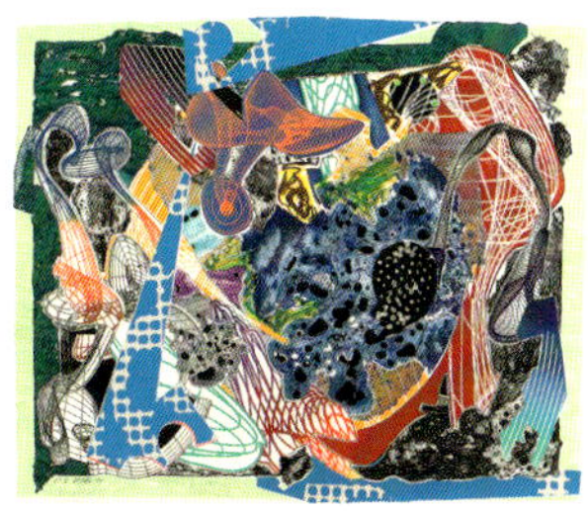

plate 27

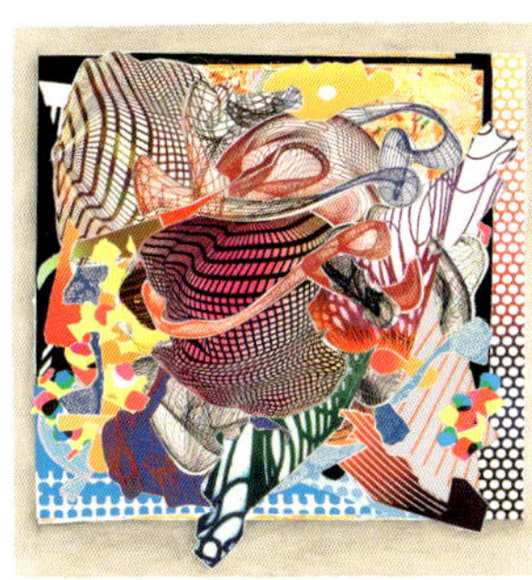

plate 28

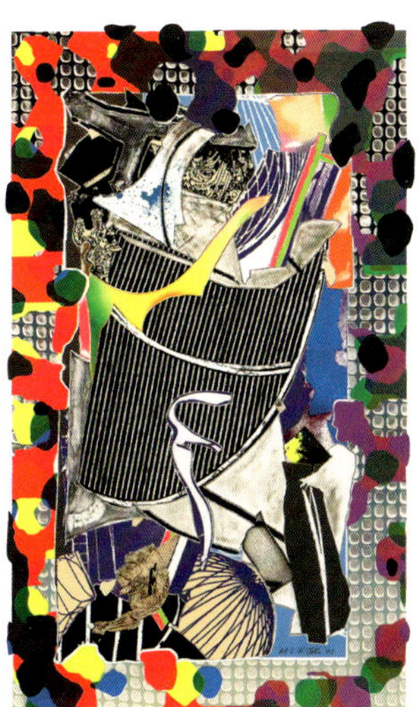

plate 24

22 *The Cabin. Ahab and Starbuck (Dome)*, 1992
From the series *Moby Dick Domes*
Etching, aquatint, relief, and engraving on molded handmade paper, 185.4 × 134.6 × 15.2 cm; Publisher: Tyler Graphics, Mount Kisco, New York; Axsom 209; Collection of Preston H. Haskell, Class of 1960

23 *Jonah Historically Regarded (Dome)*, 1992
From the series *Moby Dick Domes*
Etching, aquatint, relief, engraving, screenprint, stencil, hand-coloring, on molded handmade paper, 186.7 × 134.6 × 15.2 cm; Publisher: Tyler Graphics, Mount Kisco, New York; Addison Gallery of American Art. Tyler Graphics Ltd. 1974–2001 Collection, given in honor of Frank Stella (2003.44.300)

24 *The Battering Ram*, 1993
From the series *Moby Dick Deckle Edges*
Lithograph, etching, aquatint, relief, engraving, screenprint, and collagraph on handmade paper cut to image, 151.4 × 90.5 cm (irregular); Publisher: Tyler Graphics, Mount Kisco, New York; Axsom 214; Collection of Preston H. Haskell, Class of 1960

25 *The Affidavit*, 1993
From the series *Moby Dick Deckle Edges*
Lithograph, etching, aquatint, relief, engraving, and screenprint on handmade paper cut to image, 156.8 × 115.6 cm (irregular); Publisher: Tyler Graphics, Mount Kisco, New York; Axsom 220; Collection of Preston H. Haskell, Class of 1960

26 *The Monkey Rope*, 1993
From the series *Moby Dick Deckle Edges*
Lithograph, etching, aquatint, relief, engraving, and screenprint on handmade paper cut to image, 60.3 × 173.4 cm (irregular); Publisher: Tyler Graphics, Mount Kisco, New York; Axsom 218; Collection of Preston H. Haskell, Class of 1960

Imaginary Places, 1994–99

27 *Swoonarie*, 1995
From the series *Imaginary Places*
Etching, aquatint, relief, screenprint, lithograph, and woodcut on handmade paper, 106.7 × 132.1 cm; Publisher: Tyler Graphics, Mount Kisco, New York; Axsom 225; Collection of Preston H. Haskell, Class of 1960

28 *Feneralia*, 1995
From the series *Imaginary Places*
Screenprint, lithograph, etching, aquatint, relief, and collagraph on handmade paper, 116.8 × 106.7 cm; Publisher: Tyler Graphics, Mount Kisco, New York; Axsom 228; Addison Gallery of American Art. Tyler Graphics Ltd. 1974–2001 Collection, given in honor of Frank Stella (2003.44.294)

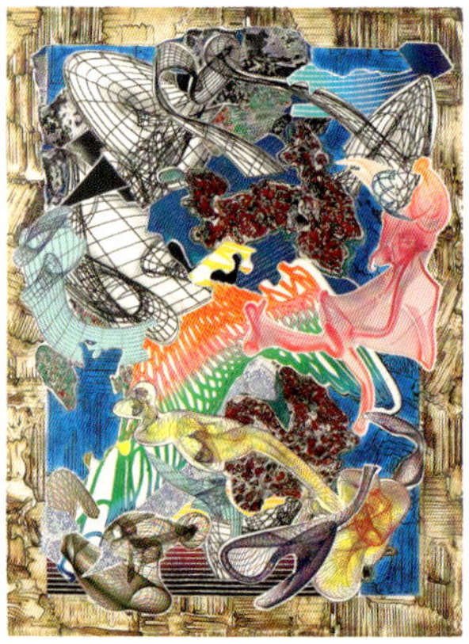

plate 29

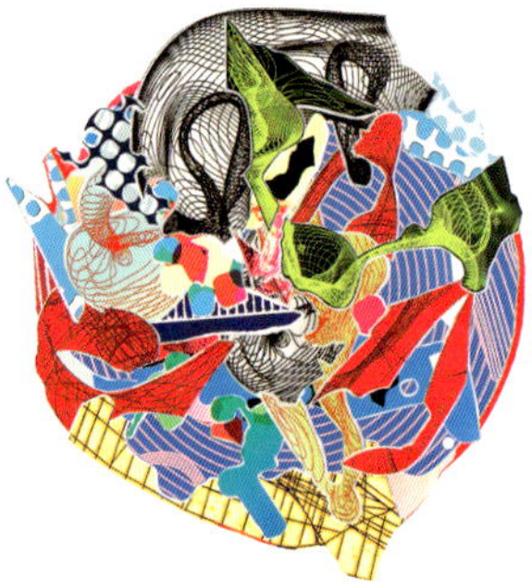

plate 32

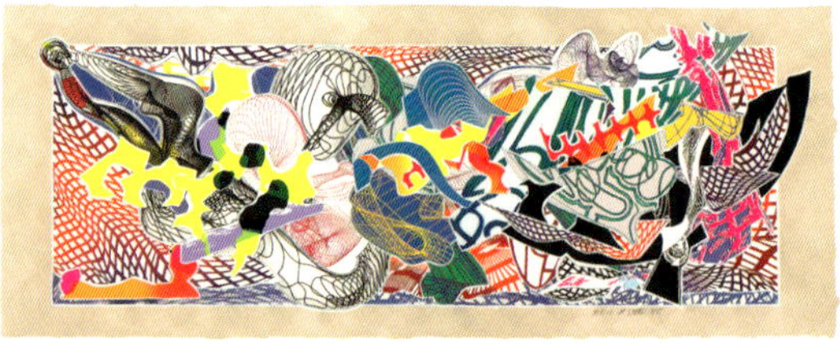

plate 30

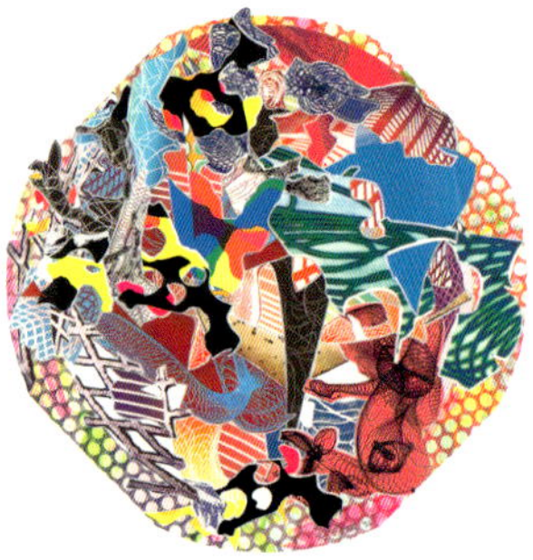

plate 33

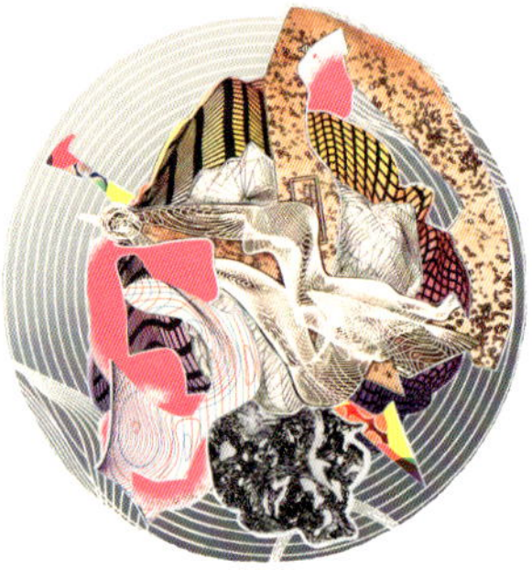

plate 31

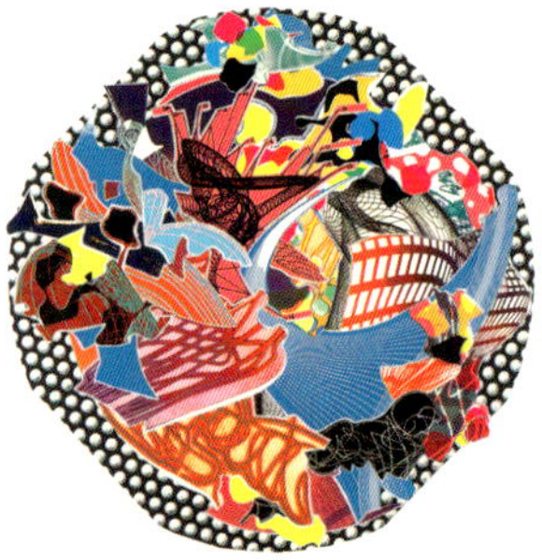

plate 34

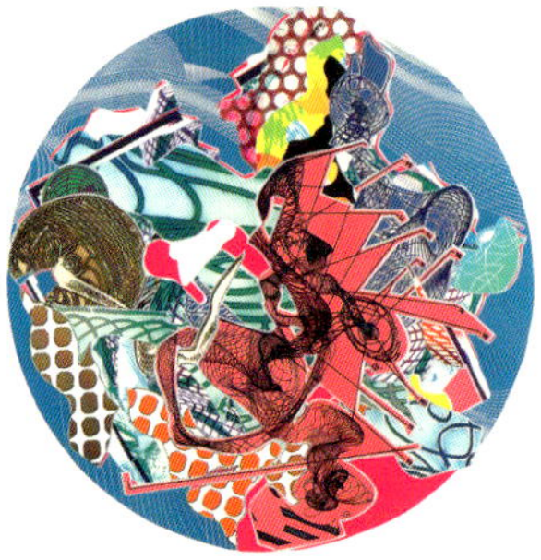

plate 35

29 *Fanattia*, 1995
From the series *Imaginary Places*
Etching, engraving, relief, lithograph, stamping, woodcut, and mezzotint on handmade hand-colored paper with metalized silver foil, 138.4 × 104.1 cm; Publisher: Tyler Graphics, Mount Kisco, New York; Axsom 230; Collection of Preston H. Haskell, Class of 1960

30 *Despairia*, 1995
From the series *Imaginary Places*
Screenprint, aquatint, etching, relief, lithograph, engraving, and mezzotint on handmade paper, 50.8 × 132.1 cm; Publisher: Tyler Graphics, Mount Kisco, New York; Axsom 231; Collection of Preston H. Haskell, Class of 1960

31 *Atvatabar*, 1996
From the series *Imaginary Places II*
Lithograph, screenprint, etching, aquatint, and relief on handmade paper cut to image, diam. 66.7 cm (irregular); Publisher: Tyler Graphics, Mount Kisco, New York; Axsom 236; Addison Gallery of American Art. Tyler Graphics Ltd. 1974–2001 Collection, given in honor of Frank Stella (2003.44.290)

32 *Dubiaxo*, 1996
From the series *Imaginary Places II*
Lithograph, screenprint, etching, aquatint, relief, and stamping, with metalized silver foil on handmade paper cut to image, diam. 73.7 cm (irregular); Publisher: Tyler Graphics, Mount Kisco, New York; Axsom 239; Addison Gallery of American Art. Tyler Graphics Ltd. 1974–2001 Collection, given in honor of Frank Stella (2003.44.284)

33 *Fattiburg*, 1996
From the series *Imaginary Places II*
Lithograph, screenprint, etching, aquatint, relief, engraving, and stamping, with metalized silver foil on handmade paper cut to image, diam. 81.3 cm (irregular); Publisher: Tyler Graphics, Mount Kisco, New York; Axsom 242; Collection of Preston H. Haskell, Class of 1960

34 *Fattipuff*, 1996
From the series *Imaginary Places II*
Lithograph, screenprint, etching, aquatint, and relief on handmade paper cut to image, diam. 82.6 cm (irregular); Publisher: Tyler Graphics, Mount Kisco, New York; Axsom 243; Collection of Preston H. Haskell, Class of 1960

35 *Perinthia*, 1996
From the series *Imaginary Places II*
Lithograph, screenprint, etching, aquatint, and relief on handmade paper cut to image, diam. 68.9 cm (irregular); Publisher: Tyler Graphics, Mount Kisco, New York; Axsom 245; Collection of Preston H. Haskell, Class of 1960

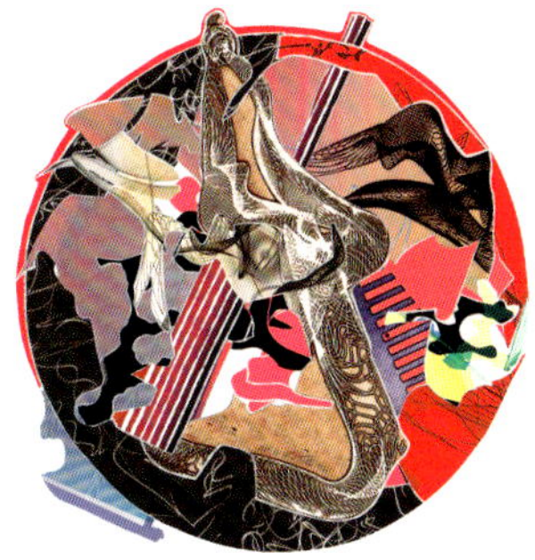

plate 36

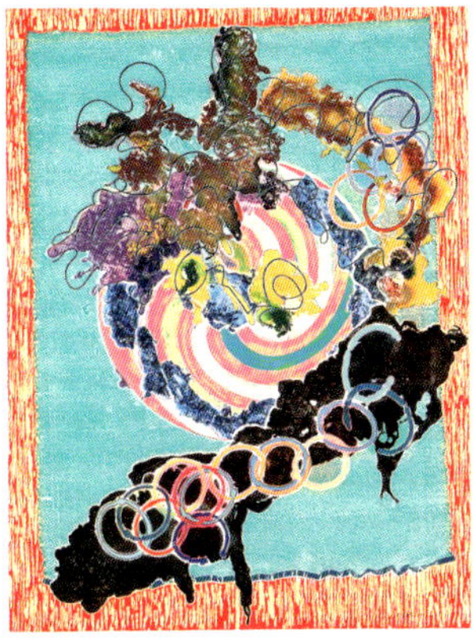

plate 37

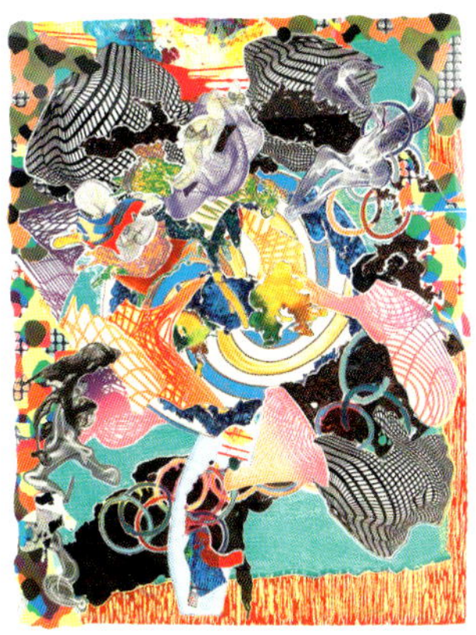

plate 38

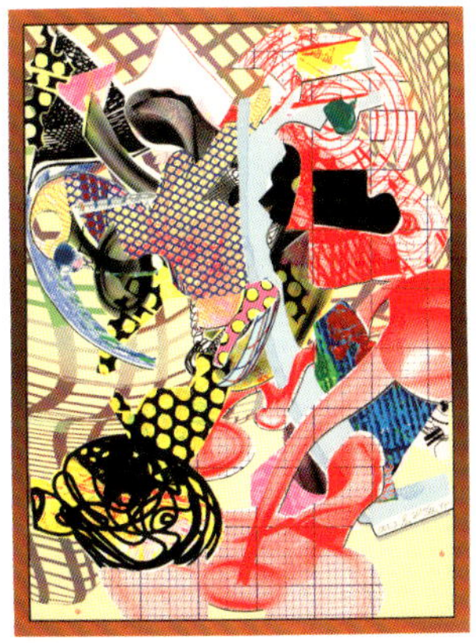

plate 39

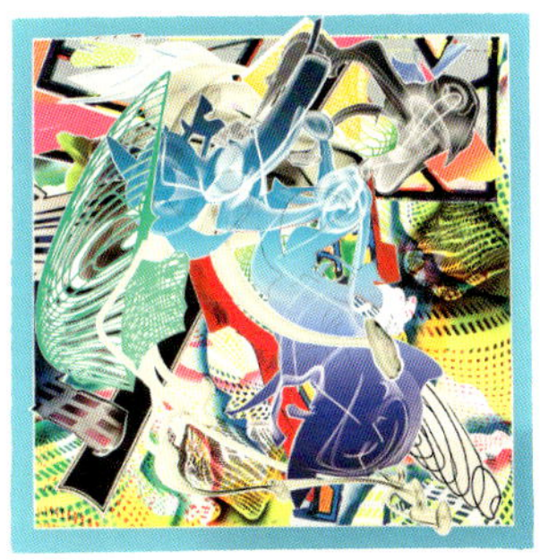

plate 40

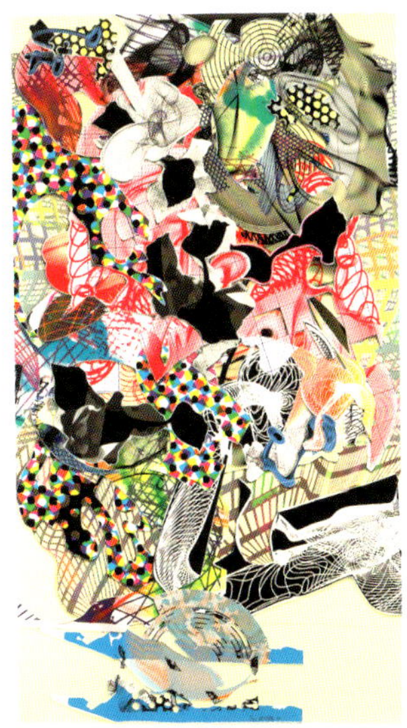

plate 41

36 *Sanor*, 1996
From the series *Imaginary Places II*
Lithograph, screenprint, etching, aquatint, relief, and engraving on handmade paper cut to image, diam. 73.7 cm (irregular); Publisher: Tyler Graphics, Mount Kisco, New York; Axsom 247; Addison Gallery of American Art. Tyler Graphics Ltd. 1974–2001 Collection, given in honor of Frank Stella (2003.44.286)

37 *Juam, State I*, 1997
From the series *Imaginary Places II*
Relief, woodcut, etching, aquatint, and hand coloring on two overlapping sheets of shaped, hand-dyed, and painted handmade paper, 198.8 × 152.4 cm (overall); Publisher: Tyler Graphics, Mount Kisco, New York; Axsom 248a; Addison Gallery of American Art. Tyler Graphics Ltd. 1974–2001 Collection, given in honor of Frank Stella (2003.44.273)

38 *Juam*, 1997
From the series *Imaginary Places II*
Relief, etching, aquatint, lithograph, screenprint, woodcut, and engraving on two overlapping sheets of shaped, hand-dyed handmade paper cut to image, 201.9 × 156.2 cm (overall, irregular); Publisher: Tyler Graphics, Mount Kisco, New York; Axsom 248; Collection of Preston H. Haskell, Class of 1960

39 *Coxuria, State I*, 1997
From the series *Imaginary Places II*
Screenprint and lithograph, 81.3 × 61.0 cm; Publisher: Tyler Graphics, Mount Kisco, New York; Axsom 249a; Collection of John Gutman, Class of 1983

40 *Cantahar*, 1998
From the series *Imaginary Places III*
Lithograph, screenprint, etching, aquatint, and relief on handmade paper, 133.4 × 133.4 cm; Publisher: Tyler Graphics, Mount Kisco, New York; Axsom 251; Addison Gallery of American Art. Tyler Graphics Ltd. 1974–2001 Collection, given in honor of Frank Stella (2003.44.274)

41 *Stranz*, 1999
From the series *Imaginary Places III*
Screenprint, 195.6 × 110.5 cm; Publisher: Tyler Graphics, Mount Kisco, New York; Axsom 257; Collection of Preston H. Haskell, Class of 1960

Bibliography

Abramsky 1966

Abramsky, Chimen. "El Lissitzky as Jewish Illustrator and Typographer." *Studio International* 172 (1966): 182–85.

Armstrong 1987

Armstrong, Elizabeth, ed. *Tyler Graphics: The Extended Image*. New York: Abbeville Press, 1987.

Auping 2015

Auping, Michael. "The Phenomenology of Frank: 'Materiality and Gesture Make Space.'" In *Frank Stella: A Retrospective*, ed. Michael Auping, 15–39. New Haven: Yale University Press, in association with the Whitney Museum of American Art, New York, and the Modern Art Museum of Fort Worth, 2015.

Axsom 1983

Axsom, Richard H. *The Prints of Frank Stella: A Catalogue Raisonné, 1967–82*. New York: Hudson Hills Press; Ann Arbor: University of Michigan Museum of Art, 1983.

Axsom 2016

Axsom, Richard H. *Frank Stella Prints: A Catalogue Raisonné*. New York: Jordan Schnitzer Family Foundation, in association with the Madison Museum of Contemporary Art; New York: D.A.P. / Distributed Art Publishers, 2016.

Barber 1998

Barber, Lynn. "Spent: An Interview with Frank Stella." *Observer Life Magazine* (London), June 14, 1998, 4–8.

Bezanson 1953

Bezanson, Walter E. "Moby-Dick: Work of Art." In *Moby-Dick Centennial Essays*, ed. for the Melville Society, 30–58. Dallas: Southern Methodist University Press, 1953.

Calvino 1980

Calvino, Italo. Introduction (1980) to *Italian Folktales*, xv–xxxii. Translated by George Martin and Catherine Hill. New York: Harcourt Brace Jovanovich, 1980. Originally published as *Fiabe italiane* (1956).

Chanin 2002

Chanin, Clifford. *Frank Stella, The Polish Village Series*. New York: Legacy Project, 2002.

De Duve 1990

De Duve, Thierry. "The Monochrome and the Blank Canvas." In *Reconstructing Modernism: Art in New York, Paris, and Montreal 1945–1964*, ed. Serge Guilbaut, 244–310. Cambridge: The MIT Press, 1990.

Dimock 2014

Dimock, W.C. "Epic Relays: C.L.R. James, Herman Melville, Frank Stella." *Comparatist* 38, no. 1 (2014): 148–57.

Dye 1937

Dye, Daniel Sheets. *A Grammar of Chinese Lattice*. 2 vols. Cambridge: Harvard-Yenching Institute, 1937.

Engberg and Stella 1997

Engberg, Siri, and Frank Stella. *Frank Stella at Tyler Graphics*. Minneapolis: Walker Art Center, 1997.

Fried 1998

Fried, Michael. "Art and Objecthood." In *Art and Objecthood: Essays and Reviews*, 148–72. Chicago: University of Chicago Press, 1998.

Friedberg 1986–87

Friedberg, Haia. "Lissitzky's Had Gadya." *Jewish Art* 12–13 (1986–87): 292–303.

Gilmour 1986

Gilmour, Pat. *Ken Tyler—Master Printer, and the American Print Renaissance*. New York: Hudson Hills Press, in association with the Australian National Gallery, 1986.

Gilmour 1987

Gilmour, Pat. "Kenneth Tyler: A Collaborator in Context." In Tyler 1987, 9–29.

Gilmour 2001

Gilmour, Pat. "Frank Stella's 'Moby Dick.'" *Print Quarterly* 18, no. 4 (December 2001): 414–36.

Glaser 1995

Glaser, Bruce, ed. by Lucy R. Lippard. "Questions to Stella and Judd." In *Minimal Art: A Critical Anthology*, ed. Gregory Battcock, 148–64. Berkeley: University of California Press, 1995. Originally published in *ARTnews* 65 (September 1966): 55–61; and broadcast asv "New Nihilism or New Art?," WBAI-FM, New York, February 1964.

Goldman 1983

Goldman, Judith. *Frank Stella: Fourteen Prints, with Drawings, Collages, and Working Proofs*. Princeton: Princeton University Art Museum, 1983.

Goldman 1987

Goldman, Judith. "Kenneth Tyler: The Artisan as Artist." In Armstrong 1987, 13–37.

Goldman-Ida 2014

Goldman-Ida, Batsheva. "The Path of Abstraction: Alois Breyer, El Lissitzky, Frank Stella." In *Wooden Synagogues: Alois Breyer, El Lissitzky, Frank Stella*, 121–42. Tel Aviv: Tel Aviv Museum of Art, 2014.

Greenberg 1973

Greenberg, Clement. "Modernist Painting." *Art and Literature* 4 (Spring 1965). Reprinted in *The New Art: A Critical Anthology*, ed. Gregory Battcock, 66–77. New York: Dutton, 1973.

Guberman 1995

Guberman, Sidney. *Frank Stella: An Illustrated Biography*. New York: Rizzoli, 1995.

Hansen 1995

Hansen, Trudy Victoria, ed. *Printmaking in America: Collaborative Prints and Presses, 1960–1990*. New York: Harry N. Abrams, in association with Mary and Leigh Block Gallery, Northwestern University, 1995.

Hobbs 2011

Hobbs, Robert. "Connecting Past and Present." In *Frank Stella: Connections*, ed. Ben Tufnell, 16–31. Ostfildern, Germany: Hatje Cantz, 2011.

Judd 1975

Judd, Donald. "Local History." *Arts Yearbook* 7 (1964). Reprinted in Donald Judd, *Complete Writings 1959–1975*, 148–56. Halifax: Press of the Nova Scotia College of Art and Design, 1975.

Kantor 2015

Kantor, Jordan. "Frank Painting/Some Aspects on Stella's Work." In *Frank Stella: A Retrospective*, ed. Michael Auping, 41–51. New Haven: Yale University Press, in association with the Whitney Museum of American Art, New York, and the Modern Art Museum of Fort Worth, 2015.

Kimball 1983

Kimball, Roger. "Frank Stella at Harvard." *The New Criterion* 2, no. 4 (December 1983): 86–88.

Kramer 1970

Kramer, Hilton. "Art: A Retrospective of Frank Stella." *New York Times*, March 25, 1970.

Leider 1970

Leider, Philip. "Abstraction and Literalism: Reflections on Stella at the Modern." *Artforum* 8, no. 8 (April 1970): 44–51.

Leider 1978

Leider, Philip. *Stella Since 1970*. Fort Worth: Fort Worth Art Museum, 1978.

Leider 1990

Leider, Philip. "Shakespearean Fish: Frank Stella Meets Moby Dick." *Art in America* 78 (October 1990): 172–91.

Manguel and Guadalupi 1980
Manguel, Alberto, and Gianni Guadalupi. *The Dictionary of Imaginary Places.* New York: Macmillan; Toronto: Lester & Orpen, 1980.

McCartney 2014
McCartney, Stella. "Frank Stella." *Interview*, November 10, 2014, https://www.interview-magazine.com/art/frank-stella.

Melville 1930
Melville, Herman. *Moby-Dick; or, The Whale.* 3 vols. Illustrated by Rockwell Kent. Chicago: Lakeside Press, 1930.

Melville 2003
Melville, Herman. *Moby-Dick.* 1851. Reprint, Mineola, NY: Dover, 2003.

Mickenberg 1995
Mickenberg, David. "Multiple Purposes: Collaboration and Education in University and Non-Profit Workshops." In Hansen 1995, 96–111.

Monduit 1889
Monduit, Louis. *Traité théorique et pratique de la stéréotomie: Au point de vue de la coupe des pierres.* Paris: Ch. Juliot, 1889.

Moshenson 1986
Moshenson, Edna. *Frank Stella: Had Gadya, after El Lissitzky: A Series of Prints, 1982–1984.* Tel Aviv: Tel Aviv Museum, 1986.

Museum of Modern Art 1936
Museum of Modern Art. *Cubism and Abstract Art.* New York: Published for the Museum of Modern Art by Arno Press, 1936.

Olson 1997
Olson, Charles. *Call Me Ishmael.* 1947. Reprint, Baltimore: The Johns Hopkins University Press, 1997.

Perloff 2004
Perloff, Nancy. Introduction to *Had Gadya: The Only Kid; Facsimile of El Lissitzky's Edition of 1919*, ed. Arnold J. Band, iii–vi. Los Angeles: Getty Research Institute, 2004.

Preziosi 2010
Preziosi, Donald. *Rethinking Art History: Meditations on a Coy Science.* New Haven: Yale University Press, 2010.

Rosenberg 1970
Rosenberg, Harold. "The Art World: Young Masters, New Critics." *New Yorker* 46, no. 12 (May 9, 1970): 103–16.

Rubin 1970
Rubin, William S. *Frank Stella.* New York: Museum of Modern Art, 1970.

Rubin 1987
Rubin, William. *Frank Stella, 1970–1987.* New York: Museum of Modern Art, 1987.

Russell 1984
Russell, John. "Art View: Frank Stella at Harvard — The Artist as Lecturer." *New York Times,* March 18, 1984.

Salus 2010
Salus, Carol. "Frank Stella's Polish Village Series and Related Works: Heritage and Alliance." *Shofar: An Interdisciplinary Journal of Jewish Studies* 28, no. 2 (Winter 2010): 139–56.

Schultz 1995
Schultz, Elizabeth A. *Unpainted to the Last: Moby-Dick and Twentieth-Century American Art.* Lawrence: University Press of Kansas, 1995.

Stella 1986
Stella, Frank. *Working Space.* The Charles Eliot Norton Lectures, 1983–84. Cambridge: Harvard University Press, 1986.

Stella 1989

Stella, Frank. "1989 Previews from 36 Creative Artists." *New York Times,* January 1, 1989.

Stella 2000a

Stella, Frank. "Grimm's Ecstacy (1991)." In *Frank Stella at Two Thousand: Changing the Rules (Contemporary Art)*, ed. Bonnie Clearwater, 57–69. North Miami: Museum of Contemporary Art, 2000.

Stella 2000b

Stella, Frank. "Melrose Avenue (1995)." In *Frank Stella at Two Thousand: Changing the Rules (Contemporary Art)*, ed. Bonnie Clearwater, 81–91. North Miami: Museum of Contemporary Art, 2000.

Storr 1985

Storr, Robert. "Frank Stella's Norton Lectures: A Response." *Art in America* 73, no. 2 (February 1985): 11–15.

Tomkins 1984

Tomkins, Calvin. "Profiles (Frank Stella): The Space Around Real Things." *New Yorker*, September 10, 1984, 53–97

Tyler 1987

Tyler, Kenneth E. *Tyler Graphics: Catalogue Raisonné, 1974–1985.* With a foreword by Elizabeth Armstrong and an essay by Pat Gilmour. Minneapolis: Walker Arts Center; New York: Abbeville Press, 1987.

Wallace 2000

Wallace, Robert K. *Frank Stella's Moby Dick: Words and Shapes.* Ann Arbor: University of Michigan Press, 2000.

Photography Credits

pp. 33, 40
Digital Image © The Museum of Modern Art / Licensed by SCALA / Art Resource, New York

pp. 19, 35
Photo: Avraham Hai

p. 24
Photo courtesy Princeton University Library / © 1930, Lakeside Press

pp. 37, 44, plates 1–12, 16, 18–20, 22, 24–27, 29–30, 33–35, 38–39, 41
Photo: Princeton University Art Museum, Jeffrey Evans

p. 44
© 1937, Harvard University Press

p. 48, top left, top right, bottom left
Photo: Marabeth Cohen-Tyler

p. 48, bottom right
Photo: Steven Sloman

plates 13–15, 17, 21, 23, 28, 31–32, 36–37, 40
Photo: Addison Gallery of American Art, Phillips Academy, Andover, Massachusetts / Art Resource, New York